OKLAHOMA'S BENNIE OWEN

OKLAHOMA'S
BENNIE OWEN

Man for All Seasons

GARY KING

Foreword by Jay Wilkinson

The History PRESS

Published by The History Press
Charleston, SC 29403
www.historypress.net

First published 2015

Manufactured in the United States

ISBN 978.1.62619.949.1

Library of Congress Control Number: 2015931716

This book is dedicated to all the Owen clan but especially to Dorothy.

Contents

FOREWORD

Few football traditions can rival the consistency of excellence of the University of Oklahoma Sooners during the past seventy years.

My father, Bud Wilkinson, is usually given credit for the genesis of the OU football tradition that continued through Coach Barry Switzer and remains with Coach Bob Stoops today. That's because most people don't think about what happened before World War II. People tend to forget that over one hundred years ago, the University of Oklahoma built an enviable program under Coach Bennie Owen that laid the foundation for the modern-day tradition.

When my father, at the age of thirty-one, became the head football coach at OU in 1947, he knew this. He was grateful that Owen had not only created the finest athletic facilities he had ever seen but also generated statewide support for the OU football program. He publicly thanked Owen for the opportunity to inherit the tradition that he had built. Then with the return of many World War II veterans, the modern-day Sooner tradition began.

History is an important facet of every American's life. Gaining a better understanding of the past helps us to value and appreciate the people who paved the way for others. Such a person was Bennie Owen, who not only built a prominent program but was also responsible for the development of OU's first football stadium and the student union building.

Foreword

By writing this important book, Gary King has made an enormous contribution to Sooner fans throughout the country. He takes us back to a century ago and makes us feel that we were actually there.

Bennie Owen deserves to have a book written about him. Thank you, Gary, for bringing his story to life.

Jay Wilkinson

Acknowledgements

Harold Keith! I must begin with his name because he deserves the lion's share of the credit for this book. The late Mr. Keith was the sports information director at the University of Oklahoma from 1930 to 1969. In addition to his coverage of OU sports, Keith won numerous awards for excellence in children's literature, including the Oklahoma Book award, the prestigious Newby Medal and a couple Spur awards from the Western Writers of America.

In 1948, Keith published a book entitled *Oklahoma Kickoff* that James Gregg Jr. of the *Pittsburg Press* thought was the best book ever written on the game of football. This book is the source of most of the information about Bennie Owen and his Oklahoma teams. Keith conducted numerous interviews with Bennie's former players (all of whom are now deceased) in order to get their unique perspective on their beloved coach and the games they played for him. Thus, unless otherwise noted, all direct quotes of Bennie's OU players come from Keith's wonderful book.

There were, of course, newspaper accounts of the games, and I made use of these as best I could. But in those days, sports reporting was nothing like it is today. There were no postgame interviews with players and coaches. For these, I had to rely on Keith's reporting. Without *Oklahoma Kickoff*, we would not know the real story of the bloodbath that was the game between the University of Oklahoma Territory and the Haskell Indians in 1905 or of Lee Field's race against the train or of Sabe Hott's glass eye, among many others. Somehow, I do not think that Keith, gracious gentleman that he was, would object to the retelling of these old tales, especially when they enhance the legacy of his good friend Bennie Owen. I believe he would be glad they were passed along to a new generation of OU fans, which was my goal.

Ultimately, however, Harold Keith's book was a book about OU football. This is a book about Bennie Owen. Keith said very little about Bennie's life before he came to the University of Oklahoma, and to this end, I spent many hours in the state of Kansas—in such places as Lawrence, Topeka, Lindsborg and Arkansas City—researching yearbooks, reels and reels of microfilm and local history tomes in pursuit of new information. Also, there was nothing in *Oklahoma Kickoff* about Owen's years as OU's baseball and basketball coach or about his life after he retired from coaching. I tried as best I could to complete the record in this regard.

I must thank Jackie Reese of the University of Oklahoma's Western History Collection for all her help in processing the photographs that appear in this book. And I certainly owe a tremendous debt of gratitude to Becky LeJeune, my editor at The History Press, for her guidance and her patience with me in bringing this project to fruition.

I must also thank my wife, Patricia. Her contributions as proofreader and research assistant were invaluable to me. And last but certainly not least, I want to express my enormous appreciation to Bennie's daughter, Dorothy Bryan; to his grandchildren, Sandy Trudgeon, Ann Stussi, Jan (Page) Howard, William Gilbert Page and James Bessent Haynes; and to his wife, Anne, who graciously shared their scrapbooks and memories of Bennie with me. I hope that they will all be pleased with the book.

INTRODUCTION

Beauty pawed the dirt, tossed her head back and flared her nostrils. "Easy girl," Bennie said. "The gun will sound in just a minute, and then we're gonna race."

It was almost noon on Saturday, September 16, 1893. Bennie Owen and his black mare, Beauty, were waiting at the south border of Kansas for the start of the Cherokee Strip Land Run. It was the largest land run in American history. The U.S. government was offering forty thousand parcels of free land in what is now northern Oklahoma. The Cherokee Strip contained more than six and a half million acres. It was larger than the states of Delaware, Connecticut and Rhode Island combined. Any U.S. citizen (male or female) who was at least twenty-one years old and had not previously benefited from the Homestead Act was eligible to stake a claim. Native Americans, whose ancestors had hunted on this land for at least ten thousand years, were not considered U.S. citizens and were not allowed to race.

By nightfall, every acre had been claimed. The intrepid settlers built sod huts and tried to farm the dry land, but conditions were so unforgiving that only 25 percent of those who filed claims were able to survive for six months in order to satisfy the residency requirement and receive their official deeds.

Bennie's family lived on a farm near Arkansas City, Kansas, which was only three miles from the northern starting point for the land run. On the day of the race, it was estimated that 100,000 people were in town. Three days later, only 5,000 remained. For months, Bennie had watched them come. Some came on horseback. Others came in wagons with their families. Still others came on foot. It was a time of great hope and high adventure.

Bennie had ridden Beauty deep into Oklahoma Territory many times while chasing coyotes and jackrabbits. He knew the area well. He was one of fifty thousand who lined up on the northern border of the Cherokee Strip that day, and there were at least that many on the southern boundary. A few shameless mercenaries at the starting line were charging a nickel for a drink of water, and many were willing to pay it to choke down the dust; dust so thick, by one participant's account, that you could not see more than three feet in front of your face.

Bennie was only seventeen years old and therefore ineligible to file a claim, but he was not about to miss this adventure. When the shotgun blast sounded, he and Beauty raced among the leaders for four miles before he reluctantly pulled up and turned for home.

It was not yet time for him to live in this untamed land. Twelve years later, he would move into the very heart of this windswept prairie, and he would play an important role in shaping the history of the young state and the destiny of the new university in Norman.

Bennie Owen made such an impact on Oklahoma that the most valuable and best-known acre of land in the state now bears his name. This acre is, of course, Owen Field, the turf on which the University of Oklahoma football games are played. He was afforded this honor because Benjamin Gilbert Owen was a coach. He is best remembered as the mentor of the University of Oklahoma's football team from 1905 through 1926, but he also coached basketball at OU from 1909 to 1921 and baseball from 1906 until 1922. Truly, he was a man for all seasons.

On October 16, 1907, Bennie Owen lost his right arm in a hunting accident. He was soon back at work and doing everything a man with two arms could do and more. He hunted and fished. He shuffled, dealt, held and played cards with one hand. He drove his old stick shift Buick all over Norman with reckless abandon. He even tied his own shoelaces. His good friend Phillip Kendall observed: "Bennie didn't know he had only one arm. I think he made himself forget it, and he made you forget it too. He was the most complete and well-rounded person I've ever known."

During the first ten years that Owen coached at Oklahoma, there were many rule changes in football. Owen used these new rules as an opportunity to add to his offensive arsenal. J. Brent Clark wrote in *Sooner Century: One Hundred Glorious Years of Oklahoma Football*, "Nowhere in America was there a more skilled or creative mind than Bennie Owen of Oklahoma." He split his ends out, unbalanced his line and ran the "tackle-around" play. The "tackle-eligible" pass is one of the oldest plays in football, but Bennie's tackles didn't just catch passes; they also threw them. He developed the "long punt" formation, which was an early prototype of the single-wing, and he was the first OU coach to have a spring practice.

Bud Wilkinson, in the 1950s, ran the "fast break," reeling off plays as fast as he could, and in 2008, Bob Stoops installed the "no huddle" offense. Owen ran both fifty years before Bud and one hundred years before Bob. Charlie Orr, a 117-pound quarterback who won his letter in 1912, said, "In those days, we didn't hold any conferences [huddles] behind the line of scrimmage after each play. We called signals, and we called 'um fast. I've called many a signal flat on my back thirty yards from the ball."

However, Owen is probably best remembered for the innovations he made in the passing game. It might surprise fans who remember OU football before Bob Stoops—back in the days of Wilkinson and Switzer, who both disdained the pass—to learn that Bennie Owen's teams were throwing the ball thirty to thirty-five times a game before World War I. Forrest "Spot" Geyer, the first Sooner to be picked as an All-American, consistently threw for over two hundred yards a game between 1913 and 1915. Geyer could easily heave the ball fifty-five yards in the air, even though the ball they were using in those days more closely resembled a pumpkin than the streamlined missile quarterbacks hurl today.

In a 1914 game, OU scored five passing TDs. That same year, Ad Lindsey, a halfback for Kansas who later succeeded Owen as OU's coach, said, "Oklahoma bewildered us with forward passes." The venerable Harold Keith wrote in *Oklahoma Kickoff*, "Oklahoma appears to have been the first team in America to go in consistently for mass production of aerial play and to prove that the forward pass could be a major unit of the offense in every game on the schedule with the forward passing yardage usually surpassing the running yardage."

Owen's twenty-two-year tenure is the longest of any coach in OU history. He won 122 games, lost 54 and tied 16. If these numbers don't seem all that spectacular in comparison to some of the coaches who followed him, it must be remembered that his players were walk-ons—all of them. He did not recruit players, and he gave out no scholarships. He thought the reason for going to college was to get an education and that football was an extracurricular activity. "All we got out of football was the fun," said Sabe Hott, a tackle for Owen from 1910 to 1913. "It was sport and that's why we played. If Bennie had offered me board, room and tuition, I wouldn't have played for him."

Owen had three all-victorious seasons, 1911, 1915 and 1918, and his 1920 team was undefeated with one tie. Even though he would never have tried to embarrass an opponent by running up the score, his teams scored more than one hundred points eight times and more than eighty on four other occasions. Such lopsided victories were unavoidable since his starters had to play almost the whole game because he seldom had more than fifteen men on a squad.

Bennie Owen was always noted for his fine sportsmanship in a time when sportsmanship was not exactly commonplace. Dewey "Snorter" Luster, captain of Owen's unbeaten 1920 team and later OU's head coach, said, "Bennie was a sportsman in every sense of the word, a true sportsman. He knew how to win and lose like a gentleman." Ivan Grove, an outstanding quarterback for Henry Kendall College in 1917, recalled, "Oklahoma absolutely had the cleanest team of all the teams we ever played."

In this regard, Oklahoma teams clearly reflected the personality and values of their coach. No one led a "cleaner" life than Bennie Owen. He did not drink, smoke, chew tobacco or use profanity. His favorite expression was "Gee Cly!" But if he was really upset, he might shout out "murder, murder, murder!" Page Belcher, a guard for Owen in 1918, said, "Bennie was clean as a pin himself and wouldn't let us swear, either in practice or in a game. If some player sang out in disgust, 'Hell, I dropped it!' Bennie would stop practice in a flash and call the whole squad in. 'We don't use that kind of language around here,' he'd tell everybody. 'You're men now, and men don't talk that way.'"

When Owen stepped down as head football coach in 1926, OU president Dr. William Bennett Bizzell said, "For more than twenty years, Bennie Owen has stood for good sportsmanship and high ideals. No man identified with athletic activities in this country has contributed more than he has to the wholesomeness of athletics."

But Owen was much more than a coach. He was also a visionary and a builder. As director of athletics from 1907 to 1934 and later as intramural director from 1934 until his retirement in 1950 at the age of seventy-five, he was the driving force that produced Owen Field, the field house, the Memorial Union building, the men's swimming pool, the baseball field and bleachers, the concrete tennis courts, the nine-hole golf course and the intramural playing fields.

Bennie Owen died on February 26, 1970, at the age of ninety-four. Upon hearing of his death, University of Oklahoma president emeritus George

Lynn Cross said, "His contributions to the university athletic program can never be measured. He was a legend in his own time and the name of Bennie Owen will always be synonymous with football."

This is his story.

1

A Childhood Well Spent

St. Louis, Missouri, 1888

Bennie had a plan, and when Bennie Owen explained one of his plans, his buddies paid attention. The plan was that they would all go out to Sportsman's Park early while the Brownies were still taking batting practice. Bennie was going to stand outside the ballpark on Dodier Street, a half a block up from Grand. Another boy would stand on the corner of Dodier and Grand Streets, and a third boy was to line up a block or so farther south on Grand. Then, when one of the Browns hit a foul ball over the roof of the stadium, Bennie would grab it and throw it to the second boy who would relay it to the third. This last boy would stash the ball at his house, and Bennie's gang would have a new baseball for their sandlot games.

Bennie Owen was thirteen years old and small for his age, but he was a good athlete and the acknowledged leader of his gang. Bennie loved the Browns, and he loved to play baseball in the sandlots of St. Louis. He had learned the game from his father, George, who had been a barehanded catcher for the Covington, Kentucky professional team, and he had the crooked fingers and swollen knuckles to prove it. His nose had been broken several times because he played without a mask.

Bennie's parents understood that a boy as vibrant and energetic as Bennie was had to have time for sports and play but only after the chores were done. And if he should come home from the streets or sandlots bruised and bleeding, as he often did, he could expect no sympathy. He and his four brothers and two sisters learned from their mother that they were not to complain about physical pain. Only a broken bone, if even that, got any attention in the Owen household. Bennie would later employ this Spartan attitude both as a college athlete and coach.

Bennie watched his beloved Browns play at every opportunity, and a great team they were. Their owner, the colorful Chris Von der Ahe, put together a club that captured the American Association championship four years in a row (1885–88). At this time, the AA was the "Major League" of baseball. Von der Ahe, a St. Louis saloon owner, initially had no interest in the sport, but he began to notice that the baseball fans liked to stop by his establishment for a beer after the games. So, long before Jacob Ruppert or "Gussie" Busch, he saw the natural link between beer and baseball.

The teams that Bennie watched featured several great players. Their leader was Charles Albert Comiskey, who later, as owner of the Chicago White Sox, became one of the founding fathers of the American League. Comiskey was the Browns' first baseman and manager. His plaque at Cooperstown says that he was the first man at his position to play away from the bag.

Bill Gleason was a good defensive shortstop and a reliable hitter, but the Browns' best batsman was outfielder James Edward "Tip" O'Neil. O'Neil must have been a colorful character because one nickname was not enough for him. Tip was also known as the "Woodstock Wonder." O'Neil by any nickname was a great hitter. In 1887, he won the only Triple Crown in the history of the American Association, hitting .435 with fourteen home runs and 123 RBI.

The team's best pitcher was Elton "Ice Box" Chamberlain. In 1888, he won 25 games, lost 11 and had a 2.19 ERA. The following year his stats were 34-15, 2.97.

Bennie was quite the resourceful lad and not at all bashful. He devised a scheme that allowed him not only to see the game but also to make money while doing so. His ploy was to get out to the ballpark early, usually without a cent in his trousers, and grab a choice spot in the queue of fans that were waiting for the ticket office to open. Then as the line grew longer and longer, he would sell his spot for fifty cents to someone who did not want to endure the wait at the back of the line. Then he would buy a seat in the bleachers for a quarter and have two bits left over to spend any way he wished.

Or if he did not finish his chores in time to get out to the old Sportsman's Park early enough, he might just scale a telephone pole and place a board across the spikes sticking out of the pole. Then he could watch the game from what Dodger announcer Red Barber years later might have called "the cat bird's seat."

Comiskey and his men were great heroes to Bennie and his friends. In fact, most people in St. Louis idolized them. They were great athletes, and more importantly, they were winners. Thus, Bennie witnessed at an early age the kind of notoriety that success in athletics can bring.

Earlier

Both of Bennie's parents, Olivia Ring and George Henry Owen, were born in upstate New York—George in 1848 and "Ollie," as she was known, two years later. They both moved south, met and married in 1872 in Covington,

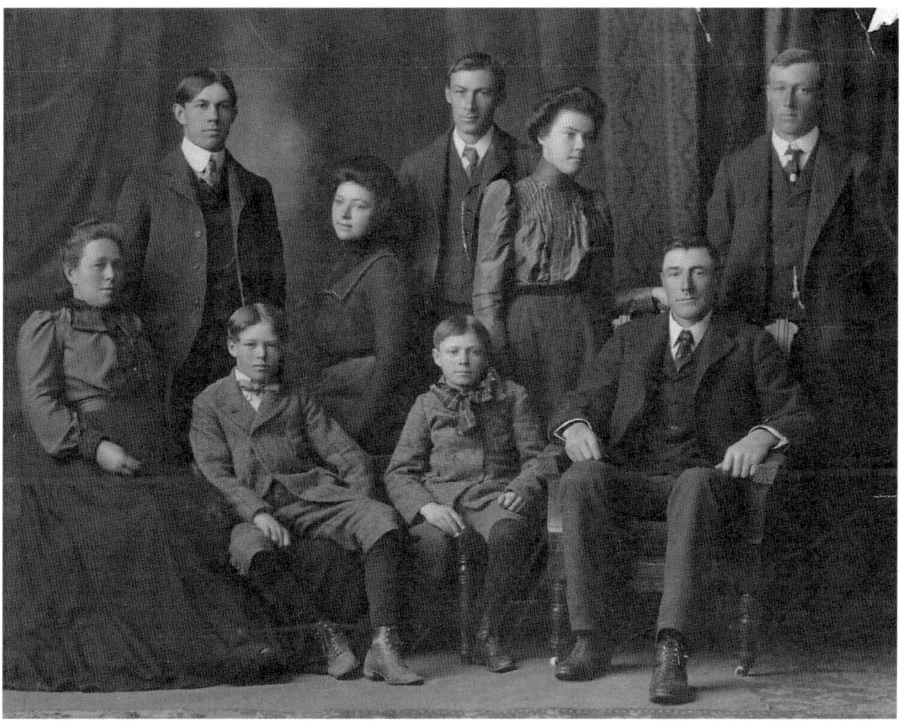

Bennie's family circa 1894. *Back row, left to right*: Bennie, Roberta, William, Olivia (Olive) and Arthur. *Front row, left to right*: Bennie's mother, Olivia; George; Ted; and Bennie's father, George Henry. *Courtesy of Jan Howard.*

Kentucky, where George was batting the old horsehide around. Soon after their wedding, the couple moved to Chicago, which then had a population of less than thirty thousand.

After the great fire of 1871, Chicago became one of the world's most economically important cities, the "broad shouldered hog butcher to the world" that Carl Sandburg would write about years later. Chicago took the raw materials that were shipped in from the West—grain, cattle, hogs, lumber and iron—processed them and shipped them east. George, working as a heater in a steel mill, was a part of this process.

Ollie gave birth to the first of her seven children in 1873. The child was a boy, whom she and George named William. Benjamin Gilbert Owen, born on July 24, 1875, was their second child. When Bennie was still a very young baby, his family began traveling south by southwest on an odyssey that would take them to St. Louis and later even farther southwest to a farm in Kansas.

Their first move was only about 20 miles, to Aurora, Illinois. It was here that another boy, Arthur, was born in 1877 and also their first daughter, Roberta ("Birdie"), in 1879. Next, the Owen clan, now six strong, moved 260 miles almost due south to Centralia, Illinois, where Ollie gave birth in 1883 to her namesake, Olivia, who became known as "Olive." Then, three years and 60 miles later, another son, George, was born in Belleville, Illinois. From there, it was just another short jaunt of 20 miles to St. Louis, where their last child, Ted, was born in 1889. It was here that Bennie spent his adolescence.

1889: Back in St. Louis

When Bennie and his buddies were not playing baseball or watching baseball and the weather was warm enough, they could most likely be found swimming in the Mississippi River. They quickly learned as much about the majestic old river, with its shifting sand bars and fickle currents, as any character ever invented by Mark Twain.

They liked to climb up to the second story of a grain elevator that extended out over the river and dive off. Usually, they would swim out to one of the many lumber barges floating in the river, climb aboard, ride it back to the shore and repeat the process.

At least, that's what most of the boys did. Bennie liked to swim much farther out into the river, where he could surf the waves kicked up by the steamboats.

Sometimes, Bennie would swim really far out into the river, and the current would carry him downstream so far and so fast that his friends would lose sight of him. If the current was stronger than he thought, he did not panic. He just relaxed and rested, floating with the current and conserving his energy. He was confident that he would eventually get back on land. He would never admit that he might have pushed things too far. Those who knew him would confirm that throughout his life, Bennie Owen had a stubborn streak at least as wide as the river he was swimming in.

If his friends became concerned about him, they would start walking south until they spotted their young friend, tan as a piece of saddle leather and grinning like he had just hit the game-winning home run. Of course, they never let on like they were ever worried about him, and soon, he began teasing them about being too scared to swim very far out into the river.

Bennie attended Henry Clay High School in north St. Louis, where he played on the baseball team. At this time in his life, he had never even seen a football or a basketball game. College football had barely advanced farther west than the Hudson River let alone the Mississippi in the late 1880s, and basketball had not yet been invented. When Bennie was in high school, the Great American West was still a pretty wild place. Geronimo, Sitting Bull, Buffalo Bill Cody and Wyatt Earp were all still very much alive.

SOUTHEASTERN KANSAS, SEPTEMBER 1893

In 1892, Bennie made one more trip south by southwest with his family. This time, they traveled about 450 miles from St. Louis to a farm that was about 12 miles west of Arkansas City, Kansas, near the small hamlet of Guelph. George decided to settle here because he thought this would be good land for growing wheat.

About a year after the Owen family had moved to the farm, hoards of hardy adventurers began to descend on the area. Bennie watched them come on horseback, on mule back, in wagons, on trains and on foot. He heard them talking about things like the last great land run, Boomers and Sooners and the closing of the West. Although he did not really understand the significance of these things at the time, he was caught up in the drama and excitement of the great Cherokee Strip Land Run.

Fred Wiley and John Blake, a couple of Bennie's neighbors, were planning to take part in the big event. They knew that Bennie was too young to stake a claim, so they asked him if he would do a favor for them. They planned to file a claim on a piece of land near the Hackberry Crossing on the Chikaskia River, and they wanted Bennie to drive their supply wagon down to meet them on the day following the race.

Bennie agreed to help the two men. He was familiar with the spot they were talking about because he had ridden his pony all over that country chasing jackrabbits and coyotes. He was glad they wanted him to bring the wagon on the day after the race because that meant he could line up with the others and be a part of the largest land run in the nation's history. An adventurous boy like Bennie was not about to miss anything this exciting. So, at noon on Saturday, September 16, 1893, Bennie and his black filly, Beauty, were at the starting line choking back the dust and ready to race. The next day, the *Guthrie Daily News* described this historic event as follows:

> *When the signal sounded at Orlando and the crowd, like a mighty torrent, burst over the line into the land which to them had been so long a mystery, there went to the skies a roar so far reaching and prolonged that the very sense of hearing was stunned and the faculty of thought for the time seemed paralyzed. I have heard the roar of artillery—sixty batteries playing on the enemy at one time, have listened to the federal yell and rah coming up from 50,000 soldiers' throats, have listened to the fiercest peals of thunder as it rattled amid the lonely pines of the Black Hills...but never in all my life did I hear a cry so peculiar—a roar of such subdued fierceness like to the awful agony of a mighty ocean in the storm throes of madness, as that which rose on the morning of that fateful day of September 16, 1893. It seemed to me as if all the mad passions of an army of devils was let loose...and in dense and horrid clouds of sand and dust, were sweeping down upon some world upon which they had planned to wreck a dire and awful vengeance.*

A quarter of a section, 160 acres, was what these intrepid settlers were racing for. There were around forty thousand of these parcels, and over 100,000 optimistic souls were competing for them.

If they were not trampled to death (as some were) or seriously injured in the race, and if they were fortunate enough to file a claim, they were still not home free. They would have to construct some kind of dwelling place that would allow them to survive a brutal winter, get their crops in the ground in the spring and make a successful harvest. Three out of every four who filed claims did not complete the six-month residency requirement to receive their official deeds.

Bennie witnessed the drama and the "mad passions" of this spectacular event, but after racing for about four miles, he reined Beauty in and turned back north, back to his family's farm. About a dozen years later, he would return to this territory and make his home much farther south, south of the tall grass prairie and west of the Cross Timbers on the bank of the sandy South Canadian River at a place called Norman, where they were building a university. There he would hear a lot more about the Boomers and Sooners.

THE GOOD DOCTOR

Bennie was quite a busy young man during his five years in southeastern Kansas. His primary task was to help his father with the wheat harvests. George Owen brought the first harvesting machine, or "header," to Cowley County. This was rich farmland, a sort of "Middle America Mesopotamia" lying between the Arkansas and Walnut Rivers. Bennie earned five dollars a day walking behind the horse-drawn header and stacking the freshly cut grain with a pitchfork.

Once the crops were planted, the Owen clan always found time for their real love—baseball. Bennie and his father and brothers laid out a diamond in a corner of their pasture and began teaching the game to the local farmers. Soon teams were coming on Saturday afternoons from nearby towns such as Guenda Springs, Ashton and Arkansas City, a tradition that continued long after Bennie and his family moved away.

Bennie did not neglect his education. Three days a week, he saddled Beauty and rode her eight miles into Arkansas City, fording the Arkansas River along the way, to study at the Hendershot Academy. This was apparently a sort of prep school that derived its name from C.P. Hendershot, the local superintendent of schools. After his classes, Bennie somehow found the time to coach boxing and wrestling at the Arkansas City YMCA.

On one of his many trips to town, Bennie became acquainted with a frontier physician named S.B. Parsons. The bay mare that pulled his buggy around the countryside was the mother of Bennie's beloved Beauty. It is easy to envision Dr. Parsons as a character similar to Galen Adams of *Gunsmoke* fame, treating patients and taking his payment in chickens, eggs and hogs.

Parsons, who earned his medical degree at the University of Michigan, was infatuated with frontier life and started his practice in Arkansas City in 1883. Impressed with Bennie's sharp mind and indomitable work ethic, he began tutoring the young boy in the art of medicine. Harold Keith wrote in *Oklahoma Kickoff*, "For three years the boy went with the old doctor about the country rendering him whatever aid was needed from giving anesthetics to helping deliver babies, for now it was his ambition to become a doctor."

Although Keith did not mention it in his book, apparently Bennie lived with the Parsons in Arkansas City for at least some of the time he was attending Hendershot. The doctor's daughter, Mary wrote, in her memoirs, which were published in a book entitled *Between the Rivers: Stories of the Eighties and Nineties in Arkansas City, Kansas*:

> *Father and Mother decided to ask Ben to come live with us while he was in high school.* [Presumably, she meant the Hendershot Academy.] *He was bright, very likable, eager for an education and was such a help at home. He proved to be much better than the usual 'hired girl.' He fitted into our family life and we children were delighted to have him as a big brother. He went on to the university, was active in athletics, and after graduating was coach at the University of Oklahoma. He was considered the finest the school ever had, and indeed he made quite a name for himself in all Oklahoma.*

Dr. Parsons was not the only colorful character Bennie came to know in Arkansas City. There was another whose influence on Owen's life would prove to be even more important than the old frontier physician's.

The Iceman Cometh to Arkansas City

When Bennie learned that a coach was putting together a football team in Arkansas City, he became curious and stopped by the city park one day to watch practice. After watching the scrimmage for about half an hour, Bennie decided he would like to get in on the action, so he asked the coach for a tryout.

The player-coach of the team was a man with the aristocratic-sounding name of Arthur St. Leger Mosse, but most of his friends just called him "Texas." When the burly Mosse was not coaching or playing football, he earned his living as Arkansas City's iceman. He was doubtful that Owen—at five feet, seven inches tall and 130 pounds—would make much of a player, but he needed more bodies and agreed to let him try out. It did not take him long to see that Bennie was a superior athlete, but what surprised him most was the little guy's aptitude for tackling.

Bennie was not at all intimidated by the bigger and stronger but decidedly slower players. He attacked the sport with reckless abandon and quickly became a starter at halfback for Mosse. He soon became so infatuated with the sport that the following fall, both he and Mosse journeyed north 220 miles to Lawrence, Kansas, because they heard the university there was looking for football players.

2
Rock Chalk a Jayhawk

Contrasting Coaches

Bennie Owen and Arthur Mosse were among the three hundred freshmen who matriculated at the university atop Mount Oread in the fall of 1897. Bennie's goal at this time was to follow in the footsteps of his mentor, Dr. Parsons, and become a physician.

To that end, he enrolled in a premed curriculum, featuring courses in Latin and pharmacy. Based on an evaluation of his transcripts from the Hendershot Academy, the registrar gave Bennie one semester credit in Greek, German, algebra, trigonometry and Latin.

Bennie's coach for his first two years at the University of Kansas (KU) was Dr. Wylie Woodruff, who had an outstanding football pedigree as well as a medical degree from the University of Pennsylvania. Wylie was the younger brother of George Woodruff, who was one of the great pioneers of the game.

George played at Yale from 1885 to 1888. His teammate for all four years (during which the Bulldogs compiled a record of 38-1-1) was Amos Alonso Stagg, and their coach for their senior year was Walter Camp. At Yale, George was also captain of the crew team and earned a letter in track and field. Gifted academically as well, he was a Phi Beta Kappa student and won the Winthrop Award for excellence in Greek and Latin. George came to the University

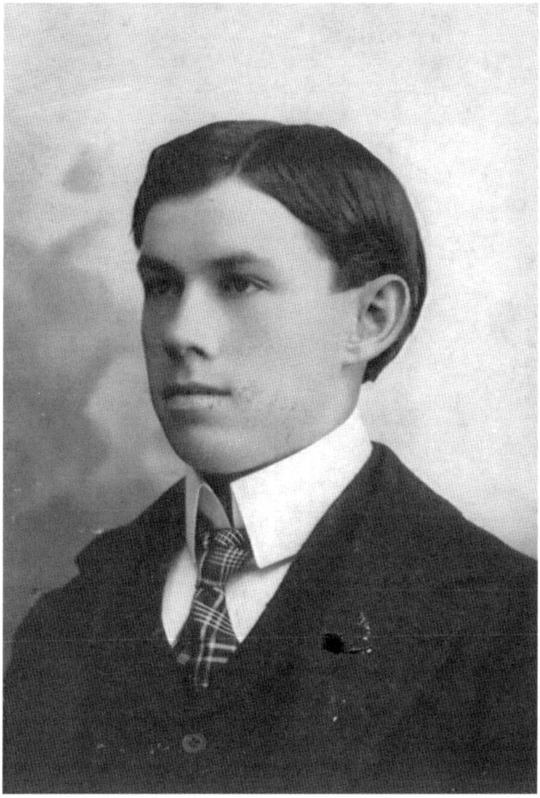

Bennie at age twenty. *Courtesy of Jan Howard.*

of Pennsylvania in 1892 to study law and obtained his LLB in 1895. He also coached the Penn football team from 1892 to 1901, fashioning a record of 124-15-2. John Heisman was one of the many greats he developed at Pennsylvania. After leaving Penn, he coached at the University of Illinois in 1903 and the Carlisle Indian School in 1905. He is credited with developing the "guards back" formation and the "delayed pass" play. He was named to the College Football Hall of Fame in 1963.

Wylie learned most of his football from his illustrious brother. As a thirty-year-old guard on George's 1896 Penn squad, Wylie was selected as an All-American by both Walter Camp and *Harper's Weekly*. The following season, he was in Lawrence to coach the Jayhawks.

In an article entitled "We'll Play like Pennsylvania," the August 2, 1897 *Kansas University Weekly* opined, "There has never been a brighter prospect for a foot ball team at Kansas University than there is this fall." Apparently, Woodruff agreed because he told the reporter, "I think with hard work and systematic training we will be able to show our superiority over any team in the world not by a slight margin but by a good big score which will gain us recognition both North and West." He then proceeded to expound on the coaching philosophy he intended to employ in order to produce such a juggernaut:

> *Foot ball is the one most manly sport of modern times; a sport that brings out all that is noble and intellectual in a young man's nature…I want foot*

> *ball players to be good students…Athletics should raise and not lower the standard of scholarship. Any man who plays can be as good and in fact a better student than the majority of those who do not play if he has the desire to be a good student…The eye must be bright and keen, the head clear, the body free from deformity, the legs and arms strong and well padded with muscle, and above all a mental courage which knows not defeat—which laughs at pain…What makes the clear head, keen eye, mental courage, strong limb, prompt quick thoughts, and gives the endurance? It all depends on training; training not only on the field but every hour of every day…Then comes the training to great many the most trying, (I might almost say cruel) and that which shows the man from the fellow; the breaking off from established habits such as smoking, drinking, chewing, and staying out late at night to see friends or sweetheart. On these points I am absolute. I will not coach any man and expect to win universally, and allow him to break any of the above rules, and a man who is heart and soul into football will willingly forego these pleasures for a few months to become a champion…Why not make up your minds, you sons of Old Kansas, to come to me this fall with the thought, "I will make the season one of glorious memory."*

Woodruff concluded this bombast by saying, "I want to say football and other college sports are not to make cripples and to slay the young men of the land, but if you have carefully followed me, to make them more manly, noble, more self-reliant, braver and men of brains who may know how to properly honor their fathers and mothers and respect and defend the state at whose institution they are imbibing that knowledge for which mankind has so long been in search."

In reality, football under Woodruff was not nearly as highly principled and chivalrous as he claimed. A proponent of a smash-mouth style, he liked his players big and strong. A bit of a mean streak was fine, too. He wanted his men to run over, not finesse their way around, opponents. His motto was, "Hurdle the wounded, step on the dead." However, Harold Keith wrote,

> *Sometimes his players became so fiercely preoccupied in their work that they stepped on everybody, living and dead alike. His Kansas team aimed to overpower its opponents, hammering them so cruelly in the first half that they couldn't stand up in the last half. For example in the Iowa game of 1897 the score at intermission was a deadlock, 0–0. However the homicidal Jayhawkers had taken so much out of their opponents that they romped to a 56–0 win over the dispirited Hawkeyes in the last half.*

Woodruff employed his brother's "guards back" formation, in which Mosse and the 250-pound "Shorty" Hammill lined up in the backfield directly behind the tackles. This was a maneuver very much in keeping with Woodruff's philosophy of straight-ahead power football, as it stacked two additional blockers in front of the ball carrier.

Early in the season, Woodruff was skeptical of Bennie because of his lack of size and used him only sparingly. Although he did not win his letter that year, by the end of the season, Owen had become one of the Jayhawks's stalwarts. In the final game of the 1897 season, KU squared off against its bitter rivals, the Tigers from the University of Missouri, at Exhibition Park in Kansas City on Thanksgiving Day. The gridiron was covered with a thick layer of ice and sleet—so much so that the hash marks had to be painted on with lampblack. Bennie fielded a Missouri punt and ran, slid and skated seventy-five yards over the slippery turf for a TD that sealed a 12–0 win for the Jayhawks. This victory wrapped up an 8-2 season for Woodruff's men. They failed to score against the Kansas City Medics and lost 2–0, and when a KU extra point try went awry, Nebraska escaped with a 6–5 victory. (At this time, touchdowns counted 5 points.)

In 1898, the Jayhawks won seven games and lost only once, an 18–6 slugfest to a Nebraska squad coached by Fielding Yost. That season, one of KU's favorite plays was the "Quarterback Toss." At this time, the forward pass was verboten in college football, so instead of throwing the football, they threw Bennie. After Owen received the snap from center, the huge Hammill would grab him by the seat of his pants and heave him over the line of scrimmage—a perfectly legal maneuver in those days. Sometimes, Bennie would land on his feet and scamper for several more yards, and sometimes, he found himself at the bottom of a dog pile.

The 1898 season was the last Woodruff would coach at KU or anywhere else. He gave up the gridiron to pursue a career in medicine. Three years later, a very curious article appeared in the *New York Times*:

> *Wylie G. Woodruff Arrested: Famous Football Player Taken to Jail in Portland Ore.—Charged with Kidnapping.*
>
> *Portland, Ore., May 31, 1901—Dr. Wylie G. Woodruff of Philadelphia, one of the star football players at the University of Pennsylvania five years ago, was arrested today at the Union station, together with Mrs. Edith Moyer of Lawrence, Kan., on a charge of kidnapping Mrs. Moyer's baby daughter, Myrtle. Dr. Woodruff, Mrs. Moyer and her baby were lodged*

> *in jail. The arrests were made on telegraphic instructions from Chief of Police Hayes of Lawrence, Kan.*
>
> *"I do not understand what the matter is," said Dr. Woodruff. "I came here to make my home in Oregon. This arrest is an outrage and I propose to make someone suffer."*

It is not known whether Dr. Woodruff was able to follow through on his threat to "make someone suffer," but apparently, he did not suffer either, as there is no record of his being convicted on these charges. He continued to practice medicine in Portland until his death on June 21, 1930.

During the summer of 1898, Bennie Owen worked in a drugstore in Arkansas City. When the store closed at 6:00 p.m., there was still a lot of daylight left—enough, Bennie thought, for a baseball game. A commodity as precious as daylight should not be squandered, he believed. So, ever the energetic and enterprising young man, he talked to his brothers in the Elks Lodge and the businessmen in Arkansas City and convinced them that it would be a good idea to organize a twilight baseball league. The city fathers went along with the idea, and a six-team league, comprising primarily men who worked in the railroad shops, was formed. Bennie charged a dime for admission to the games and soon had enough to build a grandstand and a board fence around the field. "Bennie's Field," as it were, was to last several years in the south-central Kansas town. This would not be the last athletic facility Bennie Owen would build.

MR. YOST

"Hurry Up" was his nickname, and "Hurry up" was his game, as he explained in his book, *Football for Player and Spectator*: "Hurry up and be the first man to line up. Hurry up all the time. Football is not a slow or lazy man's game. Hurry up, football is a game of hurry, hurry, hurry. Hurry up and get into every play. Football is played by eleven men. Spectators are not wanted on the field; their place is in the grandstand."

It was at the University of Michigan where Fielding Harris Yost fashioned the career that would lead him to the College Football Hall of Fame, but for one golden football autumn, he led Kansas University to the greatest season in the history of that august institution. On the first day of practice in the fall of 1899, at the foot of Mount Oread, the Jayhawks quickly realized that their new coach's philosophy of football was quite different from the wily Woodruff's.

Woodruff's game was predicated on the idea of simply overpowering his opponents physically. Yost relied on speed and stealth. He pioneered the "no-huddle" and "fast break" offense. When a play was blown dead, he wanted his quarterback—whether he was twenty yards away from the line of scrimmage or under a pile of players, or both—to shout out the signals for the next play immediately. Then he wanted his men to hurry up and line up and run another play as quickly as they could. His teams would do this over and over again until their opponents were dropping from exhaustion trying to keep up. The *Kansas University Weekly* reported that the Jayhawks reeled off eighteen plays in 4.0 minutes against Nebraska in 1899, an average of 13.3 seconds per play. This is at least twice as fast as modern teams run plays.

Yost was the first coach to use linebackers in his defense. He was a great teacher of football techniques: blocking, tackling, stiff-arming, side-stepping and kicking—especially kicking. His prize pupil that fall was his diminutive quarterback and team captain, Benjamin Gilbert Owen. Harold Keith referred to Bennie as "Yost's Boy Wonder."

Before the forward pass was legalized in 1906, many teams used "onside kicks" in much the same manner as modern teams use the passing game. In those days the rules allowed the punting team to retain possession of the ball if one of their men recovered the kick. Thus, if a kicker was skillful enough to place the punt (i.e., onside kick) in a certain spot on the field, one of his backs or ends could run to that place and recover the ball for a twenty-, thirty- or forty-yard gain. Yost worked with Bennie for hours on end until he was able to kick the old pumpkin of a football they played with in those days almost as accurately as a modern-day quarterback can throw the ball, thus enabling KU to gobble up huge chunks of yardage.

Bennie Owen is prominently mentioned in accounts of the 1899 games as reported by the *Kansas University Weekly*, which described him to be "as reliable a quarterback as could be wished." The paper also tells of Bennie's blocking a punt against Ottawa, making "great gains" versus Haskell, ripping off "a beautiful twenty yard dash, sidestepping and dodging" against Washburn and booting a seventy-yard punt in the Missouri game.

A few days before the Emporia game, Bennie developed severe boils on his kicking foot. Despite the painfully swollen foot (he normally wore a size six shoe but, on this day, had to have a size nine), he played every minute of the 35–0 KU victory. His mother must have been proud.

After their perfect 10-0 season, the Jayhawks were honored at a banquet sponsored by the Merchants' Athletic Club of Lawrence. Coach Yost gave a short address entitled "Our Reasons for Winning," in which he said that "every man had kept his eye on the ball" and that they had "worked harmoniously together throughout the season." Then Dr. James Naismith, who had invented the game of basketball and was currently the Kansas coach, spoke of "the true athlete," saying he was "a gentleman who takes pleasure in sport for sport's sake." Bennie Owen was asked to speak, but he limited his remarks to thanking the Athletic Club for their hospitality.

The Jayhawks had originally scheduled an eleventh game that season. Their opponent was to be the University of the Territory of Oklahoma, then coached by the scholarly English professor Vernon E. Parrington, who had learned the game at Harvard. However, only a few days before the contest was to be played, the Oklahomans received word from the Kansas football manager that the varsity team had disbanded for the season and the game would have to be canceled. But he went on to say that if he were advanced enough money to cover their travel expenses to and from Norman, he would guarantee that a team he called the Kansas Stars, composed mostly of varsity players with a few KU students as subs, would come south to Indian Territory and play the game.

The Oklahomans quickly forwarded the money only to learn three days before the agreed-on date that this game, too, had been canceled. The KU manager offered no explanation, nor did he refund their money. So, Parrington (or perhaps it was university president David Ross Boyd) fired off a letter to Professor Adams, chairman of the University of Kansas athletic association, demanding an explanation. Adams replied that the matter would be brought to the attention of the association. This was the last anyone in Norman ever heard about the game.

After the 1899 season, Bennie returned to play with the Arkansas City town team on weekends in December (as he had done in 1898). On both of these occasions, his opponents, very much aware of his quarterbacking skills, demanded that he play only in the line. So the 130-pound Owen played guard and gained valuable knowledge of line play that served him well when he became a coach.

However, before closing the book on the Jayhawks' season, there is one more affair that merits discussion, *l' affaire Krebs*, as it came to be known. This is important because it is illustrative of the state of college football at the turn of the twentieth century not just in Kansas but also across the nation.

The gist of the Krebs affair is that apparently, Yost sought the services of a hired gun in hopes of defeating KU's greatest rivals, Nebraska, Washburn and Missouri, which he did, by scores of 36–20, 23–0 and 34–6, respectively. Rollo Krebs, a strapping six-foot-three, 210-pound man, starred in all three games. In the season finale, the tenacious Teutonic tackle sent three Missouri men to the hospital on stretchers.

The party line on Krebs was that he had recently moved with his parents from Trinidad, Colorado, to Birmingham, Kansas. He decided to enroll at KU in the fall of 1899, and since he had played "a little" high school football in Trinidad, he thought he would try out for the varsity squad. Yost explained that he did not let Krebs play until the eighth game of the season because of his "inexperience."

However, when KU students turned out to welcome their heroes home after the Missouri victory, Krebs was nowhere to be found, and rumors began to circulate that he may not have been the raw rookie Yost claimed. Harold C. Evans wrote, in an August 1940 *Kansas Historical Quarterlies* article entitled "College Football in Kansas":

> *The Krebs mystery was solved at last in 1934. The "phantom tackle" at that time 62 years of age and a mining engineer at Charleston, West Virginia, came back to Lawrence the day before the Missouri game as guest of honor at a belated celebration. Krebs admitted that he had never been a resident either of Trinidad, Col. or Birmingham, Kan. His gridiron experience before his brief Kansas career consisted of five years' varsity competition at the University of West Virginia* [which, perhaps not coincidentally, just happened to be Fielding Yost's alma mater] *and a year in the professional ranks. He explained his disappearance at the conclusion of the 1899 campaign by stating tersely that he came to KU to play football, not to acquire an education.*

A Jayhawk in Paris

In the spring of 1900, Bennie Owen earned a letter in both baseball and track and field. He played second base on a Jayhawk team that finished 12-4. In track competition, he ran the mile; threw shot put, despite weighing only 135 pounds and, according to the KU yearbook, took first place in the running high jump with a leap of five feet, one and a half inches in an April meet.

That summer, Bennie and two of his football teammates, Fay Moulton (who would later win a bronze medal at the 1904 Olympics in the sixty-meter dash) and Antonio Buzzie, journeyed across the Atlantic to visit the Paris Exposition. Unfortunately, very little was recorded about this trip. Harold Keith had one sentence about it, and neither Bennie's daughter, Dorothy Bryan, nor any of his grandchildren recall him ever mentioning it. Whatever the details may have been, one can imagine three young men from America's heartland must have had a great time in Paris.

Alexandre Gustave Eiffel's tower was eleven years old when Bennie visited Paris, and it is a good bet that he climbed every one of its 1,740 steps to reach the highest platform, from which he could view a panorama—forty-two miles in all directions—of the French countryside. The World Exposition of 1900, which was visited by fifty million people, was located just west of the Eiffel Tower at a point where the Seine veers southward. It was billed as a "review of the century" and intended to showcase the greatest achievements in technology, science and art over the past one hundred years. However, critics thought the planners overreached. The web page of the "History of World Expositions" proclaimed it a "bombastic, thoughtless dissipation of energy" and reported, "The exhibition offered so much of everything that it was given the nickname 'World Junk Shop.'" Perhaps this is why Bennie Owen did not say much about it.

The one thing that is known for sure about this trip is that it exhausted the funds Bennie had set aside for his education, and there were no athletic scholarships in those days. Now, he had a decision to make.

3
Ichabods, Wolverines and Terrible Swedes

What Is an Ichabod Anyway?

When Bennie got back to Arkansas City, he planned to work until he had saved enough money to complete his premed studies. Then he got a job offer from Washburn College. The school needed a football coach, and it thought the twenty-five-year-old Bennie Owen was just the man to do the job.

It might be overstating the case to call this *the* turning point in Bennie's life but then again, perhaps not. He had to weigh a future in medicine, which had been his goal for at least five years, against a career in coaching. Clearly, he loved athletics, but then, as now, the coaching profession did not promise great job security. No one knows how he arrived at his decision, but whatever his thought process (perhaps he believed he could always go back to school if coaching did not work out), he agreed to go to Topeka and coach the Ichabods.

Washburn was established in 1865 and named for its benefactor, Ichabod Washburn. Washburn gave the school—which admitted blacks and women at a time when this was not fashionable—$25,000, hence the soubriquet Ichabods for the university's athletic teams. Bennie guided Washburn to a record of 6-2 in 1900. His best player was Fred Roberts, who also played an important role in establishing football at the University of Oklahoma (OU).

Roberts grew up on a farm near Mayfield, Kansas, which is about thirty miles (as the meadowlark, the state bird of Kansas, would fly) northwest of Bennie's hometown of Arkansas City. His cousin Lum Roberts was the captain of the University of Oklahoma Territory football team in 1899, and Lum convinced Fred to come and play for the Rough Riders that season. It did not take folks in Norman long to realize that the five-foot-ten, two-hundred-pound Roberts was an exceptional athlete. "He was a cat and a locomotive combined," one of his teammates said. This is how Harold Keith described him: "[He had] sloping shoulders, a low slung torso and calves that bulged like maple ten pins. Because of his long exposure to the Kansas sun and wind in the harvest fields, his skin was burned a deep copper red. When he rolled his sleeve back from his wrist, his arm popped out as big as the average man's thigh."

In his first game, Roberts ran over, around and through the Arkansas defense for two touchdowns, prompting one of the Razorbacks to say, "That big Oklahoma halfback destroyed our hopes of victory. He destroyed our will to win. After trying to stop him we realized it was no one man job." Bill Owen, Bennie's brother, played for an Arkansas City team that defeated the Rough Riders 17–11 that year, but he had high praise for Roberts, "He was a wildcat, fast and good."

When Roberts learned that Bennie Owen would coach at Washburn in 1900, he returned to his home state because he thought this would be a great chance to learn from a man who really knew the game. But when Owen moved on, Roberts came back to Norman as a player-coach for the Rough Riders in 1901. Then he returned to Kansas to devote his energies full-time to farming. However, in both 1902 and 1903, he was lured out of retirement to play in a couple critical contests for the Rough Riders, nevermind that he was not enrolled at the university. His coach for those games, Mark McMahon, said of him, "Fred Roberts was as great a half as I ever saw." He was quick as lightening and strong as an ox, weighed about 200, was never hurt, and could think in action. I played against him in the Texas-Oklahoma game of 1901 and he was great."

Try as they might, after the 1903 season, the Oklahomans could not entice Roberts to leave his wheat fields for football. However, for several years, whenever OU was to face a tough opponent, the cry of "Let's go get old Fred" would reverberate around the campus. Forty years after Roberts played his last game, there were old-timers around Norman who still proclaimed him to be the best halfback who ever played there.

RUNNING BETWEEN ROWS OF CORN AND DODGING STALKS

Roberts was by no means the only arrow in Bennie's quiver. Wade Moore was a hard-running halfback as well as a good punter and place kicker. A player identified only by his surname, Gill was a strong blocker and a good tackler. He also gained a lot of yardage on the "tackle around" play, a maneuver that Bennie would employ with great success later at OU, the rules allowing linemen to carry the ball then. Six-foot-seven, 286-pound guard "Fatty" White did not run with the ball, but he ripped open large holes for those who did.

Just before the season opener, the *Washburn Review* proclaimed, "The very best material available will be used in the [football] suits and the jerseys will be a work of art. The members of the team will be beautiful to behold." Perhaps this is why Fred Roberts always wore his blue Washburn jersey in 1901 when he played at Oklahoma.

The article further stated, "Owen, the coach, at KU for two years, the last year as captain and quarter back, has the reputation of being one of the fastest and headiest gentlemen of the gridiron. He possesses keen judgment in picking material and in discerning a man's possibilities. We invite the University of Kansas to watch Mr. Owen's business methods win and beware."

KU should have heeded this last remark because the highlight of the 1900 season was the Ichabods' two victories over the Jayhawks. In the first game at Lawrence, Roberts scored two touchdowns, and Washburn gained its first victory ever over Kansas. In the return match at Topeka, Gill and Moore scored two TDs each, and this time, the score was 24–0. Roberts didn't tally in this game but the *Topeka State Journal* reported, "For Washburn, Fred Roberts played a wonderful game and repeatedly took the ball for long gains." It must be noted that Bennie did not achieve these victories at the expense of his former coach Fielding Yost. After spending just one year at Kansas, Yost moved west to lead the Stanford Cardinal.

The Ichabods' two losses came at the hands of the Denver Athletic Club and the Haskell Indians. The Denver game was especially noteworthy. For the one and only time all season, Bennie Owen quarterbacked the Ichabods and, by all accounts, played a stellar game. The *Washburn Review* reported that on one defensive stand "Bennie manages to soar high enough in the air to strike the giant with his shoulder; he nearly capsized one of the giant's floating ribs." For some reason, the newspapers referred to the Denver players, both as a team and individually, as giants with a small *g*.

The game hinged on two highly controversial plays. In the first half, the Ichabods thought they had held Denver on a goal line stand, but the refs inexplicably gave the giants an extra down, which they took advantage of and pushed across the game's only TD. Then, with time winding down in the fourth quarter, Bennie reeling off plays in rapid fire fashion à la the Yost "hurry up style" and the mammoth Smith opening huge holes in the Denver line for his backs to break through, Washburn advanced to the Denver three. A touchdown would have given the Ichabods a tie, and if the normally reliable Moore could have converted the extra point, they would have won. But before the Ichabod center could snap the ball for the next play, a Denver player by the name of Gallagher snatched it out of his hands and started yelling that he had recovered a fumble. The refs awarded the ball to Denver, who ran out the clock and preserved the 5–0 victory.

The Washburn fans and players thought they had been cheated, and even the Denver sportswriters agreed with them. The *Denver Post* wrote, "And to be candid Gallagher stole the ball and claimed to have got it on a fumble but as no one saw it the play went on."

The *Denver Times* also clearly thought the Ichabods had outplayed the giants:

> *These big husky corn-fed farmers worked with the precision of a piece of machinery and the fierce attacks they made upon the Denver Athletic Club was by all odds the feature of the game. The great DAC line which has been vaunted as invulnerable went down before these farmers. It not only went down, but it was mowed down and swept out of the way or trampled underneath by these husky collegians who got their idea of the game running through rows of corn and dodging stalks from ten to twenty feet high. They dodged around the big men in the Denver line just as if they considered them stalks.*

In any case, the Ichabods did not have much time to dwell on the loss because they had to play another game against Colorado College in Colorado Springs three days later. Bennie had scheduled the games so close together in order to conserve on travel expenses, something he would do later at Oklahoma several times.

The day before the game, Bennie and his players visited Pikes Peak and the Garden of the Gods and enjoyed a reception sponsored by the coeds of the college. The game was played on a field blanketed with snow, but this did not slow down the relentless Wade Moore, who scored three touchdowns and led Washburn to a 29–0 victory. The *Washburn Review* was quite pleased with the road trip. It wrote:

> *The Denver people freely admit that the Washburn football team is the best college team that ever played on Colorado soil. Our play was so fast that the DAC men scarcely had time to find their positions. Their so-called giants were frequently compelled to stop and recuperate. Owen supplied the team with ginger, made lightning passes* [read passes here as laterals], *and was in every play.*
>
> *Washburn used no substitutes…Coach Owen's training has accomplished wonders. It is certainly marvelous that in these two games in Colorado not a single Washburn man was seriously hurt. The Denver game was the hardest that our boys ever played, and then only three days later the game with the strongest college in Colorado was played in a blinding snow storm.*

Owen said, "The trip as a whole was a success. Although we were defeated at Denver, our boys outplayed them and showed better training. They did not consider themselves beaten and proved they could play good ball by defeating Colorado College, the strongest college team in the state, by a score of 29–5."

The Ichabods' other loss came at the hands of the Haskell Indians with a score of 11–5. Haskell always fielded one of the best teams on the prairies in this era. In fact, Bennie had many titanic struggles with the team after he took over the reins at OU. Washburn had defeated the Indians 11–0 in the season opener, which proved to be Haskell's only loss that year.

Bennie wanted to quarterback the Ichabods in the rematch, but the Indians would not stand for it. Whether that was the reason or not, Bennie's boys clearly did not have their usual zip that afternoon. The *Topeka State Journal* reported:

> *It was the hardest fought game since the historic bloody battle between KU and Baker in 1893. The Indians were never known before to play football as they played Saturday.*
>
> *The Indians were in better training and showed it in the second half when the Washburn players began to exhibit signs of fatigue and took the time limit for rests after each play. At the end of the game the braves were as full of spirit and play as at the beginning while Washburn showed the effects of the play more than in any other game of the season.*

The following week, the Ichabods returned to form and beat Ottawa 16–0 on Thanksgiving Day. Although Ottawa was not a strong team, finishing the year at 2-4-2, for some reason, this game attracted an overflow crowd of two thousand, by far the largest of the season at Topeka. They came on horseback, in carriages and on foot. Some people climbed on the roofs of their houses, and others shinned up telephone poles to watch the fray. A few hardy young men even sat atop the barbed-wire fence that surrounded the field. Moore fractured his ankle on the first play of the game, but Roberts and Gill tallied TDs so that the outcome was never in doubt.

In its recap of the season, the *Washburn Review* stated, "In the football world Washburn College has taken huge strides toward the front. With interest the people looked on our growth, and with amazement they watched Bennie Owen's business methods win…Never before has Washburn had such a well trained team."

Bennie spent the following summer umpiring in the Missouri Valley Baseball League. This was a Class D league, composed of teams with very colorful nicknames, including the Iola Gasbags, Jefferson Convicts and Nevada Lunatics. It was too bad it lasted only three seasons. Some time that summer, Bennie got a call from his old coach Fielding Yost who had fled Palo Alto to become the coach of the Michigan Wolverines. He needed an assistant and wanted to know if Bennie was interested. He was, and in the fall of 1901, Bennie was reunited with his mentor in Ann Arbor, Michigan.

THE POINT-A-MINUTE MEN

Fielding Yost coached at Michigan for twenty-five seasons. His record was 165-29-10. From 1901 through 1905, his Wolverines played fifty-six consecutive games without a loss. The only blemish on this record was a 6–6 tie at Minnesota in 1903. A 2–0 loss to a University of Chicago team coached by Amos Alonzo Stagg in the final game of the 1905 season ended the streak. During these years, the Wolverines outscored their opponents 2,821–40 which means the average score was 50–1, hence the appellation "point-a-minute men."

Yost did not accomplish this by playing a bunch of Humpty Dumptys. If their losses to Michigan were not counted, Yost's opponents would have had a combined winning percentage of .695, and three of these teams would have posted perfect records.

His greatest team was the 1901 squad, which posted a record of 11-0, defeating Stanford 49–0 in the first-ever Rose Bowl game. That season, the maize and blue outscored opponents by a cumulative total of 550–0, thus stating a pretty strong case for being the greatest team in the history of college football. This powerhouse was led by two All-Americans who would later be voted into the College Football Hall of Fame: fullback Neil Snow and halfback "Willie" Heston.

The five-foot-eight, 190-pound Snow was a great all-around athlete. He won ten letters at Michigan, four each in football and baseball and two in track. The New York Giants tried to ink him to a baseball contract, but Snow declined, preferring to go into business instead. Walter Camp said of him, "No college ever developed a better all-around athlete," and the venerable sports scribe Grantland Rice called him "a football marvel, hurdler, jumper, and shot-putter and one of the best [base] ball players Michigan ever produced." Rice also considered him among the three best all-around college athletes ever along with Jim Thorpe and Elmer Oliphant.

Willie Heston, at five feet, eight inches tall and 185 pounds, was built like Snow but probably possessed more foot speed. Michigan legend has it that he regularly beat Archie Hahn (the "Milwaukee Meteor" and winner of gold medals in the sixty-, one-hundred- and two-hundred-meter sprints at the 1904 Olympics) at distances up to forty yards. His 72 career touchdowns still stand as a Michigan record. Yost always maintained that he actually scored 106 TDs and that on several occasions he rushed for over five hundred yards in a single game.

The toughest opponent for the Wolverines that season may well have been the scrub team they scrimmaged against every day in practice, and this is where Bennie Owen fits into the picture. Bennie coached and quarterbacked the scrubs, who regularly pushed the varsity players to their limits. A reporter from the *Detroit News* watched an early season scrimmage and filed this report:

> *The scrubs kicked off and Sweeley made a dodging runback of fifty yards. The scrubs held their opponents at the center of the field. At this point the celebrated Bennie Owens* [sic] *went in at quarter to run the scrubs. The scrubs simply tore the varsity defense to pieces. Then Owens gave a fine quarterback kick and Hincks saved it. The scrubs worked the ball to the varsity 25-yard line and then lost it on downs. Heston ran it out of danger. Back and forth the leather was shoved...The practice was the fiercest struggle seen on Regents Field this year.*

This was probably not the first and certainly not the last time Bennie's surname was misspelled. Long after he had retired from coaching, some writers were still adding an *s*.

Polo Matches and Chariot Races

In 1901, the Tournament of Roses Parade Committee thought something more exciting than the usual polo match was needed to enliven the festivities. Ultimately, the committee decided to hold a football game on January 1, 1902. Committee chairman James Wagner invited the "best team in the west," Fielding H. Yost's Michigan Wolverines. Their opponent was to be Stanford University, "the champion of the Pacific Coast universities." On December 17, when the Wolverines boarded the train for Pasadena, there were six inches of snow on the ground. When they arrived eight days later, they were greeted by sunny skies and temperatures in the eighties.

Stanford's record going into this game was 3-1-2. More telling still were the facts that it had never scored more than twelve points in any one game and had managed a total of only thirty-four points for the whole season. Michigan usually scored that many points in the first half. Thus, the 49–0 shellacking Stanford absorbed from the Wolverines should not have come as a surprise to the Rose Bowl Parade Committee. Yet the committee was so upset with this outcome (even though it made a handsome profit of $3,161.86) that it did not schedule another football game for sixteen years. The following year, it opted to stage a "Roman-style" chariot race.

In this first-ever Rose Bowl football game, Neil Snow and Willie Heston put on quite a show for the eight thousand fans who had crowded into Tournament Park. Snow rushed for 107 yards and scored twenty-five points on five touchdowns, both of which are records that stand to this day. Heston did not score, but his 170 rushing yards (on eighteen carries) was a record that stood for fifty-nine years. With eight minutes remaining to be played, the Stanford Cardinal captain Ralph Fisher walked over to Yost, shook his hand and conceded defeat.

It was a great experience for Bennie Owen to be a part of such a memorable season, but he was by nature a head coach, not an assistant. He liked to be the man in charge. So, when Bethany College offered him the chance to once again lead his own team, he quickly accepted.

Gentlemanliness and Good Feeling

A river runs through the rolling fields of wheat in central Kansas, the Smoky Hill River. On this river once stood the Smoky Valley Mill, where prize-winning flour from hard winter wheat was ground. The river runs south and then bends back east of the town of Lindsborg—or "Little Sweden," as it is known. Bennie Owen spent three years there coaching at Bethany College, and he loved every minute of it. Why wouldn't he? It was, and is, a beautiful place where time is measured in seasons—planting and harvesting—rather than in hours and minutes.

The reverend Dr. Carl Aaron Swensson and a few other Swedish Lutherans founded Bethany Academy on October 15, 1881. The first classes were held in the sacristy of the Bethany Lutheran Church with ten students attending. The school grew rapidly, and in 1889, it became known as Bethany College.

Bethany played its first football game on November 14, 1893, against Kansas Wesleyan University. According to Robert A. Lundgren in *A Century of Bethany Football*, the boys from Bethany were "coached" by Professor Kjellstrand, who "gave instructions as to the latest tactics of the popular game." Luther Dahlsten started the game at quarterback but was soon moved to left end by Kjellstrand, who took over at quarter. A couple of other faculty members also played for the Swedes, V.A.C. Henmon and J.E. Welin.

Although the Lutherans were slaughtered 48–0 by the Methodists, the locals did not seem to be too disappointed. The *Lindsborg News* described the contest as "an interesting affair. Taking time and practice into consideration, the Bethany boys distinguished themselves in a creditable manner." And the *Bethany Messenger* complimented the team for "playing a plucky game throughout, although they were no match for the Wesleyans. The game was characterized throughout by gentlemanliness and good feeling." A few weeks later, the same paper observed, "Football seems to be the craze, tennis, croquet, and baseball have been crowded out."

This was the only game Bethany played in 1893. The following year, the school played only two games, both of them against Wesleyan. The Swedes won the first 24–12 in Salina, but the Methodists captured the return match 16–6 in Lindsborg. Then Bethany took a six-year hiatus from the sport.

According to Emory Kempton Lindquist in *From Bethany in Kansas: The History of a College*, on February 2, 1895, the following resolution was passed by the college's board of directors:

> *Whereas, the sport of Foot Ball has caused much unfavorable comment among our friends and patrons, and, Whereas the board is assured that Foot Ball is not a suitable game for our students giving occasions for brutality and other base passions, and often accompanied with painful and dangerous accidents, therefore be it Resolved, that Foot Ball is hereafter prohibited at this institution.*

In a letter to the *Topeka Capitol*, President Swensson explained that the college had banned the sport because "it is brutal; it is dangerous; it is a poor substitute for gymnastics; it causes students to become negligent in studies; it includes noisy boisterousness, savage all-penetrating yelling, free and unpleasant exhibition of unrestricted lung power."

Conditioning, Innovation and Motivational Leadership

However, in May 1901, a faculty committee submitted a petition to Swensson urging him to reinstate football at Bethany. The committee claimed, "The game promotes courage and manliness; it exercises the mental faculties; it arouses college spirit and enthusiasm; it develops keenness and accuracy of thought; it attracts to our school the healthiest and most robust students; the sentiment of our community seems to be entirely favorable to the game." This last statement was certainly true. It seems to have been only the hierarchy of the Lutheran Church that was so adamantly opposed to football.

Apparently swayed by these arguments, Swenson agreed to give the sport another chance provided the following conditions were met: (1) If the student is a minor, he shall procure the consent of his parents or guardian; (2) He must submit to a medical examination as to his physical soundness; and (3) Each student desiring to be on a contesting team must do his work in his classes so that it is satisfactory to the faculty. Thus, in the fall of 1901, a "team" composed of faculty and students played eight games, winning five, losing two and tying one. The following year, Swensson decided to make a greater commitment to the sport, so he brought in Bennie Owen to coach the Swedes and teach chemistry at a salary of $500 a year. Although he was one semester shy of completing his bachelor's degree when he left the University of Kansas, Bennie certainly seemed to be well qualified to teach chemistry, having taken courses in pharmacy, pharmacognosy (the study of medicines derived from natural sources), general chemistry, microscopic examination of drugs, organic chemistry, physical chemistry and urinary analysis and toxicology.

Harold C. Evans, in "College Football in Kansas," wrote:

> *The early 1900s were marked by the rise of the Haskell Indians and "Terrible Swedes" of Bethany College, Lindsborg...Bennie Owen was engaged at the*

> *Lindsborg school and the fruit of his efforts was a delight to residents of the Smoky Hill Valley…Owen's debut at Lindsborg was heralded in* The Lindsborg Record *as follows, "We are particularly fortunate in securing the well known Bennie Owen as coach at Bethany this year. All lovers of the gridiron sport remember his magnificent work at quarterback with KU…His name has a permanent spot in the football history at the university. As coach for Washburn the year they were in their glory and swept the state his work is well remembered. Owen served last year as an assistant coach for the University of Michigan and contributed liberally to the success of their great team." What Owen did to make the Swedes terrible is not definitely known, but they certainly performed in a fashion that struck fear from Lawrence to the Rocky Mountains and to the plains of Oklahoma.*

Actually, we do know quite a bit about how Bennie was able to make the Swedes so terrible. Owen's success as a coach can be attributed to three major factors: conditioning, innovation and motivational leadership. Owen implemented the "hurry up" offense he had learned from Yost. In order to run this for an entire game, his teams had to be in peak physical condition, and he made sure they were. After the daily scrimmage, Bennie would have his team run two miles out to the Smokey Hill River and back.

Bennie did not just stand on the sidelines and blow his whistle. He pulled on his moleskins and got into the scrimmages to demonstrate technique, and he always ran with his team on their cross-country jaunts. His quarterback in 1903–04, Quince Banbury, told Harold Keith several years later:

> *Many's the time Bennie would start practice by making us run two or three miles out of town to some cow pasture and then say, "Well it's getting late. You'll have to hurry back to town in time for dinner." And run us back. But Bennie always ran with us. Once when we were coming home on the train from a game, Bennie asked the conductor to stop the train two miles from Lindsborg and we all climbed off, Bennie too, and trotted the rest of the way to work the stiffness out.*

Besides wearing down opponents, Owen's rigorous conditioning paid off in another respect, as Robert G. Lundgren wrote in *A Century of Bethany Football*: "No one has ever received injuries amounting to more than bruises or sprains in any game played on the local gridiron."

It was at Bethany that Bennie first began to exhibit his genius for innovation. He started a training table and always ate with his players.

He devised plays and formations that had never before been seen on the windswept western prairies. He used both a balanced and unbalanced line. He ran spinners, cross bucks and "possum" plays. This is how Banbury described the quarterback spinner:

> *We would run three or four plays off tackle until they thought that was all we had. Then we put the spinner on. If we were going to the right, I would take the ball from the center and fake it to our left half who would dive low and hard into the line, pulling everything in to stop the tackle smash. But this time I would keep the ball and staying low, spin to my left and come out into the open behind our left end as a personal interferer and make a long run to the right. Thus I had five interferers if we were using tackle back formation, and four if we were using our regular formation. Either way it was a surprise play but just to make sure the defensive right tackle or right halfback didn't spoil it (the defensive right end would be hepped out too far to reach it) Les Petterson, our left tackle, would use the cartwheel block* [a maneuver outlawed years ago], *checking the linesman in front of him with his body hurling his leg out behind him to discourage the defensive right tackle or right half. The cartwheel block was plenty wicked. After a defensive player got a foot in his face, he didn't come in so fast.*

The "possum play" required one of Bennie's ends to do a little impromptu acting. If the Swedes ran a play to the right side of the field, the right end would feign an injury and lie on the ground writhing in pain instead of lining up for the next play, which would be an end sweep to the other side of the field. Then, on the ensuing play, the quarterback would execute an on-sides kick (a maneuver Bennie had perfected at KU) to the right. The "injured" end would miraculously be healed, jump up, catch the ball and usually run for a long gain.

Probably the most lethal weapon in Bethany's arsenal was the cross buck, which he would also run with great success at Oklahoma. When the ball was snapped, the fullback would smash into the line behind the right guard, and the quarterback would fake the ball to the left half, who was following him into the hole. This usually pulled the defense to the right side of the formation. Then the quarterback would hand the ball to the right halfback, who had delayed a count and then hit into the line behind his left tackle. If the back got cleanly through the line of scrimmage, he would cut to the sideline away from the defensive pursuit. As mundane as this and the spinner play may seem today, they represented a great departure from the straight-ahead power football most teams used one hundred years ago.

In *Smoky Valley People: A History of Lindsborg, Kansas*, Emory Kempton Lindquist wrote, "Bethany's teams under Bennie Owen played fast, hard and clean. Officials and spectators everywhere praised the fine conduct of the 'Terrible Swedes.' They played with alertness and knew exactly what they wanted to do. Training rules were observed with strict concern. The teamwork was outstanding. Bennie Owen was a leader of men. An enthusiastic team played to win for coach and Alma Mater."

If there is one sentence that describes the coaching career and, indeed, the life of Bennie Owen, it would be, as Lindquist wrote, "Bennie Owen was a leader of men." From the days of his childhood in St. Louis to his college years at KU and everywhere he coached, though not a large man, Bennie was always the pack leader, the alpha male. He had about him a quiet confidence, a self-assurance that inspired confidence in others. He also knew how to use his considerable stubbornness to his best advantage. The Reverend Kenneth Feaver would later say about him, "Genial man that he was, he made it clear to all about him that he knew who he was and who he was not, and no one should question this. With a grace that could disintegrate any would-be challenger, through the ripples of a smile across his face he communicated with utmost clarity that he believed in himself and no one, with impunity, debated this. It was a fascinating suggestion of strength."

Rockar! Stockar!

After winning his seventh World Series championship with the New York Yankees in 1958, Casey Stengel magnanimously said, "I couldn't a done it without my players." And neither could Bennie Owen. At Bethany, he was not lacking for talented players. Quince Banbury was a swift and crafty quarterback, and under Bennie's tutelage, he mastered the art of the onside kick. His brother Win was a hard-running halfback. The Swede's fullback was Luther "Human Battering Ram" Stormquist. Bennie's best lineman was the 224-pound Leslie Petterson. Les's three brothers—Dave, Alfred and Andrew—were also husky Lutheran farm boys and tough competitors. "They were all fine clean boys and loved football so well that they would have got up early to play before breakfast," Bennie said. What more could a coach have asked for?

The Swedes' hard hitting on the gridiron belied a gentle nature. Les Petterson preferred knitting socks and mittens on train trips rather than playing card games, and there were other Terrible Swedes who liked to crochet. Bennie Owen never coached a finer, more dedicated squad of student athletes than these young men.

On September 21, 1902, the *Lindsborg News* stated, "Since the arrival of Coach Owen, football has attracted more attention at the college than ever before. Practice games are played every afternoon and everything possible will be done to make the Bethany ball club the best in the state." And it was. The Swedes outscored their opponents 371–22 en route to a record of 8-1-1. Their only loss came at the hands of Washburn, with a score of 12–11, when a last-second Bethany field goal bounced off the cross bar. However, the Swedes avenged this defeat a month later by walloping the Ichabods 72–0. They fought to a 0–0 tie with the rugged Haskell Indians at midseason and then beat them 11–0 in the season-ending rematch. They also pounded the Kansas Aggies 40–0 that season.

The year 1902 was when the famous "Rockar Stockar" cheer was written. It seems a group of students, including E.O. Deere, who later became the college dean, had grown tired of the old "Rah! Rah!" cheers. In the fall of 1902, some of these students were taking a class in Swedish mythology and learned of the legend of Thor flying through space in a chariot pulled by goats. In this same course, they studied the myth of a certain Swedish jarl (a Scandinavian noble ranking just below a king) who loaded all his possessions on a raft and set out to cross the Baltic Sea. He vowed that he would build a great city wherever the raft came ashore. Combining these two stories, the students came up with "Rockar! Stockar!" Emory Lindquist published this cheer and its English translation in *Smoky Valley People*:

> *Rockar! Stockar! (The Jarl wore a jacket or coat—a* rockar. *He was on a log raft, or* stockar, *braving the perils of the Baltic, floating to the peninsula where he founded Stockholm.)*
>
> *Thor och hans bockar! (Thor going forward with lightning speed, driving his goats from pinnacle to pinnacle, irresistibly through all opposition.)*
>
> *Kor igenom! Kor igenom! (Drive on through! Drive on through!)*
>
> *Tju! Tju! Tju! (A Swedish interjection)*
>
> *Bethania (Bethany)*

In 1903 the Swedes were 7-1-1, tying Glasco 0–0 and losing to Washburn 12–6. In *A Century of Bethany Football*, Robert Lundgren said of the Washburn game:

> *The only loss in 1903 was to Washburn 12–6 in a very controversial game officiated by students from Topeka. No penalty was called on the home team, while many holding and off side calls were assessed* [to] *the Swedes, particularly when Bethany was about to score. The corrupt officiating infuriated the Bethany players who refused to continue the game several times in protest. The final score robbed Bethany of an undefeated season, by supposedly losing to a team it had defeated 72–0 the year before. The "stolen" game in 1903 caused Bethany to drop Washburn from its schedule. The two teams did not play each other again until 1925.*

On Thanksgiving Day 1903, the Terrible Swedes met the Rough Riders of the University of Oklahoma Territory at Sportsman's Park in Oklahoma City. Two hundred Bethany fans came south on a chartered Santa Fe special to watch their champions, and it was not just the Kansans who wanted to see the Swedes. The *Daily Oklahoman* wrote, "The Terrible Swedes have never scheduled any games this far south before, but their reputation for fast and scientific football has preceded them. As a consequence, lots of lovers of the game here are glad of the chance to see them play: They want to judge for themselves whether the Swedes are all that reports say they are."

Midway through the first quarter, Win Banbury capped a 96-yard touchdown drive with a 30-yard sprint. The Swedes took a 6–0 lead and were never headed. They outgained Oklahoma 240–182 yards and won the game 12–6. Harold Keith gave this account of the game:

> *Bethany's orange and blue banners rippled gaily in the soft autumnal breeze and Bethany's yell* [Rockar! Stockar!] *shouted entirely in the Swedish tongue, was a revelation to the Oklahoma crowd. The Bethany football team was a revelation too. Splendidly conditioned, it ran its plays with frenzied speed, as though striving to sprint the varsity into exhaustion. It amazed the Rough Riders and the crowd too, with the modernity of its tactics…Of all the teams the varsity faced that year the Swedes, while not the strongest, were the fastest, the cleanest, the best behaved, and the best coached.*

Old Dan Patch

Bennie's 1904 Swedes were all victorious, outscoring their opponents 276–20 in seven games. That autumn, Bethany returned to Oklahoma City on Thanksgiving Day for the season finale. This time, the game was played in Colcord Park, where a week earlier, the great pacing horse Dan Patch had performed. The eight-year-old Dan was probably the most famous athlete alive at that time. He drew huge crowds everywhere he raced, and Oklahoma City was no exception. Five thousand people (roughly half the population of Oklahoma City) turned out to watch him. Despite racing on what Charles Leerhsen, the author of *Crazy Good: The True Story of Dan Patch*, called "perhaps the slowest racetrack in North America, a half-mile ring of ankle-deep sand," Dan turned in a 2:03 mile. While this was several seconds off his best time of 1:55, it was nevertheless a track record and the world record for a half-mile track. His owner, Marion Willis Savage, called it "the best performance of Dan's career."

This time, Bethany brought along not only several hundred fans but also a thirteen-piece band, which performed at halftime. The Swedes were even more dominant in this game, trouncing the Rough Riders 39–9. The *Daily Oklahoman* wrote:

> *The attendance at Colcord Park, where the football game occurred was even larger than the crowd that witnessed the famous performance of Dan Patch a week ago... The game was a good one to watch. No credit should be withheld from the Bethany football squad and their coach Mr. Owen. They certainly have a wonderful football machine. Every player knows the game and is in it from start to finish. It is as well to admit they are too fast for the Norman aggregation this year.*

One of Bennie's lettermen that season, Elmer T. Peterson, later became an editorial writer for the *Daily Oklahoman*. Forty-two years after this game was played he penned his thoughts on how the game had changed. "Of course football has improved scientifically since 1904, just like everything else. It has added a lot of smart know-how and 'inside stuff.' Teams are bigger and more powerful. They run faster and with better blocking when they get started. But they take too long getting started. They have lost some of the slashing spontaneity that put thrills into the old game."

After the 1904 season, the Rough Riders' coach Fred Ewing returned to medical school at the University of Chicago. Vernon Parrington,

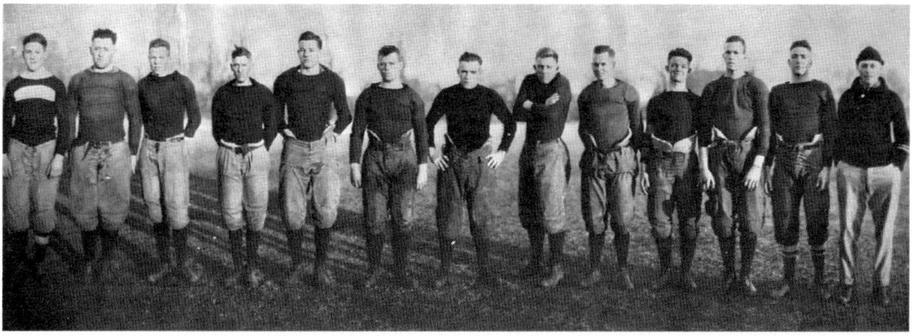

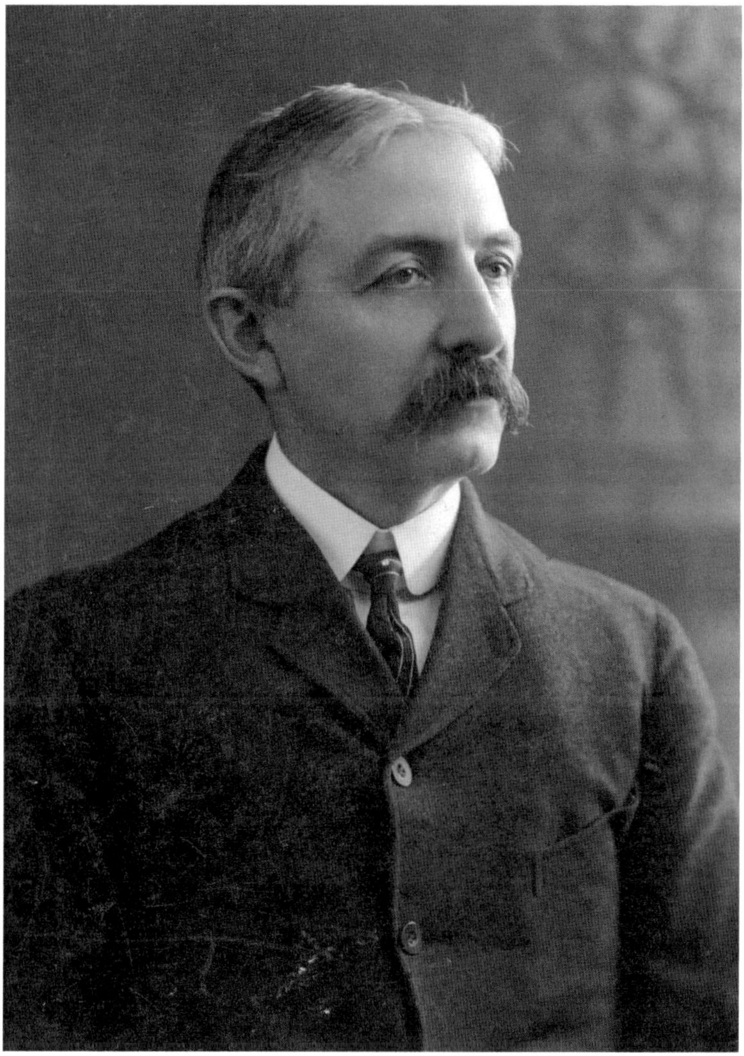

Above: The 1916 varsity football team had a record of six wins and five losses. *Courtesy of the University of Oklahoma's Western History Collection, OUPC 18*

Right: David Ross Boyd, University of Oklahoma president, 1892–1908. *Courtesy of the University of Oklahoma's Western History Collection, Boyd 10.*

Oklahoma's director of athletics, wrote to Bennie Owen and asked if he would be interested in taking over the Oklahoma team. They later met, and Parrington explained to Bennie that although the starting salary would not be large, he thought Owen would have the opportunity to accomplish great things at the Norman campus. Much to the delight and great surprise of both Parrington and university president David Ross Boyd, Bennie agreed to their offer.

4
OKLAHOMA TERRITORY

AN INSTINCT FOR ADVENTURE

In *The University of Oklahoma: A History, Volume I*, David Levy wrote:

> *One of the great mysteries in the story of Oklahoma football is why Bennie Owen decided to come to coach in Norman. Parrington, as head of the Athletic Association, could offer him only $900 for the three-month football season; there was no guarantee of a second year. At Bethany, Owen was being employed for the full academic year as coach and chemistry teacher. Moreover, the financial arrangement at Oklahoma was precarious. Money was still owed to the two previous coaches, McMahan and Ewing, and the Athletic Association was more than $700 in debt.*

And Bennie had a better offer from the University of Pittsburg. He declined the invitation, but his good friend Arthur St. Leger Mosse accepted and, with the help of five of Bennie's former Bethany standouts, fashioned a 10-1 record in 1905, losing only to Cornell, which was also the only team to score on the Panthers. Bennie would later coach against Mosse in 1912–13, when the former iceman took the reins at their alma mater, Kansas University.

It was not exactly like Bennie was moving to the garden spot of the southwest. The population of Norman in 1905 was around 2,500. There

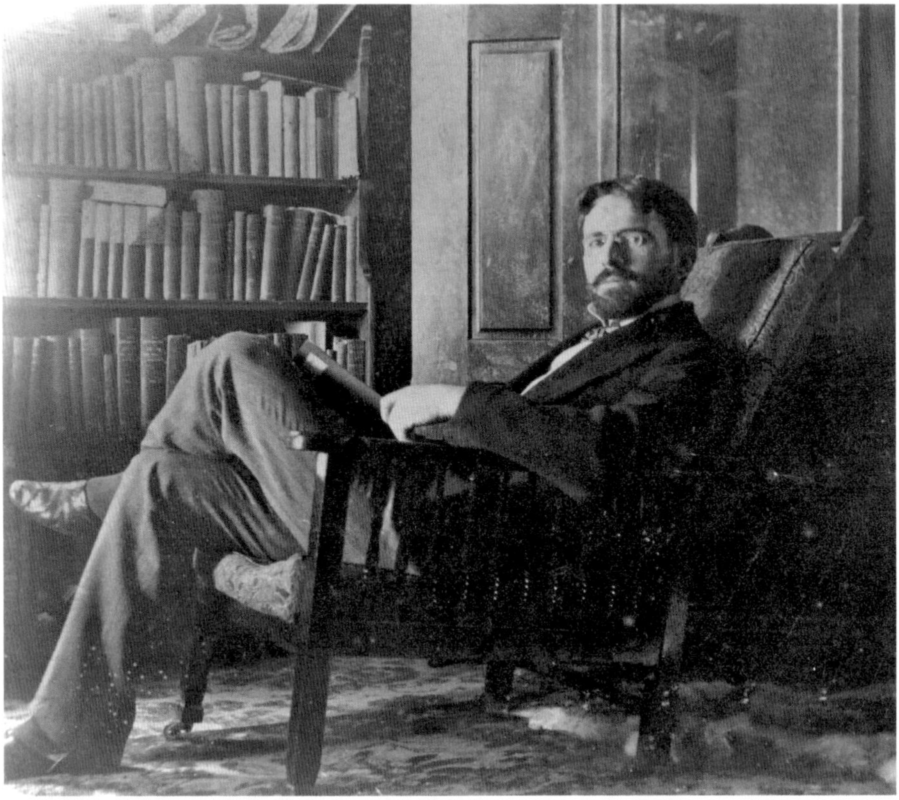

Vernon L. Parrington was the University of Oklahoma football coach (1897–1900) and director of athletics (1897–1907). More significantly, he won the Pulitzer Prize in History in 1928. *Courtesy of the University of Oklahoma's Western History Collection, Rader 8.*

were no paved streets and no bridge across the South Canadian River, and just about the only trees in town were those planted by David Ross Boyd along University Boulevard. Even those were much too small to provide any relief from the incessant wind. When Dr. Stanton Brooks, OU's third president, arrived in 1912, he said, "Norman was the only place I had ever seen where you didn't have to pay money to be shaved; the Southwest wind blew so straight off the river that all you had to do was turn you face one way, then the other, and let the blowing river sand do the job."

So why did Bennie Owen leave a secure job as the football coach and chemistry instructor at Bethany and turn down an attractive offer at an established eastern institution to come to a windswept hamlet on the plains to coach part time at a fledging university? Harold Keith thought, "It was his

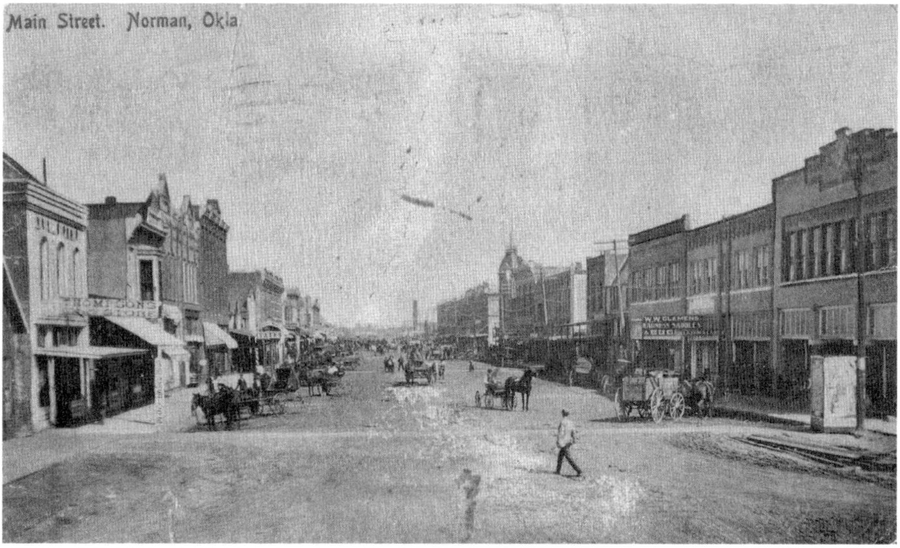

A view of Main Street in Norman, Oklahoma, in 1908. *Courtesy of the University of Oklahoma's Western History Collection, Kraettli 184.*

instinct for adventure speaking out. He was probably thinking of that dusty afternoon south of Arkansas City, when as a boy of seventeen too young to file on a homestead; he had reluctantly turned back his mare Beauty after galloping four miles with the leaders in the Cherokee Strip land run."

Another factor in Bennie's decision to leave Lindsborg may have been that with the sudden death of Dr. Swensson in 1904, Owen had lost his greatest ally against the anti-football forces of the Lutheran Church. He may have been afraid that Bethany's board of directors would convince the new president to shut down the football program, and in 1906, that is exactly what happened.

In a 1907 headline, the *Bethany Messenger* asked, "Are the Sons of Thor Extinct?" The following year, the *Messenger*'s editor made a late-night visit to the abandoned athletic field. As he walked on the dew-laden grass in the moonlight, he was suddenly startled by a strange noise.

> *Out of the still night air rang the cry, "Third down, eight to gain." Out on the bleachers from a thousand lusty throats the yell, "Stone Wall, Stone Wall, Bethany." Distinctly above all the rest could be heard one well-known voice saying, "Play fast, tackle low!" It was Bennie* [Owen] *urging his men to victory. The Swedes hurled themselves like a human battering ram against their opponents' line, crossing the goal after a few minutes of play. A deafening*

> *roar ensued. The grandstand rose to a man, waving their banners and giving their* "Rockar! Sockar!" *But it was a dream. And back through the somber shadows of the night came the echo "How long?"*

The answer to this editor's question was eleven years. Bethany did not field a football team again until 1916.

When Bennie arrived in the autumn of 1905, Oklahoma University had an enrollment of 484 students, which was a 33 percent increase over the previous year. Two new buildings, the Science Hall and the Carnegie Library, had recently been added and brought the total to four. The library was the first that Andrew Carnegie had ever bestowed to a university. Stealing the tune from Yale's "Boola Boola," OU student Arthur M. Alden penned the words to "Boomer Sooner" that fall. A year later, a verse lifted from the North Carolina fight song, "I'm a Tarheel Born," was added to form the final version.

The year 1905 was also when Boyd Field was laid out on what is now the site of the Memorial Union building. Surrounded by a Bois d'Arc hedge and with a grandstand that, at that time, seated five hundred (later enlarged to accommodate three thousand), this would be the site of all OU football games, baseball games and track meets for the next nineteen years.

Owen found a lot of enthusiasm for the new sport on the prairie but not a lot of talent. Very few high schools in Oklahoma Territory were playing football in the early 1900s unlike in the eastern states and even Kansas and Missouri, where the game was much more established. His most experienced player that fall was probably Leonard Runbeck, who had been his center and placekicker at Bethany the year before. Bennie had not proselytized him, but the tall blond Runbeck was so impressed with his mentor that he left the Smoky Hill River country to follow him to the dusty plains of Oklahoma.

Primitive Aspects of Football

Owen's first year at OU was best remembered for two things: a 2–0 victory over Texas, OU's first ever over the Longhorns, and an 18–12 win over the fearsome Haskell Indians in the roughest football game anyone in Oklahoma Territory had ever seen.

The Boomers (as the university team was known from 1905 to 1907; before, they were the Rough Riders, and they would become the Sooners in 1908) began the 1905 campaign with an easy 28–0 victory over Central Normal of Edmond. Then the fearsome Haskell Indians came to town.

Haskell was founded in Lawrence, Kansas, in 1884. Its original name was the United States Indian Training School, and its mission was to provide an agricultural education for American Indian children in grades one through five. Boys took courses in tailoring, wagon making, blacksmithing, harness making, painting, shoe making and farming. Girls learned cooking, sewing and homemaking. In 1894, a "normal school" was added to provide teachers for the children's hometowns.

Today, it is known as Haskell Indian Nations University and offers bachelor degrees in elementary education, American Indian studies, business administration and environmental science. It is also the home of the American Indian Athletic Hall of Fame. Although Haskell deemphasized football many years ago, its teams of the early 1900s were the "Terrors of the Plains."

The Indians that came to play Bennie's boys in the autumn of 1905 were a formidable squad. They had won their first three games without being scored on, and just the week before, they had beaten Texas 18–0. They had beaten both Kansas and Missouri for three straight years and Nebraska in the previous season. OU's team had never beaten Kansas or Missouri, and Nebraska considered it beneath its dignity to even schedule Oklahoma. The previous year, Haskell fashioned a record of 10-1, losing only to the Carlisle Indians.

Few knowledgeable football fans could have thought the Boomers had any chance of defeating the Indians, yet on Thursday, October 12, the *Norman Transcript* implored its readers to attend the game. "Give the football game between the University and Haskell on the college campus next Monday afternoon your warmest, heartiest and earnest support. Go yourself and take friends with you. It will be a hard-fought battle: one well worth seeing and in addition you will help the boys out with your presence and patronage and influence. Everybody ought to go." Turns out, they were right on all counts.

Haskell began the scoring when its captain, Moore (accounts of games in those days often identified players by their last names only), ripped the ball away from a Boomer and took it twenty-five yards for a touchdown. Pete Hauser kicked the extra point and the Indians led 6–0. Pete and his brother Emil were the stars of this Haskell team. Both later played for Pop Warner at Carlisle and were chosen by the legendary coach on his all-time Carlisle Indian team. Moore's TD was the only scoring in the first half, although it appeared the Indians were very much in control and could probably score any time they wanted to exert themselves. So far, the play had been relatively clean, but things were about to change dramatically in the second half.

Early in the third quarter, OU's Owen Acton, a freshman from Guthrie, surprised and delighted the partisan crowd by running around the right end and following his blockers beautifully for a twenty-yard TD. Leonard Runbeck, Bennie's former Swede, kicked the extra point and tied the score at six all.

This only seemed to make the Indians mad. They took the ensuing kickoff, marched coolly and confidently down the field and, with John Aiken getting the touchdown on a short run and Pete Hauser converting, reclaimed the lead at 12–6. Then, early in the fourth quarter when Haskell attempted to punt from deep in its own territory against a brutally strong wind, the ball barely crossed the line of scrimmage. The Boomers took over, and Thomas Matthews scored a few plays later. Runbeck's extra point was good, and the score was tied again.

It was at this point, if one is to believe the Oklahoma version of things, that the Indians began attacking the Boomers like Sitting Bull attacked Custer at Little Big Horn, only without the tomahawks, bows and arrows. Harold Keith, who did not see the game and based his account on the understandably biased reports of OU fans, wrote, thirty-five years later: "Haskell's hefty warriors, experts in slugging, neck twisting, and the more primitive aspects of football, began the rough work. Some of the visiting Indians seemed to think the best defense against the swiftly-developing Oklahoma attack was a six-inch punch, a theory they were perfectly willing to demonstrate."

Haskell may have started the roughhousing, but Bennie's boys were giving back as good as they were getting. Several players on both teams were ejected from the fray. The first to go were OU's Acton and Bradley, the Haskell right end. Bennie was ambivalent about all the fighting. He had always been a proponent of clean play and good sportsmanship, but on the other hand, he was glad to see his boys were not intimidated by the bigger, stronger Indians.

When Bennie Owen got caught up in the excitement of a game, he had the nervous habit of crouching down in a catcher's stance and hopping around like a sparrow as he pulled up handfuls of grass. He must have ripped out several bales of good prairie hay during this contest.

Late in the game, the Indians seemed to be tiring just a little as OU continued to press them with its "hurry-up" style, always Owen's trademark. Boomer lineman Jim Monnett, who had been blocking on Emil Houser all day, was finally beginning to win the battle and open up big holes for his backs to run through. However, the furious pace was taking a toll on Bennie's boys as well. When he saw that his fullback, George Truesdale, was about to drop from exhaustion, he inserted seldom-used sub Clarence Reeds into the battle.

Reeds recalled years later:

> *I was just an awkward farm boy sitting on that hard splintery bench. I wasn't wearing any protective equipment of any kind, no pads nor helmet, just an old knitted sweater stuffed into my football pants. I was bareheaded and my ears stuck out like a mule's through a bridle. I remember that a new haircut I got that morning accentuated my protruding ears. When Bennie told me to go in my first reaction was to look around for a weapon. I wanted a club or a shotgun after what I'd been seeing. But I quickly forgot all that and ran right out into the middle of the roughest football game of my life.*

Some of the spectators had already armed themselves and were preparing to attack the Indians. OU student Guy Y. Williams, who later became one of the most colorful professors in the history of the university, was running around taking sticks and fence posts away from the most irate fans.

As soon as Reeds entered the game, Bill Cross, OU's quarterback, called his number on a cross buck, but the Haskell center smashed him into the turf of Boyd Field. The inexperienced Reeds was perplexed. He had run the play just as it was designed but had gotten nowhere. Cross saw the solution immediately. "Run outside the guard," he barked at Reeds. Reeds did as he was told and ripped off a big gain.

With Reeds, Harry Hughes, Matthews and Frank Long carrying the ball, the Boomers plowed down the hard, dusty field. Reeds said:

> *Down on the fifteen yard line, some big Indian, waiting each time until I fell, began grabbing my ears in his hands and trying to pull them off. He was kneading me like I was bread dough. Then the boys pushed me over for the winning touchdown, the game ended and I stood there frustrated. Everybody was pounding me on the back but I couldn't realize the game was over and we had won 18 to 12. I hadn't played but three minutes. I hadn't even gotten up a sweat. It reminded me of going out early in the morning to plow and being chased to the barn by a shower before I had had time to go one round of the field.*

If the rustic Reeds didn't quite understand the significance of the moment, everyone else at the game certainly did. The locals began a raucous

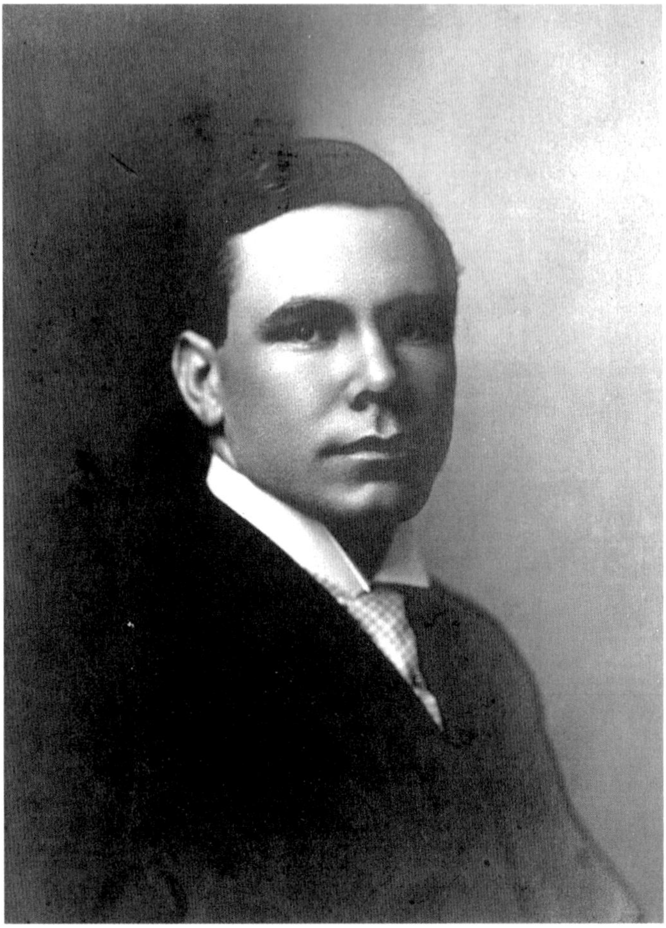

Bill Cross, OU quarterback (1904–07) and later secretary of the athletic association. *Courtesy of the University of Oklahoma's Western History Collection, Boyd 112.*

celebration that lasted well into the night. Many a cry of "Hi, Rickety, Whoop te do, Boomer Sooner, Oklahoma U" pierced the chill autumn air.

Three days later, the *Norman Transcript* minced no words in its condemnation of the officiating:

> *Oklahoma won a double victory Monday when they defeated the unwhipped Haskell Indians football team and the referee by the magnificent score of 18 to 12 and great has been the rejoicing of the students and faculty. The game was one of the fastest and most sensational ever played on*

the Oklahoma gridiron and the Oklahomans showed their superiority at every stage of the game. Coach Owen and the team are certainly to be congratulated on the fine showing they made. Much unfavorable comment has been made on the work of referee McLean of Oklahoma City who undoubtedly according to our knowledge of the game gave the Indians the best of it. He might have tried to do right, but we are of the opinion the game was just a little too fast for him—out of his class so to speak.

A FINE BEGINNING

The Texas game was the fourth in twelve days for Bennie's Boomers. Given the penurious position of the athletic budget, Owen tried in his early years at OU to economize on traveling expenses by scheduling several games on the same road trip. The previous week, he had traveled north with his squad to play Kansas University in Lawrence, where they absorbed a 34–0 loss on Monday, October 23. Two days later, the Boomers defeated the Medics in Kansas City 33–0 and then lost to Washburn 9–6 on Saturday in Topeka. At least, this is the way Harold Keith described events in *Oklahoma Kickoff*. The OU media guide gives different dates (but the same scores) for these games. The current author considers Keith to be by far the more reliable source.

Some of this confusion may arise because it was common practice then to schedule, reschedule or cancel games on a moment's notice. In fact, it was not until 1911, the seventeenth season of OU football, that the schedule was played exactly as it was originally drawn up.

The Texas game was played in Oklahoma City on Friday, November 3. Bennie's boys were battered and bruised from their grueling schedule of the previous week, and they were light, averaging only 165 pounds per man. The Sunday *Daily Oklahoman* reported, "In one of the fastest games of football ever played on an Oklahoma gridiron, Oklahoma University defeated the Texas University Team by a score of 2–0 at Oklahoma City last Friday. Between 300 and 500 Normanites attended the game and 'rooted' the boys to victory." The "Normanites" had traveled to the game, which was played at the old Colcord Park, the present-day site of the farmers' market, on the interurban train, paying seventy-five cents for a round-trip ticket.

Late in the game, with the score knotted at 0–0, Boomer halfback Harry Hughes burst through the line. When the Texas safety came up to stop him, Hughes, a hurdler on the track team, leaped over him. This maneuver brought the OU fans to their feet as it now appeared their man had a clear path to the goal line, but alas, another Longhorn dragged him down at the five-yard line. From there, Texas held on downs, and it seemed the Boomers would have to settle for a tie. But just as time was running out, OU center Bob Severin picked up the Texas ball carrier, Don Robinson, and carried him back into the end zone (a perfectly legal play in 1905) for the game-winning safety.

The throng of Normanites stormed the field and carried their victorious gladiators off on their shoulders. There was great jubilation on the train back to Norman. "Hi Rickety" and "Boomer Sooner," indeed!

The final game of the season, played on Thanksgiving Day, was also played at Colcord Park. In this encounter, the Boomers achieved their first-ever victory over Bethany College by a score of 29–0, thus concluding Bennie's first season at OU with a record of 7-2, the 2 losses coming on the grueling road trip to Kansas. The little man from Kansas had made a fine beginning in Oklahoma Territory.

After the game, several OU students were making the rounds of Oklahoma City's smoky watering holes in celebration, perhaps a few even patronized some less reputable establishments. They ran upon the Boomers' coach in the lobby of the Lee Hotel and tried to entice him to join them, even offering to pay for his libations, but Bennie declined gracefully. "Boys," he said, "I feel great just the way I am about this victory. I don't drink. You don't want me with you. I don't blame you for feeling as you do, but if you must celebrate try to remember that your conduct here tonight will reflect on your school, just as the team's conduct reflected on it today." This was the quintessential Bennie Owen.

There is an old axiom in the Southwest that says a good coach can "beat you with his, take yours, give you his and then beat you with yours." That is pretty much what Bennie Owen did. When he played at Kansas, the Jayhawks beat Washburn. When he coached the Ichabods of Washburn, they beat Kansas—in fact, they beat them twice in the same year, 1900. When he coached at Bethany, the Swedes beat the University of Oklahoma. When he coached at Oklahoma, the Sooners beat the Swedes.

Well-Beloved Little Genius

The Haskell game proved to be an anomaly for Owen's teams. Throughout his long career, Owen established a reputation for clean play and good sportsmanship. Dewey "Snorter" Luster, the captain of Bennie's undefeated 1920 squad and later the Sooners' head coach from 1941 to 1945, said, "No. 1, Bennie was a sportsman in every sense of the word, a true sportsman. He knew how to win and he knew how to lose like a gentleman."

Hal Muldrow, who played for Owen the last year he coached in 1926 said, "I knew him real well. He was a fine man with the highest principles. He was the kind of a coach you would want your boy to play for. I don't know any higher compliment." Harold Keith wrote of his old friend, "As a football coach Bennie Owen was noted for his fine sportsmanship in a day when it wasn't the fashion of the times. All his teams were famous for their graciousness in defeat as well as victory and for clean play."

It was not just Bennie's players and friends who praised his sportsmanship; he drew compliments from his opponents as well. Ivan Grove, an outstanding quarterback for Henry Kendall College (which later became the University of Tulsa), in 1917 said, "Oklahoma absolutely had the cleanest team of all the teams we ever played."

After OU had defeated the Jayhawks 21–7 in 1913, the Kansas University student paper, the *Daily Kansan*, editorialized:

> *Perhaps the commonest remark about the Oklahoma defeat is "Well if we had to lose we'd rather lose to Oklahoma than anyone else." Oklahoma just walloped us and we have no excuse to offer. But when everyone knows that an old Jayhawker coached the winning team and that his greatest player* [Claude Reeds], *playing a clean game, came out of every scrimmage smiling and went through or around us for another gain—well, we've no cause for bitterness there; and there's no use trying to stop lightning, you know.*

C.E. McBride, sports editor of the *Kansas City Star*, wrote on October 24, 1915, "Owen is an exponent of the cleanest brand of football. His players are the manliest type, playing football in their own far-throwing and high-reaching fashion, saying little, doing much."

His opponents very much appreciated the fact that Bennie made no excuses when he lost. In 1912, the Sooners battled the Texas Aggies in Houston, for the championship of the Southwest Conference, a title that OU had won the previous two years. This time A&M prevailed 28–6. Following the game, the *Battalion*, the Aggies' student paper, praised Bennie's gracious acceptance of the loss. The paper, as recorded in *Oklahoma Kickoff*, quoted Owen as saying, "The best team won. Texas A&M outplayed us. We were given a good clean fight." Then it added, "This statement by Coach

Owen, the well-beloved little genius who has headed the Sooners in many a hard-fought campaign for the Southwest championship, was characteristic of him. Was the weather too warm? Was the team tired after its long trip? Was his bunch in foreign territory? Weren't three substitutes enough? Were his men handicapped by injuries? No. 'The best team won.' Bennie we take our hats off to you."

Bennie was always scrupulously honest. He did not want his teams to be given anything they had not earned. In a game against Central Normal in 1918, with the score tied at 0–0, Sooner halfback Harry "Dutch" Hill found a large hole up the middle and then veered sharply to the sidelines before cutting back to the center of the field and continuing for a touchdown. However, Charlie Wantland, Central's coach, questioned this beautiful piece of broken field running. He was certain Hill had stepped out of bounds when he made his cut to the sidelines, and he thought he could prove his point by showing the referee where Hill's cleat marks had kicked up the boundary chalk. But when he led the official over to the spot where he thought the infraction had occurred, he could not find the evidence he was looking for.

"What's wrong?" Bennie asked the ref.

"Wantland contends your man stepped out of bounds," he was told.

"Well he did, and there's his track," Owen said. Although this TD was called back, Bennie was rewarded for his integrity as the Sooners scored many more touchdowns and won 44–0.

No one led a more exemplary life than Bennie Owen, and all his teams reflected his values. He did not drink, smoke, chew tobacco or use profanity. His favorite expression was "Gee Cly," but if he got really excited he might shout out "Murder, murder, murder!" Calling someone a "big dub" was the worst epithet he was ever known to append to another person.

Page Belcher, a Sooner lineman in 1918, recalled, "Bennie was clean as a pin himself and wouldn't let us swear in practice or in games." If he heard one of his players using off color language, such as "hell," he would stop practice immediately, call the squad together and remind the players, "We don't use that kind of language around here. You're men now, and men don't talk that way."

A Fateful Day: Wednesday, October 16, 1907

Bennie and his dog, Buster, watched the chestnut mare kick up little tufts of sand as she pulled the big two-seated phaeton down the dusty street.

When John Barbour reined in his horse, Buster jumped into the back with Barbour's dog Colonel, and Bennie climbed into the front with his twelve-gauge Winchester pump and quickly reminded Barbour that they would have to start back early so that he could be at football practice.

John Barbour's drugstore on Main Street just east of the railroad tracks was the quintessential apothecary shop of the early twentieth century. It was a popular meeting spot for college students even though it was over a mile from the campus. Several large ceiling fans cooled the interior. Coeds in high-necked blouses and ankle-length skirts and young men in coats and ties gathered there to be served ice cream and Coca-Colas. Perhaps it was the popular songs of the day, such as "The Black Cat Rag," "When Love Is Young" and "Sugar Moon," that Barbour played on his Edison phonograph that attracted the young crowd.

Barbour was one of Bennie's best friends and a loyal booster of the university's football team. In 1903, when the athletic department needed to borrow $300 for train fare to Fayetteville, Arkansas, John Barbour loaned it the money. Tom Tribbey, the football manager, promised to repay Barbour with the money Arkansas University had guaranteed OU. But somehow, this "guarantee" fell through, and Barbour had to wait two years to get his money back. He never complained. When Bennie Owen needed to borrow money to buy equipment early in his career at OU, he got it from John Barbour.

Barbour made arrangements with Western Union to have play-by-play accounts of Oklahoma road games sent by telegraph to his drugstore. Huge crowds would gather in front of his store, especially when OU was playing one of its bitter rivals like Kansas, Missouri or Texas, to listen as these "accounts" were broadcast by megaphone from an open window of Dr. Hirshfield's upstairs office above Barbour Drug.

On this warm October morning, Bennie and John drove the carriage about four miles southwest of the campus to the South Canadian River. The area they liked best was near Adkins Ford, where the bridge was later built. This was not the Mississippi that Bennie had known as a boy. The South Canadian was more sand than water, and that was what made it dangerous. The natives said, "It's just a little too thick to drink and a little too thin to plow." Quicksand had trapped many a man and mule in the old days before there were any bridges, and several people had drowned when their wagons were tipped over and washed away by flash floods in the capricious old river.

At about 2:00 p.m., Bennie and John loaded the quail, dogs and shotguns into the phaeton and headed home. This time, both dogs jumped into the front of the carriage. They were covered in burrs and thrashing about recklessly on the floorboard.

Bennie saw that Buster was about to fall out of the phaeton, which had no doors. As he reached over to pull him back in, his shotgun suddenly fired. Apparently, the hammer had caught on the frame of the phaeton, discharging the shell that was in the barrel. The number-eight shot tore into Owen's right arm just below his shoulder. Barbour was startled by the noise, but he didn't realize what had happened until he heard Bennie say, in a soft voice, "Got me that time John." When Bennie saw the blood gushing out, he reached into his hip pocket for his dog chain, which he intended to use as a tourniquet. As soon as John got his frightened mare under control, he ran around to the other side of the carriage to help his stricken friend. At first he had the same idea as Bennie, to use his dog chain as a tourniquet, but he quickly decided to try his handkerchief and was able to stop the flow of blood.

Barbour told Bennie that he would get him back to Doc Hirshfield's office on Main Street as fast as he could. This was fine with Bennie, but he wanted him to drive down the alley so they would not attract too much attention.

It was almost five miles back to the doctor's office, but Barbour whipped his horse into a gallop so that they made pretty good time. Bennie walked up the stairs to Hirshfield's office, but the doctor was not in. They later learned he was out hunting quail. Barbour ran downstairs to his store and called Dr. Bobo, whose office was one block farther east. Bennie had to walk that block and up yet another flight of stairs before he could get any medical attention.

Dr. Bobo saw that Bennie had suffered extensive damage to an artery and thought that he had better call in Dr. Rolater, a specialist from Oklahoma City. Rolater and two nurses made it down to Norman at midnight on the interurban. Rolater examined the arm and determined that gangrene had set in and decided to amputate immediately. A few days later, the *Umpire* (as the university's student paper was then known) reported, "The operation was neatly performed and since Saturday night [which would have been three days after the amputation] there has been no fever."

Of course, Bennie accepted this with stoic resolve. Harold Keith wrote, "He always had a confident, insouciant manner that rarely admitted of surprise or discouragement, and with his usual pluck and assurance remarked with a grin to all his visitors. 'What do you think of a dub who'd shoot his own arm off?'"

Bennie had to miss the Boomers' next game, a 15–0 loss to the Kansas Jayhawks. This was the only loss Owen's teams suffered at Boyd Field in his first seven years at OU. There were three other "home" losses, but these games were played in Oklahoma City.

In a matter of weeks, Owen was able to resume his coaching duties and his hunting trips. He switched to a lighter Browning automatic twenty-gauge shotgun that he could wield left-handed, and John Barbour affirmed, "He could hit 'em as good as ever."

After his accident, Bennie took great pride in doing everything he needed to do with one arm, and on those rare occasions when he ran into problems, he was much too proud to ask anyone for help. His players could remember him asking for assistance only once. The team was in the lobby of a hotel in Urbana, Illinois, on the day following a game with the Illini in 1917. Bennie had just been handed the $1,700 in cash that the Sooners had been guaranteed for making the trip north. He began putting the bills into his inside vest pocket. He was in a great hurry because they were running late for their train. The players could see that he was struggling to get the bills stuffed away, but they were reluctant to offer any help because they knew how stubborn he could be about such things. Finally, he turned to guard Earl Deacon and said, with a touch of impatience, "Gee Cly, can't you help a fellow?" Owen might be forgiven for being a little frustrated because he had seen his team absorb a 44–0 drubbing on the previous day. On only one other occasion did he ever lose by such a lopsided score.

Bennie's grandsons Joe and Jim Haynes marveled at all the things he could do with just one arm and how strong he was. Joe said:

> *I remember, we had some heavy concrete slabs to move around, most of them quite large. My brother and I would pick one up and struggle along with it while Gran Gran would handle one by himself. He had more strength in his one arm than either of us had in two, and he was well over sixty at this time.*
>
> *When we went fishing, I remember him sitting on a rock with an old pair of glasses tying different flies with his one hand and his teeth. It always amazed me that he could do that. I could barely do it with both hands and my teeth. He could tie his neckties with one hand. My brother and I used to try that, and we never could get it.*

Joe recalled an occasion when he and some other boys were swimming in a lake near their home in Sandpoint, Idaho. "All of a sudden, we heard this running noise. We looked up, and here came Gran Gran, running down the dock in his shorts. And he dove into the water. We couldn't believe he could swim, too." They should have seen him in the Mississippi.

Not long after Bennie's death, his longtime friend Phillip Kendall wrote a letter to Dorothy Bryan, Bennie's youngest daughter, which read, in part:

> *I thought of Bennie Owen and recalled many of the things I had seen him do that didn't make much of an impression on me at the time, but now I can understand them—scratching his back on a door jam, putting on his coat with a body and shoulder motion, using his teeth as a substitute for a missing hand in fly-casting, and numerous other inventive ways of getting things done with one arm.*
>
> *Bennie didn't know he only had one arm. I think he made himself forget it, and he made you forget it, too. I knew him well for about forty years, but while writing this, I began to wonder which arm did Bennie lose? I couldn't remember. Neither could Dorothy or Gail, nor a friend of his I thought would remember. Evidently, those who knew him well forgot he had lost an arm because, for Bennie, it was no loss or handicap. Bennie tied his shoelaces, shuffled, dealt and played bridge with one hand. The only thing Bennie would admit he couldn't do was manicure his own nails.*
>
> *Once, when we happened to see a man with one arm, he said to me, "Look at that poor fellow. He only has one arm." The fellow was directing traffic, and Bennie wasn't making fun of him. He was genuinely sorry for him. And you soon learned not to offer help with Bennie's physical activities—he could do anything he needed to do, and many things better than those of us with no handicap. I once visited a resort in Colorado. The owner didn't know I knew Bennie, but upon learning I was from Norman said, "The best one-armed fly-fisherman I ever saw came from there." He could have left out the one-armed and still been right. He would almost always bring in the most game on a hunting party. He drove his old gear shift Buick all over Norman with reckless abandon and never dented anyone's fender that I know of. He cracked pecans by squeezing two of them together in his left hand—because it was his natural hand, his right, that he lost.*

There was one other occasion on which Bennie may have forgotten he had only one arm, and this particular situation had the potential to end badly. During World War I, the U.S. Army sent an officer to Norman to organize the university's military training program. Unfortunately, the Pentagon made a poor choice because this fellow (whose name, rank and serial number have been lost over the years) was not just a raging egomaniac but also a belligerent and unmitigated fool.

For some inexplicable reason, he believed the football team had to have his permission to practice. Thus, when he saw Owen drilling his charges one day, he decided to take it upon himself to cancel the 1918 football season. The officer summoned Bennie to his office. Owen, who had been working in his yard in an old pair of corduroy pants and a faded sweatshirt, came immediately. At first the pompous official simply ignored him. Then, suddenly looking up, he asked, "Who the hell are you?"

"I'm Bennie Owen, the football coach."

"Well, then, you're just the son of a bitch I want to see." With that entrée he launched into a litany of profane invective against Owen and his football program. Bennie, who never used such language himself, grew tired of this in a hurry.

"Now, wait a minute," he said. "I don't know where you come from, but down here in this country, we don't talk to folks that way. Now, if you're going to talk that way to me you come on out doors, and we will settle this thing right now."

The officer declined Owen's offer, but he still maintained that there would be no football on campus that fall. Owen consulted OU president Stanton Brooks, who told him not to worry. "This guy talked to me pretty much the same way," Brooks said. "We are getting a new commandant in a few days. Let's wait until I can talk to him."

The new man was Captain Fred Bachman, a much more reasonable person who liked football. He and Bennie worked out a schedule for football practice that would accommodate the military drills, and things soon were back to normal. "We all marched in our football suits and then went out for practice," tackle Paul Johnston recalled.

5

Rules and Innovations

A Boy-Killing, Education-Prostituting Gladiatorial Sport

Between 1906 and 1912, several changes were made in the rules of college football. No coach adapted more quickly or creatively to these changes than the University of Oklahoma's diminutive mentor, Benjamin Gilbert Owen.

For over a century, the myth has persisted that in 1905, President Teddy Roosevelt, alarmed at the level of violence in college football, set in motion a series of events that saved the game from oblivion. According to this canon of belief, Roosevelt was so shocked when he saw a photograph of the bloody face of Swarthmore lineman Bob "Tiny" Maxwell following a game with Penn that he immediately convened a meeting at the White House with representatives of several eastern universities. However, John S. Watterson, in a article entitled "The Gridiron Crisis of 1905: Was It Really a Crisis?" which was published in the Summer 2000 edition of the *Journal of Sport History*, explained in great detail that this story is more fiction than fact.

It is true that two days after Maxwell's injury delegates from Harvard, Yale and Princeton met with Roosevelt, but this meeting had been scheduled several weeks before the Penn-Swarthmore game, and if Roosevelt ever saw the photograph of Maxwell, he did not mention it at the meeting.

Clearly, there was reason for concern about the way football was being played in 1905. According to statistics published in both the *New York Times* and the *Chicago Tribune*, there had been 159 serious injuries and 18 deaths attributed to football games at "all levels" in that season. In college football games, these figures were 88 serious injuries and 3 deaths.

The incident that triggered the demand for rule revision (according to Watterson) was not Maxwell's bloody face but the death of Harold Moore of Union College as a result of injuries suffered in a game with New York University on November 21, 1905. A month later, a conference was held in New York City to discuss what could be done to improve the state of college football in America. President Roosevelt was not in attendance, but college presidents, coaches, faculty and athletic advisors from all over the county were. This was the first meeting of what would later become the National Collegiate Athletic Association.

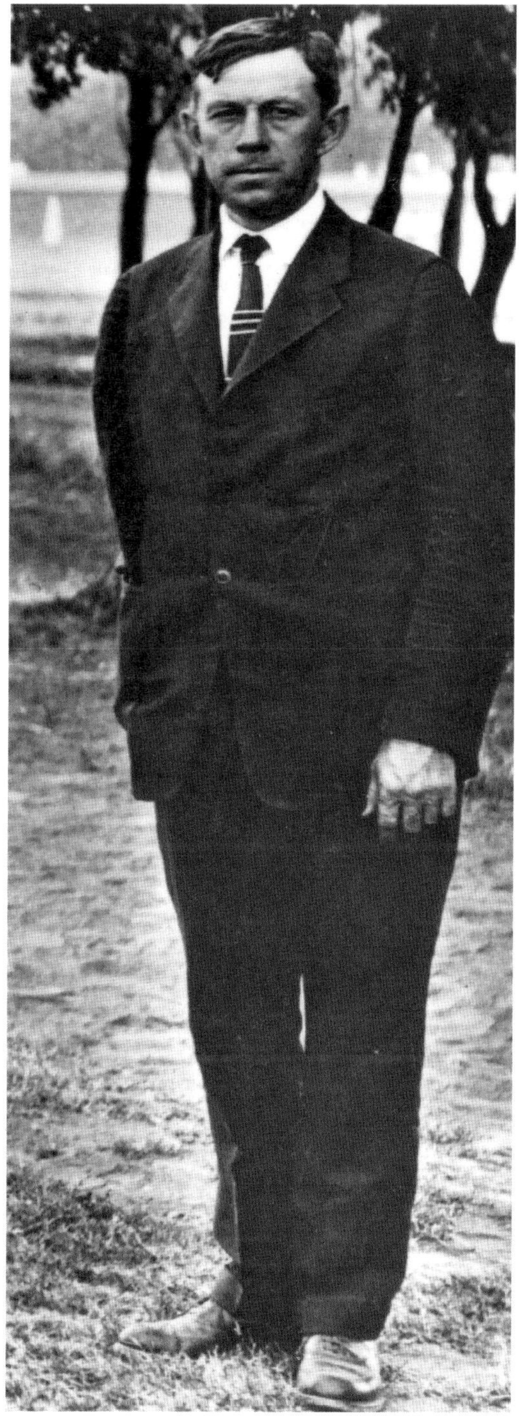

Bennie Owen circa 1910. *Courtesy of the University of Oklahoma's Western History Collection, OU 164.*

At this time, there was widespread sentiment that college football should be abolished. Nicholas Murray Butler, president of Columbia, referred to the sport as an "academic nuisance," and Shailer Matthews, dean of the Chicago University Divinity School, was quoted in the November 27, 1905 *New York Times* as saying, "Football today is a social obsession, a boy-killing, education prostituting gladiatorial sport. It teaches virility and courage but so does war. I do not know what should take its place but the new game should not require the services of a physician, the maintenance of a hospital, and the celebration of funerals."

President John W. Cavanaugh of Notre Dame thought football was too good a sport to be done away with entirely, but he advised that since most accidents occur among unseasoned players, it should not be played in high schools. Cavanaugh did not explain how a player could become "seasoned" if he did not play the sport before he came to college. Jack Wheeler, president of the University of California, said, "Football must either be made over or go." It was made over, although several schools, including Columbia, Northwestern, Union and Bethany (where only a few years earlier, Bennie Owen had enjoyed such success), did decide to abolish the sport, at least temporarily.

Football, as it was played at the turn of the twentieth century, bore scant resemblance to the game we see today. At this time, in order to retain possession of the ball, teams had three downs to make five yards. The prevailing strategy was to mass as many men as possible in front of the ball carrier, often with interlocking arms and legs, and attack straight on with brute force. Pushing, pulling and even throwing the ball carrier were well within the rules, but throwing the football was forbidden.

The rule changes that were enacted prior to the 1906 season were designed to induce the offense to take more chances and thus produce a more wide-open game. The rules committee wanted the game to become more about speed and finesse and less about raw power, thereby hopefully reducing injuries.

Some things did not change in 1906. The field was still 110 yards long. Kickoffs were executed at midfield, and a TD counted five points and a field goal four. But a lot of things did change. Games were shortened from seventy minutes to two thirty-minute halves. Locking legs was made illegal except for guards and centers. Instead of waiting for the player to shout out "down," the referee stopped play when any part of the ball carrier's body (other than his hands or feet) was in contact with the ground while he was in the grasp of an opponent.

Six men were required to be on the line of scrimmage. Not allowing any of these six to move into the backfield and act as a lead blocker would discourage, the rules committee hoped, mass power plays and thus lessen the risk of injury.

If a player was flagged for unnecessary roughness not only was he ejected from the game but his team was also penalized half the distance to their goal line. A team now had to make ten yards (instead of five) in three downs in order to retain possession. Apparently, it was thought this change would induce the offense to try more imaginative plays rather than just pounding the ball up the middle.

The most radical new rule was the legalization of the forward pass. John Heisman, who in 1906 was the coach at Georgia Tech, had for years been campaigning to add passing to the game. Phillip Brooks explained in *Forward Pass: The Play That Saved Football* that Heisman believed the defense would have to adjust to the passing game by dropping players off the line of scrimmage to cover the receivers, thus making them more vulnerable to the running game, which would lead to a balance of running and passing by offensive teams. In *Rockne of Notre Dame*, Ray Robinson quotes Heisman as saying, "It [passing] will scatter the mob. Speed will supplant bull strength. Lighter, faster men will succeed the beefy giants whose crushing weight maims or kills opponents."

However, the consequences for failure to complete a pass were so severe that the risks greatly outweighed the potential rewards. For example, if a pass hit the ground without being touched by a member of either team the defense automatically gained possession at the spot from which the ball was thrown. (In 1907, the rules committee decreed that instead of losing possession on an untouched ball, the offensive team would be penalized fifteen yards.) If the ball was touched, the offensive team retained possession, the only penalty being a loss of down. If a pass sailed out of bounds, if it was touched by an ineligible receiver or if it was not thrown at least five yards on either side of the center, the defense took over on the spot. And a forward pass completed over the goal line was not counted as a touchdown for the offense but rather as touchback for the defense. This was because there was no end zone in those days. So, rather than passing, most teams resorted to punting or executing what was then known as the "onside kick," a maneuver Bennie had used so effectively as a player at Kansas and as a coach at Bethany.

Many people were critical of the new game. Jack Wheeler, president of the University of California Berkeley, said, "I do not believe the present experiment in American college football will survive. In my opinion, the whole country will, within five years, be playing the Rugby game."

Even some of Bennie's OU players were not convinced the new rules were a good idea. Guard Key Wolf said, "We thought we would never make ten yards in three plays. It had been hard enough to make five."

While others were grousing, Bennie Owen was more optimistic, and his observations proved to be pretty accurate. "It's hard to say what effect they'll [the new rules] have," he was quoted in the *Umpire*. "Everything is new and may develop along unexpected lines. They'll certainly kill mass plays to quite an extent and call for more fast work. There also will be lots of punting. The forward pass will probably open up the game considerably. Taken all together, I believe they'll add a good deal to the game."

Although the casual observer might not have noticed that the college game of 1906 looked much different than it had in the previous year (except perhaps for more punting), it was clear that the rules committee had succeeded in its primary objectives. There were fewer injuries in 1906, and the game opened up somewhat as coaches began to look for speed and agility rather than sheer bulk. The old push and shove power game was no more.

The first year passing was legal there was only one coach brave enough, or perhaps foolhardy enough, to employ this new weapon on a consistent basis. That was Eddie Cochems of Saint Louis University. On September 5, 1906, in Waukesha, Wisconsin, Cochems, frustrated with his team's inability to run the ball against Carroll College, ordered his quarterback Bradbury Robinson to start throwing.

Robinson's first attempt fell incomplete without being touched by a player from either team, so under the rules of the day, Carroll gained possession. But when the Billikens got the ball back again, Robinson connected with Jack Schneider for a twenty-yard touchdown, and St. Louis went on the defeat Carroll 22–0. Cochems's team posted an 11-0 record that season and outscored its opponents 407–11.

Given this sort of success, one might have expected other coaches to follow Cochems's lead and mount aerial attacks; however, there were several factors mitigating this. Prior to 1906, no college player had ever run a pass route or thrown the ball across the line of scrimmage. Coaches did not understand this new weapon. They did not know how to coach passers, receivers or pass-protection blocking. Consequently, they were not convinced that spending the requisite amount of practice time learning these new techniques was worthwhile.

If, before his death, Steve Jobs had traveled back in time to 1957 and equipped a college classroom with state-of-the-art 2012 Macs and iPads, it would have taken some time for the students to learn how to use them. This is essentially the position coaches were in with respect to the forward pass in 1906.

Another problem was that the football, then, was extremely hard to throw. It more closely resembled a rugby ball than today's modern missile. Bradbury Robinson, at six feet, four inches tall, had extremely large hands and a well-developed throwing motion, having been a pitcher on his high school baseball team. Most quarterbacks in that era could not master the art of making the ball spiral. Some even tried to throw it end over end or used a two-hand basketball chest pass.

STOMP DANCE AT THE ROUNDHOUSE

The year 1906 was also the last in which Bennie Owen played in a football game. (It was the following year that he would lose his right arm.) This came about when he scheduled a game in Pawhuska with the town team in December after the Boomers had completed their collegiate schedule at 4-4. Bennie hoped to earn enough money from the game so that the athletic association could at least break even for the year. A.W. Hurley, the chief clerk for the Osage Indian agency in Pawhuska, had convinced Owen that he could expect a windfall of profit if he made the 150-mile trip north with his squad. Hurley advertised that he would run trains to Muskogee and Arkansas City to bring fans in for the game. As an added attraction, he promised that "full-blood Indians will give a stomp dance at the roundhouse the night before the game."

The Pawhuska squad included Archie Archiquette, who had played at Carlisle, and Pete Hauser, whom the Boomers certainly recalled from the previous year's battle with Haskell. Also from Haskell were Will Labodie, John Aiken, Jake Duran and E.L. Moore. Pawhuska's team was composed of ten Indians and one Caucasian, and the university team had ten pale faces and one Indian, Key Wolf.

The contest was refereed by Charlie "Chief" Bender, who had just completed a season in which he had won sixteen games for Connie Mack's Philadelphia Athletics. No one could have possibly questioned Bender's integrity or accused him of being biased in favor of Pawhuska's Indians.

Throughout his fifteen-year career in the major leagues, he was well respected by teammates and opponents alike. Rube Bressler, also an Athletics' pitcher, referred to Bender as "one of the kindest and finest men who ever lived." When he was taunted with racial epithets and war whoops, his reply would be "Foreigners, foreigners." The Chief was inducted into the Major League Baseball Hall of Fame in 1953.

With the thirty-one-year-old Owen playing quarterback in the second half, the Boomers played the Pawhuskans to a 0–0 standstill. To a man, Bennie's boys admitted after the game that they were lucky to escape with a tie. OU had managed only one first down the whole game, and that came on a penalty. Hauser had barely missed a sixty-yard drop kick field goal, and just before the game ended, the Boomers held the Indians on downs from the two-yard line.

The Santa Fe lines did not run through Pawhuska, so Bennie and his team had to travel to Nelagoney to find the nearest depot. They climbed aboard six horse-drawn wagons just before sunset and set out on the seven-mile journey to the southeast. However, the roads were so bad that all six vehicles broke down before they had gotten halfway, so all the players had to walk, carrying their luggage, to the railroad tracks where Bennie flagged down a train.

Direct Snaps and Long Passes

In 1909, the rules committee made only one significant change. It permanently set the value of a field goal at three points rather than the four it had previously been. However, the following year, the changes were so revolutionary that as soon as Bennie Owen became aware of them, he organized the first spring football practice in the university's history. He had some ideas he wanted to try out.

The new rules required seven men (instead of six) to be on the offensive line of scrimmage. The game was divided into quarters of fifteen minutes each, and if a player came out of the game, he was required to sit out only the remainder of the quarter instead of the rest of the game, as had previously been the case. Forward passes were limited to twenty yards. (Apparently, this was done to eliminate the desperation "Hail Mary" heaves that were the only passes many teams employed in those days.) And onside kicks had to travel at least twenty yards before they could be recovered by the offensive team. These were significant changes, but the emendation that really got Bennie's attention was the rule that allowed the "direct pass."

Before 1910, the rules stated that the player receiving the center snap could cross the line of scrimmage with the ball only if he did so at least five yards from the point where the ball was originally snapped. He could not cross the line of scrimmage with the ball between his own two tackles. Therefore, the man receiving the center snap (usually the quarterback) normally took the snap (handoff actually) directly from the center, as in the T-formation, and then handed the ball to another player who was allowed to run anywhere he wished—up the middle, off tackle or around end.

Bennie immediately saw that this rule change could mean several advantages for offensive football. First of all, the possibility of fumbling would be greatly reduced because now only two men (the center and ball carrier) were handling the ball as opposed to three under the old rule. Also, since the snap was going directly to the ball carrier, the play could develop more quickly, hence placing even a greater premium on speed. But the greatest benefit that would accrue was the addition of an extra blocker.

Under the new rule, the quarterback (or blocking back or whatever term one wanted to use for him) could move out from behind the center and line up anywhere he wanted. He could help his linemen block down on the defensive tackles or kick out on the ends. He could lead the ball carrier through the hole or he could drop back and protect the passer.

In the spring and fall of 1910, Owen took advantage of this new rule and began experimenting with his acclaimed long-punt formation, which was actually an archetype of the single-wing. Owen balanced his line. He unbalanced his line. He split his ends. He pulled his guards and tackles. He ran traps and reverses, and his teams would run roughshod over defenses, especially after the fourth down was added in 1912.

With the rule changes of 1912, college football became essentially the game we know today. Offenses were now allowed four downs to make ten yards in order to retain possession. The onside kick was abolished, the field was shortened form 110 to 100 yards, and the value of a touchdown permanently became six rather than five points.

By far the most significant changes in 1912 were those concerning the forward pass. Passes were no longer limited to twenty yards, and the only penalty for an incompletion was the loss of a down. Ten-yard end zones were added so passes caught beyond the goal line were now counted as touchdowns. Also, the dimensions of the football itself were changed to make it easier to throw. It became the same length and weight as the modern ball.

It was still two inches "fatter" around the middle, but certainly no longer the watermelon-like rugby ball that the game had previously known.

If Owen's teams were not the first to actually throw the football, they were evidently the first to develop a passing game refined enough to achieve the balance John Heisman foresaw between running and throwing. Harold Keith wrote, "Oklahoma appears to have been the first team in the America to go in consistently for mass production of aerial play and to prove that the forward pass could be a major unit of the offense in every game on the schedule with the forward passing yardage usually surpassing the running yardage."

Bennie Owen began taking the passing game seriously in the 1912 season once all the restrictions were removed. Before this, he had thrown the ball only sparingly. Perhaps it was the arrival on campus of one Forrest Park Geyer that sparked Bennie's interest in the aerial game. Geyer grew up in Norman and matriculated at the university in 1912. His childhood friend Hap Johnson explained, "He moved here from Forrest Park in Kansas City when he was a kid. I guess his mother must have named him after the park." Whatever the reason for his Christian name, because of his ability to throw a football, he quickly acquired the nickname of "Spot," as in "He can put the ball on the spot."

Spot, who had been an All-State fullback at Norman High, attracted attention in his very first freshman game against the University Preparatory School of Tonkawa. In this contest, he connected with his favorite target, Jess Fields, on some of the longest passes anyone had ever seen on old Boyd Field.

Although Geyer was not eligible to play with the varsity in 1912, Owen had a couple of other young men who were quite capable of throwing a football—Ray Courtright and Claude Reeds. Courtright was a star in football, basketball and baseball for the Sooners, and Reeds was one of the greatest, if not the greatest, player Bennie Owen ever coached. He could run, kick, pass and play defense. As one Sooner fan put it, "Claude done everything smooth."

The best example of OU's newfound passing prowess in 1912 came against Nebraska on November 23. The undersized Sooners were given little chance of winning this contest. The all-victorious Cornhuskers were coached by Ewald O. "Jumbo" Stiehm, who in his five years at Lincoln put up a record of 35-2, the best in the school's storied history. His teams swept across the northern plains like a tornado, crushing such rivals as Kansas, Missouri, the Haskell Indians and Washburn. In 1915, his husky Huskers defeated a Notre Dame team coached by Jesse Harper and Knute Rockne.

The Sooners struck first. Mixing running and passing, they kept the muscular Nebraskans off balance and drove seventy-five yards for a TD. The key play was a pass by Reeds to Billy Clark that carried to the Husker's twelve-yard line. Three plays later, Courtright sped around right end for the score that was the first touchdown surrendered by Nebraska all year. Their fans, shivering in a bitterly cold northwest wind, were in a state of shock. They had never seen a team rip through their stalwarts with such alacrity.

Back in Norman, Oklahoma, where it was much warmer, the throng listening to the telegraph accounts of the game were dancing, singing and shouting. The *Transcript* later reported:

> *Showing unequaled interest and great enthusiasm about six hundred students and townsmen stood in the main street of Norman Saturday afternoon and listened to the reports of the Oklahoma-Nebraska football game. For two hours traffic was almost cut off on the principal street of the University City. It being practically impossible to pass with any kind of vehicle.*
>
> *The reports were given out from a window over Barbour's drug store where the terminus of the wire was located. Such interest was shown that the entire crowd stood on the hard pavement for the entire two hours, none deserting the ranks. The girls of the university were just as loyal as the men, practically every girl being present. When Courtright made the touchdown for Oklahoma which was the first score of the game, a roar of cheers went up through the crowd, as though the crowd had been on the sidelines.*

Courtright missed the extra point, which was the first time he had failed to convert all season, and the first half ended with the Sooners leading 6–0. Trailing for the first time all year apparently got the Cornhuskers' attention, and they began to assert themselves. Harold Keith, in his inimitable style, wrote, "Now Nebraska's fury knew no bounds. Gaining the wind at the start of the second quarter, the Stiehm-roller tore the Sooner line completely apart as it moved seventy yards for a touchdown without giving up the ball. In its wake, the fighting but ridiculously light Oklahoma forwards were pressed flat as cardboard."

Nebraska also missed its conversion attempt, and there was no further scoring in the first half. But Stiehm's men took the second half kickoff and marched eighty yards virtually unimpeded. This time, they kicked the goal and led 13–7.

Early in the fourth quarter, Reeds heaved a fifty-yard aerial strike to Courtright that the Nebraska faithful testified was the longest pass they had ever seen. Courtright gathered the ball in on Nebraska's six-yard line, but before he could cross the goal, the Huskers' safety and quarterback, Max Towle, knocked the ball away from him and ran it back up field twenty yards. Thus, the score was still 13–6 when the Sooners lined up to run the game's dramatic last play.

This time, it was Ray Courtright, a great baseball pitcher who once hurled twenty-two scoreless innings versus the Oklahoma Aggies, doing the throwing. He told his end, Fred "Bink" Capshaw, "Get on your bicycle kid, I'm gonna heave this thing." And he did—a perfect spiral that Capshaw snagged on his fingertips just as the final gun sounded, but the play had to run to its conclusion. As the Nebraska fans looked on in horror and disbelief, Capshaw juked one defender and outran another. Then a collective sigh of relief emanated from the grandstand as the Nebraska captain, Own Frank, shoved Capshaw out of bounds on the twenty-three-yard line to preserve the victory.

After the game, Bennie Owen said, "We gave them a great fight, and with two minutes more to play might have won the game. The Cornhuskers had us outweighed by such a margin that we did well to hold them to two touchdowns. Oklahoma is satisfied. Going against the odds, I consider it the best game the Sooners have played this year."

Biased Effete Eastern Dopesters

Cy Sherman, sports editor of the *Lincoln Star* and incidentally the man who gave Nebraska teams the nickname of Cornhuskers (before this soubriquet caught on in 1900, they had been known as Treeplanters, Rattlesnake Boys, Antelopes, Old Gold Knights and Bugeaters), was highly complimentary of Bennie Owen and his team. This is his account as reported in *Oklahoma Kickoff*:

> *The Oklahomans are entitled to full credit. No such forward passing or receiving as was done by the Sooners was ever duplicated on the Nebraska rectangle…Cornhusker supporters came to the realization of the fact that they were inspecting an altogether new variety of football. Followers of the gridiron game in the West are assured by Eastern dopesters that Yale, Harvard, Princeton et al., are the only Simon pure disciples of all that is virile in football; that the title-holder of the East is entitled to the national*

> *championship, yet one reads in vain the accounts of gridiron combats in the effete East for mention denoting that Eastern coaches and players have sensed or solved the dazzling possibilities of the forward pass as was exemplified Saturday by the pupils of Bennie Owen, Oklahoma's one-armed mentor...the doubter is referred to the running account of last Saturday's battle between Harvard and Yale. The Crimson and the Blue, in fact, were playing archaic football—smashing at the line, running the ends or booting the oval, while on the western prairies the Sooners were shooting forward passes almost half the length of the gridiron, scoring a touchdown chiefly because of their skill in manipulating the long pass, and actually threatening to defeat a much beefier and more powerful opponent.*

Apparently, this type of eastern bias is still alive and well. In *Forward Pass: The Play That Saved Football*, Phillip L. Brooks credits the Notre Dame–Army game of 1913 with showcasing the forward pass and thus being the game that "saved football." According to the legend propounded by Hollywood and other agents of the popular media, Gus Dorias's passes to Knute Rockne propelled a small midwestern Catholic college to an upset over the juggernaut from the banks of the Hudson. This was, of course, a memorable game because of the teams and the players involved. But it was played one year after the OU-Nebraska contest that Sherman wrote about so eloquently. Unfortunately, Brooks makes no mention of the Sooners versus Cornhuskers in 1912, and the names of Owen, Courtright, Reeds and Geyer are not to be found in his book.

In 1913, Geyer was essentially an understudy to the great Reeds, and the Sooners continued to throw with good success. But with the graduation of Reeds in 1914, they really opened things up. That fall, the Sooners returned only four starters, and they were distressingly light, especially in the backfield. Geyer, at six feet tall and 162 pounds, was the largest back. The others averaged perhaps 142 pounds. Owen thought his boys were going to have to take some risks with the pigskin if they were to have any success in 1914. "We knew every major opponent we played was going to score on us, so we needed more offense than ever before," he said.

Bennie schooled all his backs, not just Geyer, in the fine art of throwing the football. He taught them to throw on the run because all the Sooner passes were designed to look like runs. He put up hoops, at about the height of a man's head, on the practice field and had his backs practice throwing the ball through these while running laterally at full speed. "All our backs had passes," Hap Johnson said. "I even threw a pass off a reverse."

The other OU backs were adequate performers, but Geyer was a virtuoso. His teammate Homer Montgomery said of him:

> *Geyer's spots were usually 40 to 70 yards from where he threw the ball. When the defensive halves moved up a little too close to stop our running game, someone noticed it and the long heave was on, even signal to the right and odd to the left, just as far as Spot could throw it after running fifteen or twenty yards toward the sideline. It was up to the receiver to get to the spot when the ball reached it and take the ball on the dead run. We never looked back while running our routes. We didn't have to. We knew the ball would be there. We practiced hour after hour with Spot trying to throw it over our heads and he didn't hold back in practice any more than he did in the games. I think the long grueling practice was the key to our success with the play.*
>
> *When "Humpy"* [another nickname for Geyer] *was rushed and had to get rid of the ball quick, he would snap out a short "Hey" that could be heard as though he were standing right at your shoulder. When that happened we forgot about the spot and deploying suddenly into the open, looked back. He usually passed to whoever was free. Then it was up to us to catch it, or see that the defense didn't catch it.*

It was a 16–16 tie with Kansas that best illustrated OU's offensive philosophy of 1914. While Kansas attempted only one pass, OU completed eleven out of thirty-five for 240 yards. "Oklahoma bewildered us with forward passes," Kansas halfback Ad Lindsey said. The Sooners also rushed for 240 yards in the contest. The *Daily Kansan* alluding to the First World War, which had just begun in Europe, suggested that the Kaiser should "put his zeppelins in the junk pile and hire one Geyer to toss his bombs on London."

C.E. McBride, the sports editor of the *Kansas City Star*, who also just happened to be the umpire of the game, later described it as "an exhibition of thrills with Oklahoma's wonderful forward passing a dazzling feature."

The Lincoln Nebraska *State Journal* chastised the eastern football establishment for ignoring Owen's passing game:

> *The Eastern writers are spinning yarns this year that their coaches sent to Canada for rugby players who drilled the Eastern players on the tricks of the forward pass. Western coaches began experimenting with the forward pass the very moment the play was grafted into the rules of football eight years ago. No coach in the country has had more success with the pass than Bennie Owen of Oklahoma. The Sooners of 1914 are probably more*

> *adept at handling the long pass than any other team in college football. It was not necessary that the East should import Canadian instructors. The Eastern chaps might better have come west to consult with Oklahoma.*

According to *Spalding's Guide* of 1914–15, as reported in *Oklahoma Kickoff*, Oklahoma led the nation in scoring in 1914, with 431 points followed by Washington and Jefferson with 369 and Texas with 358. However, in that same publication, the prominent football historian Park Davis wrote, "For every forward pass that went through for a touchdown in 1914, two forward passes were intercepted and run back for a touchdown."

Walter Camp, the old Yale coach (1888–91) and the man who has become known as the "Father of American Football," also published an article in Spalding's 1914 football guide. Camp wrote, "Someday a combination of the two [passing and running]…is likely to come. No team has yet succeeded in combining both with proper skill."

Obviously, the pompous Camp was defiantly ignorant of the fact that in 1914, Bennie Owen's Oklahoma Sooners had gained more than one mile and scored twenty-five touchdowns via the passing game.

6
The Taskmaster

Subs and Scrubs

Bennie Owen did not impose Draconian training rules on his squad. He worked his men hard, and as long as they kept up the pace, he did not make an issue of occasional training lapses such as drinking, smoking or chewing. Lineman Key Wolf (1905–08) always played with a big plug of tobacco in his mouth. Bennie also did not bore his team with bombastic motivational speeches. He preferred a more individual approach.

"Bennie was never tough with us," Page Belcher, a 1918 lineman, recalled. "He just knew how to make you feel ashamed of yourself." If he saw a player not giving his best effort Bennie would take him out of the game or scrimmage and say to him, "Now sit right down here. See that man out there in your place. He's not loafin'. He's tryin'. You're the better ball player or you wouldn't be on the first team. But you loafed. There's no room on this squad for a loafer. Now watch your sub out there. See that! See him hustle! He wants to play."

Bennie's practices were demanding. He had scrimmages every day in the preseason and three times a week once the regular schedule was underway. First the regulars went against the "scrubs," and then an hour or so later, the Norman High School (NHS) team came over to take on the varsity. Since Owen did not have an assistant coach until he hired Harry Hughes (who would later spend thirty-one years as the head coach of Colorado Agricultural College) in 1910, the scrubs were usually "coached" by one of their own.

It wasn't easy being a scrub in those days. Rarely did more than two or three subs (not scrubs) get into a game. The scrubs did not travel with the team and were never included in the team picture at year's end. If you were a scrub, you either had a deep and abiding love for the game of football or else you were an inveterate masochist.

Charlie Orr loved football. When the 117-pounder showed up for his first practice in 1909, one of the regulars sized him up and asked if he would like to be the water boy. "Shore, if it ain't too fur to the well," he replied. However, Bennie saw something he liked in the gritty little man and, in 1910, put him in charge of the scrub team.

"I had me a hell of a good scrub team," Orr declared.

> *One day early in the season after we had actually whipped the varsity in practice the day before, Bennie came walking over. I always dreaded to see Bennie coming because he always took my good players and put 'um on the varsity. Sure enough this time he took Claude Reeds, Hubert Ambrister, and Sabe Hott and my scrub team was shot to hell. The next day he came over and got me, making me a sub end for both* [Glen] *Clark and Jimmie Rogers. I made all the varsity trips that fall but I didn't get to play a minute in any of them because neither Rogers nor Clark were ever taken out. I held the linesman's chain. Bennie had promoted me to carrying the chain.*

After the varsity was worn down from scrimmaging the scrubs, Bennie sent the Norman High School team against them. This was not quite the mismatch one might expect. In the early part of the twentieth century, Norman had unquestionably the best prep team in the state. Norman High School began playing football in 1896 and, for eighteen years, remained undefeated on its home field before losing to Oklahoma City High in 1913.

Norman should have had a good team because Bennie Owen picked its coach, who installed OU's system. NHS produced some of OU's greatest players, including Claude Reeds and his brothers, Chester, Clarence and Artie; Spot Geyer; Skivey Davis; and Wallace Abbott. Abbott might possibly have been not just the best athlete Owen ever coached but also the best athlete to ever attend the University of Oklahoma. As a senior at Norman High, he was the state champion in the 100-, 220- and 440-yard sprints. He could pass with either hand and kick with either foot, and he was a vicious blocker and tackler. Had he played more than just one year (1917) at OU, he might have set scores of records.

Bennie's practices were not just about smashing bodies together in a scrimmage. He taught a lot of football technique. He taught place kickers the method he had learned from Yost. "Step through," he told them. "Lock your ankle, snap your leg, swing it through and always keep your eye on the ball." He instructed his holders to double the toe of their left foot under them so they could reach up quickly if the center snaps were high. Fifty years later, Bud Wilkinson was still teaching these same techniques at OU.

Bennie also instructed them in the finer arts of backfield play. Elmer "Trim" Capshaw, one of his backs from 1912 to 1915, said:

> *Bennie was the best backfield coach I ever saw. His backs could do everything. He taught us to use either arm as a straight-arm and to shift the ball from one arm to another so as always to have the hand nearest the tackler free to throw out as a straight-arm. Bennie also taught his backs to block. The little backs, and that included most of us, were taught to leave their feet and shoot for an opponent's knee level, turning the shoulder downward so as not to get hurt. Bennie also coached the sidestep, the change of pace and the art of dodging. All his backs were good tacklers.*

The Sooners concluded their practices by going for two-mile cross-country runs with Bennie following along to encourage stragglers.

On the first day of football practice in the fall of 1907, Charlie Wantland jogged out onto Boyd Field carrying his scarred-up leather football helmet. He had worn this headgear the previous year when he played at Castle Heights Military Academy in Lebanon, Tennessee. Wantland had heard a lot about Bennie Owen, and he was looking forward to playing for him. As he looked around trying to get a read on his new teammates and size up his competition at halfback, he quickly realized no one else had a helmet, scarred-up or otherwise. Not wanting to appear to be a softie, he quickly concealed the helmet inside the Bois d'Arc hedge that ringed the field.

Playing Practically Naked

Owen believed that the secret to avoiding injuries was to get his players into top physical condition, not to weight them down with "superfluous" equipment. All Sooners wore a light pad of quilted felt sewn into their jerseys at the shoulder and backs and small thigh pads. No one wore hip pads or back pads and the Sooners were not issued helmets until 1925. "We played practically naked," Billie "Shorty" Clark, a lineman from 1912 to 1914, said. "We wore red cotton jerseys, red stockings and reed ribs in our pants. Some of us sewed light pads in our elbows, but we had no hip pads. Our skulls were hard."

The Sooners played games in the same uniforms they used in practice, tan duck pants and thirty-eight-cent red cotton jerseys. By the season's end, the pants were torn and tattered, and the jerseys had faded to a light pink. "We were the sorriest-looking football team in the world," Artie Reeds, a 1909 letterman, said. "We didn't need numbers on our backs. The fans could recognize each man by the originality of his uniform. No two men looked alike."

Bennie taught his lightly clad minions that they could avoid injuries by relaxing when they were hit, and he instructed his backs to push their hand into the head of a tackler thus transferring part of their weight onto him while falling. He advocated a blocking technique that was designed to minimize injuries. He wanted his men to momentarily "check" an opponent or screen him out of the play rather than try to bowl him over. Harold Keith wrote, "In all his twenty-seven years of coaching Owen never had a player seriously hurt; this seems unequivocal proof of the soundness of his methods. There were of course a few broken bones, but he always held that their proportion was no greater than the number of limbs boys broke anyhow riding bicycles or falling out of trees."

Of course, if a player were injured, he received no sympathy from his coach. Owen had a way of gently chiding his players that made them feel that their injury had come about due to their own clumsiness rather just random bad luck. Therefore, a lot of players would never admit they had been hurt. Charlie Orr recalled:

> *One time big George Anderson, our sub fullback form Ardmore* [1914–15] *stepped in the middle of my back," "My ribs were torn lose. It hurt me even to talk. But I didn't want Bennie to know it. I designed a papier-mâché pad which I hung over the injured spot by means of a belt worn around my chest.*
>
> *"How's the back?" Bennie asked me a few days before the Texas game.*
>
> *"Fine," I lied, cheerfully. I was afraid he would leave me home!*
>
> *Bennie's system was never to admit an injury, therefore eliminating the need for a trainer. The only equipment he carried with him was a roll of tape in his jacket.*

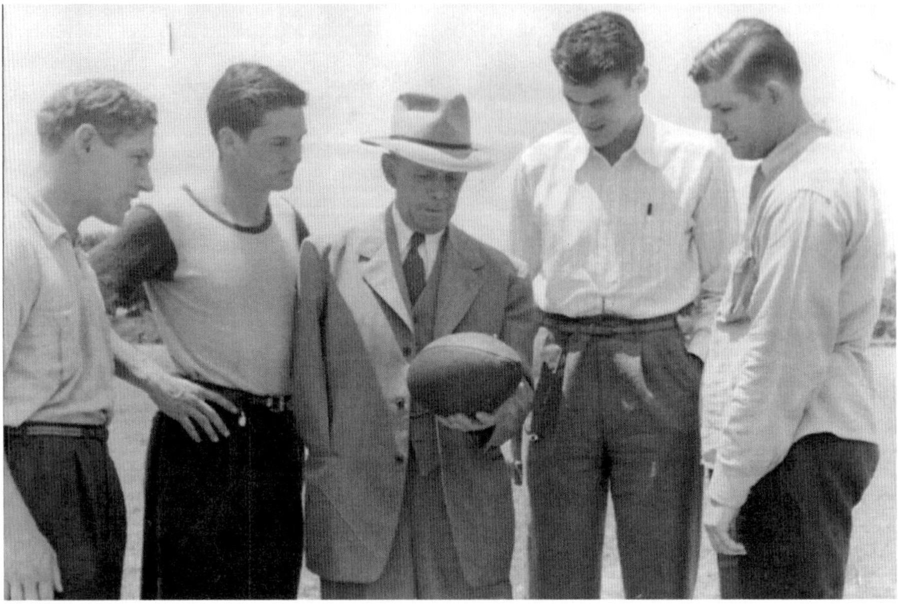

Bennie stands with some of his players, circa 1925. *Courtesy of Jan Howard.*

Orr's observations notwithstanding, Owen was quite capable of treating most of the injuries he saw. He had, after all, apprenticed with Dr. Parsons back in Arkansas City for three years.

Even the tough-minded Owen must have admired the guts and determination of his 157-pound guard Sabe Hott (1910–13), whom he did allow to wear a helmet and with good reason. While working on a wheat harvest one summer near his hometown of Wakita, Oklahoma, Hott was kicked in the head by a mule. He did not give it a second thought at the time, but when he began scrimmaging again in the fall, he started to suffer severe headaches. So, with his coach's blessing, he donned the helmet.

The following summer, Hott, who was one of the best linemen of Bennie's era, suffered an even more serious injury. A spike nail he was hammering ricocheted terribly, blinding him in one eye. When he returned to the campus in the fall of 1913, he fully intended to comply with his parents' strict orders not to play football. But as he was walking by the practice field one day, he saw the footballs in the air and his former teammates sweating, straining and stirring up dust in the warm Indian summer sun, and Bennie Owen, the man he admired above all others, was barking out commands. He could not resist. He checked out a uniform.

Bennie exercised great caution with his tackle that autumn. Hott spent most of his time jogging on the track that circled the field because Bennie held him out of scrimmages. Sabe played only against OU's greatest rivals—Missouri, Kansas and Texas—that season. Before these contests, he wrapped his knees, and then he carefully removed his glass eye and covered the empty socket with a cotton bandage, which was held in place by a long strip of gauze wrapped around his head.

7
LIFE AT 530 ELM STREET

SURROUNDED BY FAMILY

Nina Bessent looked every inch the southern belle that she was upon arriving at the ball. She was wearing a long, straight light green silk evening gown and full-length white gloves. She wore her dark hair swept up, and her headband perfectly matched her dress, as did her shoes, with their one-and-a-half-inch heels. Every man in the room took notice.

Soon, very soon, a man was approaching her apparently with the intention of asking her to dance. Her first thought was "Oh no! What does this old one-armed man want with me?" But she danced with him and saw that he had soft, kind eyes and a gentle nature. They shared several dances that evening, and she agreed to go out on a date with him.

Nina was born in Whitesboro, Texas, and moved to Norman with her family when she was a young girl. Her father, Charles H. Bessent, was one of the founders of both the First National and Security National Banks in Norman. After her graduation from Norman High School, Nina attended Ward-Belmont College in Nashville, Tennessee, and the University of Oklahoma.

At the time Bennie Owen met Nina, he was living in the Sigma Nu fraternity house at 526 South University Boulevard. The Sigma Nus had started a chapter on the OU campus in 1909 and several of Bennie's players, including Key Wolf and all the Reeds brothers—Artie, Clarence and

Claude—had become members. At their urging, Bennie became initiate No. 30 of the Delta Epsilon Chapter in 1910. Apparently, Bennie was eligible for membership because he was enrolled in some classes at OU. Bennie remained actively involved with the Sigma Nus for many years.

Living with Bennie in his basement apartment at the Sigma Nu house was his trusty bird dog Buster. Throughout the course of his life, Bennie would have several bird dogs, most of them named Buster. This particular Buster went with him everywhere, so naturally he tagged along when Bennie walked over to Nina's house to pick her up for their date. Bennie asked Mr. Bessent if he could leave Buster with him while he and Nina walked over to John Barbour's drugstore for some sandwiches and Cokes. "Is he used to staying inside?" her father asked. "Oh sure, he'll be just fine, Mr. Bessent," Bennie assured him. "I leave him in my room all the time." Unfortunately, Buster had other ideas. Bennie and Nina had not gone three blocks before they turned around to find Buster running up behind them. They later learned he had made his escape by breaking out a plate glass window.

Bennie adored Nina, and like everyone else who knew him, she grew to love the charming coach. Despite the rather shaky start to their courtship, they were married in the spring of 1912 when he was thirty-six years old and she was twenty-five. His entire football squad attended the wedding and presented the happy couple with a case of flat silver and a tray inscribed with the name of every team member.

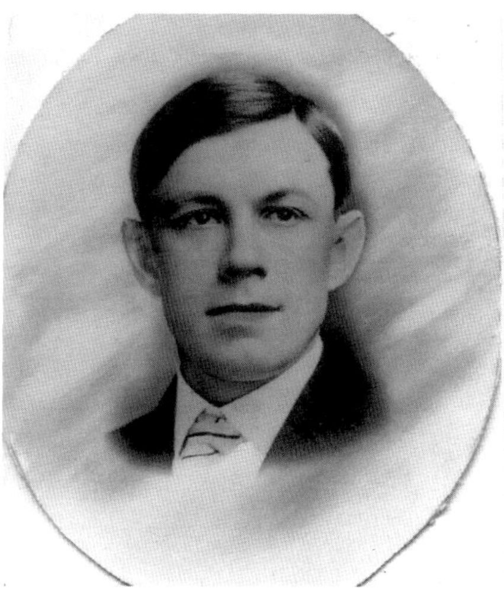

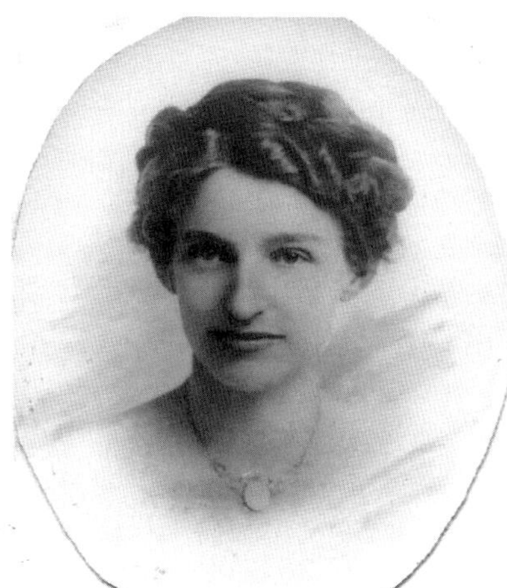

Bennie and Nina's wedding pictures, 1912. *Courtesy of Jan Howard.*

Bennie and his new bride built a home at 530 Elm Street. Their house was originally a single story with a basement, but they would later add an upstairs. Although this was not a home that would ever be featured in *Southern Living*, it was comfortable and very hospitable to their many guests. There were always guests. Nina had been a member of the Kappa Alpha Theta sorority in college and every Theta at OU knew that if she missed her curfew, she could spend the night with the Owens. And any Sooner athlete who did not have a place to stay would live in their basement.

After the renovation, their house had five bedrooms, a spacious library and a large front porch with the obligatory swing. Their friends remembered it as "the coolest house in Norman." They meant this literally because Bennie had installed a large fan on the back porch that made the severe Oklahoma summers a lot more bearable. Bennie and Nina were among the first in Norman to have a telephone. Their friends had no trouble remembering their number—seven.

Soon, they were surrounded by family. Nina's parents moved into a home just to the north of them, Bennie's folks moved next door to them on the south and Bennie's brother Ted bought a home at 525 College, which was just behind Bennie and Nina's house. Unfortunately, none of these historic old homes are still standing. They were torn down years ago so that the university could build a parking garage. Such is progress.

KINDRED SPIRITS

It must have been quite a shock for Bennie to learn only a few weeks after his wedding that he had been fired. Surely, he must have thought his job was secure since he had just posted a perfect 8-0-0 record the previous fall. However, it seems that there were several members of Oklahoma's state legislature who took a dim view of athletics, and they thought Owen's $3,500 annual salary was far too extravagant.

These misguided solons had recently fired a piano teacher at a small college because she had only one arm. They thought she was squandering tax payers' money since she could only play the piano with one hand. "You know the State University has a one-armed football coach," one of these benighted lawmakers said. "Why don't we fire him, too?" So they did. Fortunately, Stratton Duluth Brooks, who had recently replaced Arthur Evans as OU's president, rectified this fiasco so quickly that Owen did not even realize he had been fired until after he had been rehired.

Brooks and Owen were kindred spirits. Each had a strong personality and made decisions quickly and decisively, usually without seeking anyone's advice. The two men liked and respected each other. President Brooks was Owen's only boss at OU. He answered to no one else. Brooks ran the university, and Owen ran the athletic department. Each understood this. "If I had a problem I'd go see the president," Owen said. "He'd look me right in the eye and tell me what help I could count on. Then I'd go off and quit worrying. He never forgot to follow through. It would always happen like he said it would. He rarely altered any part of my program. But if there was something about it he didn't like, we always changed it to suit him."

Harold Keith wrote of Bennie Owen:

> *Owen's relationship with his athletic council in those days was a lot like Brooks' with the Board of Education: Owen regarded his council as an advisory group only. If it had any advice that was constructive, which it frequently did, he was happy to have it. But he made all the decisions and took all the responsibility. He rarely bothered with details. Owen's theory was that since he, and not the council was paid to do his job, he should be the boss. He never permitted interference by alumni, regents, newspapermen, politicians, or close friends.*

With his good friend and trusted ally in charge of the university and the debacle of his firing resolved, Bennie Owen could now get on with his mission of building OU's athletic department. And he started building a family. All three of his daughters were born in their home on Elm Street. First came Jane in 1913, then Ruth in 1915 and finally Dorothy in 1921. "I was the third child and the third daughter," she said. "I could have been a disappointment for my father, but he never made me feel that way. He was always great, wonderful; the most even-tempered man in the world. No one ever had a better dad that I did. He was always on your side."

Bennie almost lost his home in 1936. His daughter Dorothy remembered this day very well. At first, she did not know why her ninth grade classmates were staring out the window. Then she saw the black plume of smoke. Their room was in the Carnegie Building, which was one of only four buildings on campus when Bennie Owen arrived on the campus of the University of Oklahoma campus thirty-one years earlier. At first, she dismissed the smoke. It was obviously not close to their building, and she knew they were in not danger. Then she began to wonder—it was coming from the west, and their housc lay to the west.

She could not shake the nagging feeling that something might be wrong. She raised her hand, and when the teacher called on her, she asked for permission to step outside to see if her house was indeed on fire. The teacher denied her request, and she had an excruciating half-hour wait until finally, the class was dismissed.

She ran home as fast as she could. It did not take her long because her home was only about two hundred yards from the school. She arrived just a little ahead of her father, who had also seen the smoke while working at his office. By the time they got there, all their furniture had been removed from the house and was sitting out in their front lawn. Several OU students had seen the fire and had lined up and passed out chairs, tables, lamps, etc. They had even taken the legs off a baby grand piano and carried it outside. Nothing had been broken in the process. Dorothy stood with her father on the driveway and wondered what would become of their home. Would it be torn down? Would they build it back? They built it back.

A Time of Simple Pleasures

Dorothy remembered living in Norman in the 1920s as a time of "simple pleasures." "Our lives were not as structured as children's are today. We didn't really have to do anything. We were always very contented, very happy," she said. "And I always knew the rules. You will be good. You will do your homework. It never occurred to me to break the rules."

After breakfast each morning, she and her sisters would walk about five blocks to McKinley grade school. For lunch, they walked back home, where their mother usually had a bowl of soup waiting for them. In the evenings, after their homework was done, they might play cards or listen to the radio. On Saturday afternoons, they usually listened to the Metropolitan Opera radio broadcasts, or they might ride their bicycles to the Sooner Theater for a movie. None of Bennie's girls were particularly interested in sports, but Ruth was the most adventurous of the three and the most accident prone, apparently. "It seems like she was always breaking an arm or something," Dorothy recalled. "I was jealous of her because she got to have a cast. I never had a cast."

Bennie Owen taught his girls the same disregard for physical pain that he had learned from his mother and that he practiced with his football players. "If you had something to do, you got on with it. You didn't worry about pain," Dorothy explained. "Mother's shoulder would pop out of socket, and Daddy would pop it back in, which of course, he had done for a lot of his football players."

One day, Jane came running to her dad crying. "What's the matter?" Bennie asked.

"Ruth stuck her finger in my eye," she sobbed.

"Oh, well, don't cry about a little thing like that. She took it out of your eye, didn't she?" Bennie replied.

Joe Haynes (Jane's son) had very distinct memories of visiting his grandparents' home when he was a small boy in the late 1940s. "It seemed like a huge house to me at the time with a never-ending flight of stairs. The one outstanding thing I remember about the house was the basement! It had the most jumbled up mess of good things to play with a child could ever want. Anything from a bottle opener to fishing tackle to golf balls to you name it and it was there." Ten years later, the house no longer seemed so big to him, nor was the stairway "never ending." But the basement was still just as interesting.

Joe's cousin Jan (Page) Howard also had very fond memories of 530 Elm. She said:

> *I loved his house in Norman. I can picture just about all of it. It was always a big treat when we would visit my grandparents. Every time I went to Norman* [from her home in Houston], *Gran Gran would give me a big handful of change. He would reach into his pocket and pull out a bunch of coins and say, "Look at all this! Do you want it?" To me it would look like a fortune. It would be like four or five dollars in change.*
>
> *Bennie and I would play go fish. And I would win every time, and he couldn't understand how I did it. Then I told him it was because I could see the reflection of his cards in his glasses.*
>
> *I always liked to go to the OU football games in Norman. It was really exciting. It was fun to sit in the box seats with Gran Gran, but I never would have known he had been a football coach if Mom hadn't told me because he never said anything about it.*

BUILDING AND GROWING

Bennie was never one to sit around and reminisce about bygone glory days. The present was much more interesting to him than the past. If his children or grandchildren asked him about things he had done as a child or his coaching career, he would give a short answer and then ask, "OK, now what do you want to do this afternoon? Do you want to go fishing?"

Busy was the word for Bennie Owen. He was always building things and growing things. He cut down some cedar trees near his house and made a chest for each of his daughters. "There wasn't anything he couldn't do," Dorothy said. "He put up a steel beam by himself to brace the house. I'll never know how he did that. He wasn't a big man, and he did not look muscular. But he was strong. And it seemed like he never walked but always ran. I could never keep up with him even when he got older."

Joe Haynes remembered another of his grandfather's feats of strength. "We had a contest once where we placed a dime in an old-fashioned clothespin [the kind without the spring] and squeezed it shut. You had to keep the dime in the clothespin [for] three minutes. This doesn't sound hard, but it was. Gran Gran could do it indefinitely, I guess, because after five minutes we told him he could quit. The rest of us could not make the three minutes."

Bennie grew tomatoes and a lot of other things in his backyard. His pride and joy was the pecan tree he had grafted branches to. "This was his showpiece," his granddaughter Sandy Trudgeon (Dorothy's daughter) recalled. He grew mushrooms in his basement—that is, until Nina could no longer stand the stench—and he tended bees in a hive that he kept near the railroad tracks. This was about a half mile east of his house, near where he would later build OU's first golf course. This site is now officially known as Brandt Park but more commonly referred to as the Duck Pond.

Busy as he was, Bennie always had time to play with his daughters. Dorothy recalled:

> *I used to find all kinds of coins when I would go for walks. I was sixteen years old before I realized Daddy was walking ahead of me and emptying his pockets. We would go swimming in the lake at the old country club* [which was about four miles east of Norman on Alameda Street]. *Sometimes we would see tarantulas or even cottonmouth water moccasins, but they never bothered us. One time, Ruth and Jane were swimming, and I wanted to go in. But mother said I was too little. Then Daddy said he would take me, and he picked me up and walked into the water with his clothes on. He was a great swimmer with only one arm.*

HUDSONS, FRANKLINS, HUPMOBILES AND TUCKERS

Bennie loved automobiles. He got his first in the spring of 1916 as a gift from OU students and fans across the state in recognition of his undefeated season the previous fall. He had no trouble finding a parking spot for his black Hudson Super-Six Turing Sedan as only three faculty members owned autos at that time: President Brooks (Cadillac), Dr. Edwin De Barr (Paige) and Dr. Albert Van Fleet (Ford). On some days, Bennie would forget that he had driven his car to work that morning and walk home in the evening. Then he would walk back and retrieve the automobile.

Bennie's car must have been one of the very first of its kind to roll off the assembly line because the Hudson Motor Company did not receive its patent for the Super-Six until December 28, 1915. The Hudson had six cylinders (as the name would imply) and a seventy-six-horse power, 288-cubic-centimeter engine. It could hold seven passengers, and it cost $1,375, roughly twice as much as a Model-T Ford.

This engine could propel it to a top speed of seventy-five miles per hour, and it could accelerate from zero to sixty in twenty-three seconds. The fact that its gearshift was on the right side—the side of Bennie's missing arm—apparently posed no problem for him. However, it is doubtful that he ever reached the maximum speed of seventy-five miles per hour—at least not for very long because very few streets in Norman were paved in 1916. The rules of the road then were "Stay in the ruts and look out for stumps." Bennie's football players may not have been so thrilled with this new vehicle because he frequently parked it on Boyd Field and turned on the lights so that he could drill his troops long after dark.

Bennie definitely had a taste for the more exotic automobiles. He owned a Franklin and a Hupmobile. He even put in an order for a Tucker in 1948. But only fifty-one were manufactured, and he did not get one. The Franklin was considered a luxury car in its day and featured a barrel hood and an air-cooled engine. Apparently this air-cooling system did not work all that well because the engine frequently overheated and caught on fire. Bennie kept a bucket of sand in the car that he would pour on the engine in such emergencies. Such incidents were considered *de rigueur* for automobile owners in that era.

Bennie would often let one of his daughters sit on his lap and steer the car along Norman streets as he worked the pedals and shifted gears. "I was driving when I was five," Dorothy said. "Daddy would stick his left arm through steering wheel, so he had control of it, and shift the gears."

Once, just after Bennie had purchased a new Buick, he loaned it to John Jacobs, the OU track coach, who drove it to a meet at the University of Kansas. While Jacobs was busy at the track meet, the car was stolen. The problem was Jacobs was colorblind and could not give the Lawrence police a very good description of the auto, but somehow, it was recovered.

8
BASEBALL

Bennie knew baseball.

He learned the game from his father, George, the old barehanded catcher. Bennie and his friends in St. Louis played the game along the banks of the Mississippi River. They played with baseballs they snatched when one of their beloved Browns—perhaps "Tip" O'Neil, Hugh Duffy or even the great Charles Comiskey—fouled one over the roof of Sportsman's Park.

In 1891, Bennie moved with his family to the hamlet of Guelph in southeastern Kansas, and he continued to play baseball. He, his father and brothers Bill and Ted marked off a diamond in one corner of their pasture and began teaching the game to the local farmers. He lettered in baseball at the University of Kansas. Bennie also spent the summer of 1901 (two years before the first World Series was played) umpiring in the Missouri Valley Baseball League before joining Fielding Yost's staff at Michigan.

Although baseball is a game of infinite strategy, deception and even blatant larceny (stealing bases and stealing signs), its rules are simple and unambiguous at the core. A runner is either safe or out. The pitch was either a ball or a strike. The ball was either fair or foul. Bennie lived by simple, straightforward rules. He learned from his parents to do the right thing, never the wrong thing. He never ventured into foul territory.

There is also a timeless quality to baseball, as Roger Angell so eloquently describes in *The Summer Game*: "Since baseball time is measured only in outs, all you have to do is succeed, literally; keep hitting, keep the rally alive, and you have defeated time." Bennie could appreciate this. There was never a man who lived his life more thoroughly in the present than Bennie Gilbert Owen.

Bennie loved baseball.

The University of Oklahoma had a baseball team before Bennie arrived in Norman but apparently not a coach. Records show that OU fielded a team in 1898, 1899 and 1900 but not in 1901 or 1902. The school also had the sport in 1903 and 1905 but not in 1904. In 1905, the Boomers, as they were then known (they became the Sooners in 1908), played a ten-game schedule. In no season prior to that had they played more than four games, and no coach was listed for any of these years. Then Bennie took over the program in 1906, and things changed. He brought the same leadership and stability to the baseball program that he had to football.

By the early 1900s, football was well established as a collegiate sport, but this was decidedly not the case with baseball. The OU student newspaper, the *Umpire*, devoted a long article to this issue on Valentine's Day 1908, "What is the matter with baseball?" it asked. Then, quoting a person they identified as "the general manager of athletics at Kansas University," the article continued:

> *When the mid-winter sun beams down warm on the diamond and the weather conditions point to an unusually fine spring for base ball* [the sport was often written in two words in those days] *the fans began getting into their summer suits and wondering what is to come of the spring sport? Where is the schedule? Where is the team? What did I hear about ineligibility? Who isn't eligible? All these questions are the warm questions of the hour. But they can't all be answered.*
>
> *We are thinking of abandoning base ball* [at Kansas]. *Unlike football it isn't essentially a college sport. Its greatest players and greatest advocates are outside the college world. And its best exhibitions are on the professional diamond. Now when we deny men the right to play on our teams when they play on professional teams in the summer we kill the sport, for the college season of base ball barely passes the practice time of professional teams and men who play only college base ball do not become proficient enough in the sport to put up a first class exhibition of base ball, and the games are not patronized. Besides we do not like the idea of making college a preparatory school to professional base ball. Such is the sad news for college base ball in general.*

The article further stressed that although the speaker was representing the University of Kansas, the same principles applied at Oklahoma as well.

But, thanks largely to Bennie Owen, baseball not only survived but also thrived at OU. The 1909 Sooner yearbook proclaimed, "Baseball has always been a close competitor with Football for first place in athletics at the University. Although Basket ball, Track and Tennis have held prominent places in the school's activities, they have never been considered so important as Baseball, or have they received as much support from the student body."

And on April 14, 1911, the *Umpire* published the following in an article:

> *Probably the greatest baseball games of the season will be played on Boyd Field next Friday and Saturday, April 21, and 22, when the Longhorns from the University of Texas clash with the Sooners. Every student should attend this time for the purpose of strengthening the Sooners and seeing an exhibition of real college baseball. Fifty cents will be the admission fee. Most of us can afford to pay that price for these high class games and very few of us can afford to miss them.*

For the record, the Sooners and Longhorns split the two games, with Texas taking the first game 7–1 and OU prevailing 7–3 in the second. The unnamed reporter for the *Umpire* wrote, "Little enthusiasm was evoked by the first contest, but in the second, when the Sooners started their winning streak, a large crowd rushed to the side lines and carried on such a demonstration as has never been seen over a baseball game on Boyd field." Boyd Field must have seen a lot of raucous demonstrations, as it was the venue for all of OU's football, baseball and track contests from the time of Owen's arrival in 1905 until the new stadium was ready for use in 1923.

So who, besides the Longhorns, did the Sooner Nines play on this venerable old field surrounded by the Bois d'Arc hedge and its grandstand that seated five hundred? In addition to other Oklahoma institutions, such as Central State Normal, East Central Normal, Oklahoma A&M and the Chilocco Indians, OU played the University of Arkansas and the University of Kansas almost every year. In 1914, a team composed primarily of Chinese students journeyed all the way from Honolulu, Hawaii, to Norman for a two-game series with the Sooners. Hawaii shut out OU 4–0 in the first game, but Bennie's boys got their bats going the next day and prevailed 12–1.

Also during Owen's years as coach, the Sooners played several games against major-league teams. These were exhibition games for the professional clubs but not for OU. These games (all losses) counted against their record.

In April 1916, John Joseph McGraw, arguably the greatest manager to ever lace up a pair of spikes, brought his New York Giants to Norman. McGraw managed the Giants from 1902 through 1931, winning ten pennants and five World Series. The legendary Connie Mack once said, "There has been only one manager and his name is McGraw."

So, did Bennie Owen discuss the hit-and-run, squeeze play and other types of baseball strategy with the great McGraw? Surely he must have, although the newspaper accounts of the day did not mention it. Sports reporting, in those days, was not nearly as sophisticated or in depth as it is now in the twenty-first century, especially not at the college level.

In 1916, 1917 and 1918, the Sooners played the Chicago White Sox in Norman. Sox owner Charles Comiskey was a man Bennie remembered well from his boyhood days in St. Louis. Perhaps this was the connection that brought the Chicagoans to Norman so many times.

Comiskey had built a great team. Oscar "Happy" Felsch was a solid catcher. Eddie Collins was certainly the best second baseman of his time and perhaps of all time, but the Sox star player in this era was one "Shoeless" Joe Jackson. Joseph Jefferson Jackson finished his thirteen-year career with a .356 lifetime batting average, second only to Ty Cobb. The Sox also had a great pitching staff headed by Ed Cicotte, who won twenty-eight games in 1917 and twenty-nine in 1919. It must have been a wonderful treat for the local fans to see these great players toiling so far out on the prairie, even if they did administer quite a shellacking to their local heroes.

The Palehose did not win the pennant in 1916. They finished second to the Boston Red Sox, whose star moundsman was a twenty-one-year-old phenomenon named George Ruth, who won twenty-three games and had the league's lowest ERA (1.75) and most shutouts (nine).

Comiskey's men won the pennant and World Series in 1917. In 1919, they again won the American League pennant, but of course, this World Series will forever be remembered for the infamous "Black Sox" scandal. Several of the White Sox, apparently believing they were underpaid and underappreciated, conspired with gamblers, principally Arnold "Big Bankroll" Rothstein, to throw the 1919 World Series to the Cincinnati Reds. A year later, baseball commissioner Judge Kennesaw Mountain Landis levied a lifetime ban from baseball against eight members of this team, including Cicotte, Felsch and Jackson.

Shortly after the game with the White Sox in 1917, the Sooners canceled the remainder of their schedule in all spring sports because the United States had formally entered into the Great War. On April 12, 1917, the *Oklahoma Daily* reported, "With a spontaneous outburst of patriotism, 850 men students unanimously resolved to commence at once, a training camp on campus with daily universal military drill, at a mass meeting of all male students Wednesday [the previous day] afternoon."

Five days later, another article in the student paper stated:

> *The Sooner Football coach, Bennie Owen* [apparently, even the campus reporters tended to overlook his baseball and basketball coaching] *always a leader at this game has turned, for the sake of his country into a military officer with the rank of lieutenant colonel in the student regiment. As he was a leader in sports, "Bennie" unconsciously declared himself a leader in our little military world by proposing that the athletic schedule be discontinued and that Sooner manhood be worked into fighting shape.*

Apparently this "spontaneous outburst of patriotism" was short-lived as less than a month later, Owen explained that because of the recently enacted conscription bill, he would await further developments on the national scene before making or breaking any future athletic engagements. By the fall of 1917, the university seems to have resumed its normal activities, and its athletic teams played their full complement of games during the 1917–18 academic year. However, the 1918 football schedule was cut back to six games.

The same issue of the student paper that reported Bennie's comments about the conscription bill also carried a story about OU professors who were bringing their rifles on campus. They were not using the guns for military training, however. They were using them to shoot rabbits, which they then fed to their dogs. The paper called the rabbits, which made their home near the zoology building, "a splendid asset to the campus" and also said that they were "of great value here on the grounds." The paper further editorialized, "To keep boys from killing birds on the campus is the aim of the zoology department. This is hard to do when the boys see faculty members themselves in the midst of careless and ruthless slaughter of valuable animals."

In April 1918, after what had become their annual spring game with the White Sox, the Sooners played a contest against that other team from the Windy City, the Cubs. This game was held at the fairgrounds in Guthrie and over one thousand fans turned out and watched the Cubs slaughter the Sooners 13–0.

The best player on the Cub's roster, by far, was the future hall-of-famer Grover Cleveland Alexander, or "Old Pete," as he was also known. In the three previous seasons, while a member of the Philadelphia Phillies, he had won 31, 33 and 30 games. Although he battled epilepsy and alcoholism throughout his twenty-year career, he won 373 games, the third-highest total on record. Alexander threw a few warm-up pitches that day but did not play in the game. A few months later, he was fighting in the trenches of France, an experience that would haunt him for the rest of his life.

An article in the *Daily Oklahoman* the following day reported, "Guthrie treated the Cubs royally and made them an attractive offer to train in Guthrie next spring. The offer included free use of the municipal bath house." The Cubs declined.

That same article was rather unkind to the Cubs' first baseman, Fred Merkle. "Merkle today appeared to be carrying too much flesh and was slow on the bases. However, he hammered out a single and a triple, the triple going into the plowed ground beyond the left field. Had he got away from his snail's pace on the bases, the hit would have easily gone for a home run."

No doubt, every fan at the Logan County Fairgrounds that day was well aware of a play Merkle was involved in ten years earlier when he was a member of the New York Giants playing against his current teammates, the Cubs. Known forever after as "Merkle's Boner," this episode was perhaps the most famous debacle in baseball history. It unfolded as follows.

On September 28, 1908, the Giants and Cubs were battling for the pennant. The Giants were batting in the bottom of the ninth inning with two outs and the score tied 1–1. There were runners on first and third, Merkle being the runner on first. The batter hit the ball safely into left center field, and the runner on third crossed the plate with the winning run—or was it? It is at this point that things got confusing.

Moose McCormick clearly touched home plate. That much is not in dispute. The problem is that Merkle may not have touched second base. Fred said he did, but the Cubs said that when Merkle saw McCormick was certain to score he beat a path straight to the clubhouse without going near the bag. The matter has been in dispute for more than one hundred years.

When the Giant fans saw McCormick cross the plate they thought the game was over and rushed onto the field to celebrate the victory. Meanwhile, the Cubs' second baseman, Johnny Evers (as in Tinker to Evers to Chance), was screaming at his outfielder, Solly Hofman, to throw the ball to him so he could force Merkle out at second. One version of the story holds that a fan intercepted Hofman's throw and hurled the ball into the stands. The Cubs have forever claimed that pitcher Rube Kroh took the ball away from the fan and tossed it to Evers who touched second base, thus forcing out Merkle.

The umpires were so bamboozled by all the mayhem that they waited until the following day to make their ruling, which was that Merkle had not touched second base and therefore McCormick's run had not counted. The Giants had not won the game, which would have to be replayed. The Cubs won the do-over and nosed out the Giants for the pennant by one game. The Chicagoans then went on to defeat Ty Cobb and the Detroit Tigers in the World Series for the second year in a row. Over one hundred years later, they still had not won another World Series.

Merkle's teammate Fred Snodgrass stated in a book entitled *The Glory of Their Times*, edited by Lawrence S. Ritter, "As a result of what happened he took more abuse and vituperation than any other nineteen-year old I've ever heard of." All this "abuse and vituperation" came from fans. Neither Merkle's teammates nor McGraw ever criticized him, at least not publically.

In the early years, Bennie's father, George, helped him coach the Sooners. In later years, he was assisted by his brother Bill. As in other sports, Bennie stressed speed and teamwork with his hard-ballers, and he wanted them to show a fighting spirit. Upon returning from a successful road trip in 1914, Owen told his men, "You guys won because you've got the old fight and go that has made OU what she is in athletics. You won a game or two at first and got stuck on yourselves and thought all you had to do was go out on the field and the game was yours. On this trip is the first time that you've showed the Sooner spirit that makes us beat KU playing football. You've had the team all the time but lacked the fight."

The records from this era are incomplete, but it appears that Bennie's best hitters were Ray Smiser, who posted a .341 average in 1913; Neil Johnson, .341 in 1914; Charles Price, .342 in 1915; and Bryan Kirchner. The 1921 Sooner yearbook said, "Kirsch is the Babe Ruth of the Oklahoma team. His terrific smashes usually went for extra bases. He hit one at Manhattan, Kansas, that took an earthen embankment to stop. He played the sun field in Norman and played almost errorless ball."

Unfortunately, Bennie did not always have strong hitting teams. On April 28, 1918, the student paper stated, "According to unofficial figures, after playing four exhibition games and two collegiate games the Sooners have amassed the grand hitting average of .144." A month later, the paper reported that Bennie's boys had finished the season with a record of 10-6, although "it is not believed the team averaged more than .200 for the year." And his 1920 (5-8-1) team finished the year with an anemic .194 average.

Owen had pretty solid pitching and defense during most of his tenure at OU. In 1913, the Sooners allowed two runs or less in ten of their seventeen games and, the next year, two runs or less in thirteen of twenty games. Raymond Courtright, whom the Sooner yearbook described as "a pitcher having no peer in the southwest," threw a no-hitter against Missouri in 1911.

Alro "Skivey" Davis, a three-sport letterman (1917–21), was another moundsman who could always be counted on to turn in a solid performance. There were many other athletes who earned their letters with Bennie in more than one sport. Hugh McDermott, Howard McCasland, Claude Reeds and William Cox were just a few of the many athletes who accomplished this feat.

Bennie's 1915 club won seventeen games, which stood as a school record for twenty years. When he stepped down as coach in 1922, his record stood at 142-102-4 for a winning percentage of .581. He was succeeded by his brother Bill, who coached the Sooners for four more seasons before giving way to Lawrence "Jap" Haskell, who had played for Bennie in 1921–22. Haskell coached for fifteen years (1927–42) before he relinquished the helm to Jack Baer. Baer, who played under Haskell from 1936–38, coached the Sooners until 1967. Therefore, it can quite reasonably be stated that for sixty-two seasons, Bennie Owen had a profound influence on the coaching of baseball at the University of Oklahoma.

9
BASKETBALL

Bennie did not play basketball as a young boy because there was no basketball when he was a young boy. Dr. James Naismith did not hang his peach baskets in the Springfield, Massachusetts YMCA until 1891, at which time Bennie would have been sixteen years old. In Owen's sophomore year (1898–99), Kansas University, coached by the very same Dr. Naismith, played its first season of basketball. This could have been Bennie's first exposure to the sport, but somehow, he learned it well enough to guide the Sooners to three undefeated seasons and a career record of 113-49 for a percentage of .698 from 1908 through 1921.

Basketball was not the only invention Naismith contributed to the sports world. As a student at Springfield College, he played football for the venerable Amos Alonzo Stagg. One day at practice, Naismith, tired of having his ears skinned up, cut a football lengthwise and tied it on his head, thus fashioning the game's first helmet. Ironically, he was also the only basketball coach in the history of KU to have a losing record for his career.

Bennie was not OU's first basketball coach. That distinction belongs to D.C. Hall, a product of Brown University who guided the Sooners to a 3-4 record in the 1907–08 season. According to David Levy in his wonderful book *The University of Oklahoma: A History, Volume I, 1890–1917*, President David Ross Boyd hired former Olympian Hall to supervise OU's "Physical Culture" program.

Boyd also hired an attractive young woman named Kate McBride to direct the women's Physical Culture program at the university. Hall and

McBride were married in 1905. So, if Hall did not achieve great success as a basketball coach, he did so in at least one other respect.

Bennie's three undefeated seasons were 1909–10 (8-0), 1912–13 (8-0) and 1918–19 (12-0). The 1909–10 squad was led by captain Ernest Lambert. Lambert, a six-foot-tall forward, was a first team All-American and OU's first All-American round-baller. The 1909 yearbook said of Ernest, "Captain Lambert, was the star of the team. He played all over the floor, and threw more goals during the season than all the other men put together."

Early in Bennie's career, the basketball season usually did not begin until after Christmas. In 1909, the season opener was played on January 19. The Sooners trounced Central State Normal 93–7. Lambert poured in 47 points. The next day, the *Umpire* raved of his performance: "Lambert, at forward seemed to be invincible, and threw baskets at will. All that was needed to assure two points was to get the ball into his hands." In a game against Emporia State Normal later that year, Lambert made 27 of his team's 33 points.

Under the guidance of Bennie Owen, the great Lambert and his teammates sparked an interest in this new sport at the University of Oklahoma. The 1910 Sooner yearbook stated:

> *The all-victorious basket ball team of 1909–10 may well be called the Southwestern champions as well as state champions because they not only defeated the rivals of the University in this state but also Texas University and the strong Washburn teams fell before us by overwhelming scores.*
>
> *Formerly basketball was not very popular as a University activity but this year there was greater competition for the team and the attendance at the games was far greater than ever before. The future of basketball seems assured.*

Bennie's second undefeated squad (1912–13) did not have a superstar like Lambert, but it had several good athletes and great teamwork. The captain and most reliable player was Claude Reeds (of gridiron fame). The other forward, John Bell, was an accurate shooter. Frank Parsons and "Hoot" Clift alternated at the center position, and Raymond Courtright (the great pitcher) and Glen Swanson were speedy guards and deft ball handlers.

The 1913 Sooner yearbook described this team in glowing terms:

> *During the past few years basketball has gained a wonderful foothold in the West and is now generally recognized as the great college sport during the winter months. Its extreme popularity in Oklahoma is due*

> *greatly to the fact that the State University has followed the game with zeal since it was first brought westward, and has turned out some teams second to none in the Southwest.*
>
> *Coach Bennie Owen has never produced a team at the Sooner School which could equal his speedy, machine-like aggregation of the season of 1912–13. The brilliancy of this club, as exhibited by the caging battles the past season, has never been equaled by a Sooner five in the history of the University of Oklahoma. The season's schedule has seen the Sooners humble the Oklahoma Baptists in two defeats, crush the championship hopes of the Chilocco Indians in two decisive defeats, curb the southern invasion of the "Terrible Swedes" in two victories and shatter all pretensions of the Aggies and Central Normal in two of the most top-heavy scores ever recorded against an opposing team.*

Owen's third and final undefeated squad was his 1918–19 edition. No opponent even came close to beating the 1918–19 Sooners. Their average margin of victory was 29.3 points.

The captain and leader of this squad was Hugh "Scottie" McDermott, a five-foot-eight, 145-pound guard. Perhaps Bennie saw a little of his younger self in this fiery little man. McDermott and Owen were about the same size. They were natural athletes who relied more on brains than brawn, and both had the type of confident personality that made them great leaders.

McDermott hailed from Duncan, Oklahoma, where he had played four years of high school basketball. His team won the state championship in his senior year. In college, Scottie was quite a busy fellow. In addition to serving on the student council, he won a total of six varsity letters, three each in football and basketball, and he was elected captain of both sports. If all that did not keep him busy enough, he also helped coach athletics at Norman High School during his time at OU.

Complementing Mac on this team were Dorsey Boyle, a center, and Homer Risen, a forward. Both men were just a shade over six feet tall, which was plenty tall enough for centers and forwards in that era. Bennie never had a player taller than six feet, two inches, and Phil White of his 1920 team, at 195 pounds, was thought to be the heaviest man in the Missouri Valley Conference.

In addition to those previously mentioned, Bennie had two other very outstanding basketball players at OU, Howard McCasland and Ed Waite. McCasland, who was also an excellent end for Bennie's football team, was the captain of the 1915–16 team. He seemed to have springs in his legs.

Fans claimed that throughout his senior season the six-foot center controlled every jump ball. In this era, having a center who could control the jump balls was extremely important because until 1936, after each made field goal or free throw, the teams lined up again at center court and the game restarted with a center jump.

McCasland typically accounted for about half of his team's points in each game. Former OU president Dr. George Lynn Cross, in his book *The Seeds of Excellence*, wrote of McCasland, "During his senior year, 1915–16, as center and captain of the basketball team, he scored a total of 407 points—a school record that was not broken for more than twenty-five years."

Cross further said of him, "With a personal fortune amassed relatively early in life, Howard was determined to repay the society that had made his success possible. He organized the McCasland Foundation to handle his charitable contributions, and he made his extraordinary organizational and leadership talents available in public service. The University of Oklahoma benefited greatly from his contributions of money and time."

Charles Edwin Waite was the center for Bennie's last basketball team in 1920–21. He led the Sooners in scoring that year and was voted second team All-Missouri Valley. The following year, he made the first team. The 1921 college yearbook said of him, "Ed was the mainstay of the team for he was always able to start the ball in the right direction from the jump off. He got the tip on every center he played against including Williams, the University of Missouri's All-Valley center for 1920."

The uniforms of the day were quite different from what we see now, one hundred years later. The tops were basically cut the same as the modern jerseys, but they had no lettering to identify the player by name or number or even what school he played for. OU's tops were red with one thick white horizontal stripe that ran from just under the armpits to the bottom of the rib cage. Their stockings were red and came up just below the knees. The pants were white, and the shoes were leather high-tops with very thin soles.

This would describe the Sooner uniforms from 1908 to 1913. Then, for some reason, from 1914 to 1918, they began wearing pants that looked suspiciously like their football moleskins. These pants were well padded and came down below the knee. Given the impecunious state of the athletic department during this era, it is highly probable that Bennie used the same pants for both sports in order to conserve money. However, photographs of OU's teams from 1919 to 1921 in the yearbook show that they had ditched the moleskins and gone back to the more traditional basketball shorts. Perhaps their finances had improved enough to allow them to buy some new equipment.

From 1908 until 1918, Bennie's teams played their games in the original gymnasium, which was built in 1903 just north of what is now the Memorial Union building. The old gym was a one-hundred- by one-hundred-foot wooden structure that was divided into eight rooms. The Sooners played their games in what was then referred to as the main "classroom." This room was forty feet wide, sixty feet long and twenty feet high and could accommodate only two hundred spectators. Twenty-five cents would purchase a ticket to sit in the bleachers, which ran along the west side of the court.

As primitive as this old gym may have been, it was better than a lot of places the Sooners played on their road trips. In the early 1900s, many schools did not have a gymnasium, so they played their games at the local YMCA, which typically would have no bleachers and could accommodate far fewer patrons than OU's building.

In 1917, Bennie and his team took the train south to Dallas for a game with SMU. When they arrived on campus, they were surprised to learn that they would be playing outside on a dirt court, and to make things even worse, it rained heavily during the contest. The Sooners lost that one 47–20, but they recovered their form the next day and defeated the Terrell Training School by a margin of 40–19. This contest was played indoors at the Dallas YMCA. The OU student paper reported on the game as follows: "As was the case in the last game Ponder was the strong man. He substituted in the last half for Risen and threw good goals. Bennie Owen's men did unusually good at passing and grabbing the ball and their speed enabled them to run rings around the Dallas five."

As will be noted in that brief example, sports reporting in that era was not what one has become accustomed to hearing on *Sports Center*. Here is another example from the *Oklahoma Daily*. This is an account of play in the second half of the OU–Kansas State game in 1917:

> *Waite got the tip-off. Bunger took the ball on a weak pass after a flight up and down the court and lobbed a goal. McDermott got one. Leo Waite passed one to Ed Waite directly under the ring and the latter dropped it in. E. Waite repeated on a toss-out, White scored, Bunger threw one and started a string of Aggie scores. Jennings put one through with a clear field. Hinds then rolled in one as W. Cowell put the ball in play. Cox scored again.*

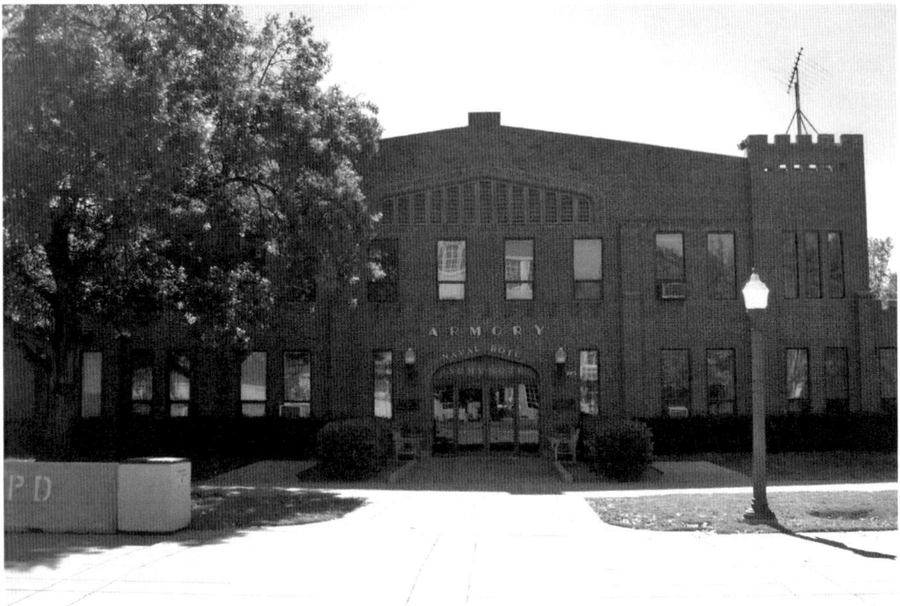

The Armory was the site of OU basketball games from 1920 through 1927. *Courtesy of Patricia King.*

In the 1919–20 season, the Sooners began playing their games in the new Armory. This sturdy three-hundred-foot-long brick fortress still stands just a few feet northwest of the football stadium. It could accommodate four thousand spectators and was a great improvement over the old gym. However, the lighting was so poor that the games had to be played in the afternoon. In one of the first contests held there, Bennie Owen became upset with a few fans who were smoking in the building. "This was terrible for the players!" he lamented.

OU usually played each opponent twice during the season but not on a home and away rotation. If the Kansas Jayhawks came to Norman, they would play two games on consecutive days, usually Friday and Saturday. The following year, OU would journey to Lawrence, and they would do the same thing. This helped to cut down on traveling expenses, but it sometimes led to some tough road trips because when the Sooners traveled, they would try to pack the games as close together as possible to further conserve funds.

In Bennie's final season as coach, the Sooners took this concept to the extreme. The coach and his nine-man traveling squad departed on Friday, January 28, 1921, and returned on Sunday, February 6. During this stretch, they traveled around 1,500 miles by rail and played seven games in eight days.

The first game on this odyssey was a 27–16 loss to Creighton in Omaha, Nebraska, on Saturday, January 29. Then after resting on the Sabbath, they moved on to Lincoln, where they lost two games to the University of Nebraska, 34–20 on Monday and 32–22 on Tuesday. Then it was north to Des Moines, Iowa, where they took the first of two games from Drake 35–32 but lost the second 22–16. They closed out the trip on a positive note with victories on Friday and Saturday night at Grinnell, Iowa, 29–22 and 23–20.

The coverage of this northern campaign in the student paper gives one considerable insight into the state of basketball at OU and on the other campuses of Missouri Valley schools. The *Oklahoma Daily* reported:

> *The Sooners made it fifty-fifty in the conference clashes and lost to Creighton in the non-conference clash. The men report excellent treatment and real sportsmanship at the hands of every school visited with Grinnell probably leading in the good fellowship.*
>
> *Without exception every one of the four schools visited on the trip have far superior athletic plants and equipment than the University of Oklahoma is able to boast of. Drake is the poorest of the four but their plant seemed adequate and spacious compared to the long-cramped Sooners.*
>
> *One of the noticeable features of the trip was the price of admission charged. The uniform rate was seventy-five cents for students and one dollar for others. Oklahoma has not come up to that price.*
>
> *In explanation of the seven games Captain* [William] *Cox summarizes somewhat as follows: Creighton stands for the rough and ready bordering on the football type of basketball, but their players are good fellows, fair despite their roughness. Nebraska was the classiest club met and hospitality was extended in true Cornhusker style. Drake played hard and consistent basketball and deserved the split in honors. Grinnell displayed a friendly rivalry for the cellar championship, courteous in treatment and liberal with enthusiasm for brilliant court work regardless of the side from which it came.*

Coach Owen appeared to be well pleased with the results of the trip. He pointed out, "Basketball is a young sport at Oklahoma while it has been long established at the other Valley schools. It takes time to build a winner in basketball and this is really our first year in the conference since we joined last year after the basketball season was well begun."

Bennie Owen's influence on basketball at the University of Oklahoma spanned the decades from Theodore Roosevelt to Dwight Eisenhower, from David Ross Boyd to George Lynn Cross. When he stepped down as coach after the 1920–21 season, he handed his whistle and sneakers to Hugh "Scottie" McDermott, whom he had mentored in both football and basketball. McDermott coached the Sooners until 1938 before deferring to Bruce Drake. Drake, who had been a star player for McDermott from 1927–29, remained at the Sooner Helm until 1955.

Thus, because of the dynamic leadership of Benjamin Gilbert Owen, the University of Oklahoma was able to establish a winning tradition in football, baseball and basketball. Truly, he was OU's man for all seasons.

10

Great Teams, Great Players

Tremendous Tackles

Bennie Owen had four undefeated football teams at the University of Oklahoma—1911, 1915, 1918 and 1920—but his first great team was the 1908 squad, which compiled a record of 8-1-1. The '08 Sooners—and this was the first year they were known by that appellation—featured the blocking and running of what may have been the greatest pair of offensive tackles ever to play at OU: Ralph Campbell and Willard Douglas.

Yes, runners. Campbell and Douglas were both dangerous ball carriers on Bennie's "tackle around" play, which was a legal maneuver at the time. The two men played together for only one year, but they certainly made the most of it, combining to gain more than a mile of real estate and score twenty touchdowns. Campbell, a strappingly handsome young lad of 195 pounds, was the fastest man on the team. He ran a leg on OU's mile relay team and could cover one hundred yards in 10.2 seconds.

Douglas, the right tackle and 175 pounds, was not quite the physical marvel that Campbell was, but he was tough and understood the game. Campbell was a step faster than his running mate and a slightly better ball carrier. Douglas, who also caught several passes that season, was the better blocker and defensive stopper. However, Campbell could block, and Douglas could run. Both were elusive in the open field and quite adept at stiff-arming would-be tacklers.

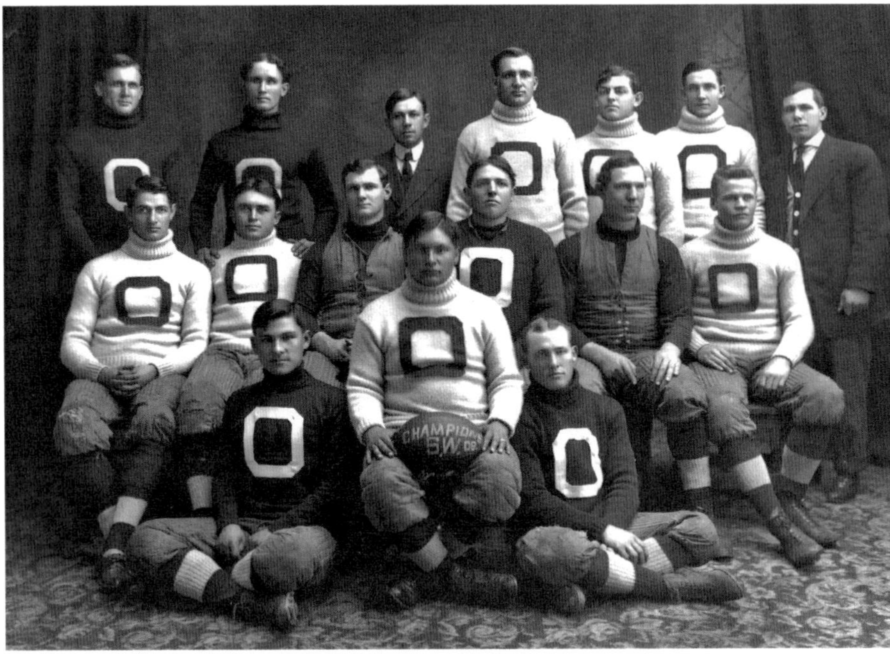

The OU 1908 varsity football team had a record of eight wins, one loss and one tie. *Courtesy of the University of Oklahoma's Western History Collection, OUPC 6.*

The old "tackle around" play, also known as the "tackle sweep" and the "tackle help," was designed to look like an end run. The quarterback took the snap and then turned his back to the defense and faked a handoff to one of his backs running wide and being escorted by the other two backs. Then the QB would spin the other direction and hand the ball off to one of his tackles who had pulled out behind the line of scrimmage. When Campbell toted the hog bladder, Douglas opened the hole and vice versa.

The strength of the '08 Sooners was their line, which averaged a hefty (for the times) 180 pounds per man. In addition to their two great tackles, the Sooners had Key Wolf, the team's captain, at guard and Ralph Campbell's younger brother Roy at center.

Key Wolf, a five-foot-seven, 210 pound fire plug, was as wild and tough as the bison his Chickasaw ancestors had hunted on the surrounding prairies not so many years before he matriculated at the University of Oklahoma Territory in the autumn of 1905. At his enrollment, Wolf was told he would have to take Latin. "I don't want to take Latin," he said. "I already know two languages, English and Chickasaw, and I don't need to learn another one."

He argued his point so passionately that the professor relented and dropped the Latin requirement.

Roy Campbell was probably the most powerful man Bennie Owen ever coached. His teammates were in awe of his strength and aggressiveness. "He was the roughest human being to ever put on a suit," Charlie Wantland said. Owen Acton called him "the most powerful man I have ever seen in a football uniform." "Crush you and would" is the way Artie Reeds summed him up.

The mainstays of Bennie's backfield were the senior Wantland, who was generally regarded as the best running back in all the Southwest, and a sixteen-year-old, 145-pound freshman named Fred Capshaw. Despite his slight stature, Capshaw did not back down from anyone. He loved to block and tackle, and he ran with almost berserk abandon. "Give him a foot of daylight, and he'd be through the line in a flash," Wolf said. "I've had him nearly knock me over just hitting me in the back."

The only two blemishes on OU's record that season were a hard fought 11–0 loss in Lawrence to an all-victorious Kansas team coached by Dr. Bert Kennedy and Bennie's old friend Arthur St. Leger Mosse and a disappointing 6–6 tie with Washburn in Topeka on a muddy field, which neutralized the Sooners' speed. The *Umpire* wrote of the game with the Ichabods, "Once when within a yard of the goal line the ball was given to [Charley] Armstrong but in some way a Washburn man got it away from him. He was speedily shoved over the line for a safety which ordinarily counts two points [for OU] but not so according to the referee who brought the ball out the ten yard line and gave it to Washburn." These two contests notwithstanding, 1908 was the year it became obvious to friend and foe alike that Bennie Owen was building a solid football program at the University of Oklahoma.

The game which best showcased the prowess of Campbell and Douglas was played on Friday, November 13, 1908, which just happened to be the coldest day Norman had seen in ten years. OU games were played on Fridays in those days because Norman merchants closed their doors during the games, and they preferred shutting down on Fridays rather than Saturdays, when the local farmers drove their buggies and wagons into town for Trades Day.

The contest began with Ralph Campbell running down a Texas back and making a touchdown-saving tackle just short of the goal line. On the final play of the game, OU fumbled the ball on the Texas ten, and the Longhorns' fastest back, Ben Dyer, scooped it up and set sail for the Sooner goal line 100 yards away (the field being 110 yards long in those days). With no one in his path, it looked like he was sure to score. But Willard Douglas, who had been in the game for every play, took off after him. With the frozen spectators cheering him on, the tackle began to gain on the smaller man. Finally, after a ninety-yard sprint, Douglas reached out with a meaty paw and pulled the Texan down at the ten yard line. After the game, the Longhorns' coach, W.E. Metzenthin threw up his hands and exclaimed, "When big tackles like those run down my fastest backs from behind I give up!"

These two spectacular defensive plays were only a small part of the damage Campbell and Douglas inflicted on the Longhorns on that frigid afternoon. Oklahoma rushed for the amazing total of 778 yards. This becomes even more incredible when one realizes that in 1908, a team had only three downs instead of four to make ten yards and retain possession. Of this 778 total, the two awesome tackles accounted for 401. Douglas led all Sooner ground gainers with 220, and Campbell was second with 181. The tandem rushed thirty-six times for an average of 11.1 yards per carry. Campbell tallied two touchdown and Douglas one. The final score was OU, 50; Texas, 0, and this was in an era when a touchdown counted 5 points rather than 6. Also, Owen and Metzenthin agreed to stop the slaughter with seven minutes left to play. Bennie's only comment after the game was, "I am more than satisfied."

Three days later, the the *Umpire* opined:

> *To say that the outcome of the game was a surprise would be putting it mildly. Such wagers as were laid were even or with the odds in favor of Texas and not even the Sooner team had expected such an easy victory. True enough; before the game Captain Wolf was not exactly gushing with confidence. His assessment was, "Whatever happens they are going to know that they have been in a football game before we get through with them."*

This was regarded as the greatest football victory in the history of the university at that time. It was especially satisfying when one realizes Oklahoma had beaten Texas only once previously in ten tries and that by a score of 2–0 in 1905. This remained the largest margin of victory over the Longhorns for ninety-five years until Bob Stoops's troops beat them 65–13 in 2003. Bud Wilkinson is justifiably given credit for building the Sooner dynasty that has won more games than any other collegiate team since World War II. However, forty years before Bud achieved his first conquest of Texas, Bennie's team had stirred as much pride in the breasts of Normanites, town and gown alike, as any of Wilkinson's wins ever would.

Neither the brutally cold weather nor the dark of night could stop the Sooner fans' celebration. Students spontaneously began to send up shouts of "Hi, rickety, Whoop te do, Boomer Sooner, Oklahoma U" from all parts of the campus. Then the thumping of a big bass drum called them to the steps of the library. From there, students and faculty began a snake dance that proceeded into the teeth of the fierce north wind nine blocks up University Boulevard to Main Street. At a spot near the railroad tracks, a bonfire was lit, the university band played and speeches were made by football players, professors and Norman businessmen. The celebration lasted well into the night. Harold Keith wrote of this spectacle, "It was an eloquent demonstration of the wild, free, by-gone college spirit that made young people so blissfully oblivious to the worries of the day."

SPEED FIENDS

Bennie Owen had not had a particularly good season in 1910, but he did have some good players returning for the 1911 campaign. Sabert "Sabe" Hott and Jimmy Nairn were back for their second and fourth seasons, respectively, as tackles, and while they were hardly the equals of Campbell and Douglas, they were certainly steady players. The guards, "Six Shooter Bill" Moss and Roger Berry, were also crafty veterans. A somewhat apocryphal legend has it that Moss, who had begun his football career at the University of Texas, drove a herd of cattle north across the Red River into Oklahoma and found the young state so much to his liking that he decided to stay there and study law.

The backfield—or the "Speed Fiends," as they were known—was thought to be the best the university had yet produced. The quarterback Hubert Ambrister, a junior, was small (140 pounds) but smart, and he clearly had the respect of his teammates. The fullback was sophomore Claude Reeds, one of the greatest players of this era. Senior captain Elmer "Trim" Capshaw held down one halfback spot, and the other was manned by Ray Courtright, a freshman who would fashion quite a career for himself in three sports before he graduated.

The assistant coach, Harry Hughes, whom Bennie had hired only the previous year, left to begin a long career as the head coach of Colorado A&M. However, he was ably replaced by Cleve Thompson, the 1910 captain, and Charlie Wantland, a halfback on Bennie's 1908 squad. After graduation, Wantland became the superintendent of schools in Bradley, Oklahoma, and

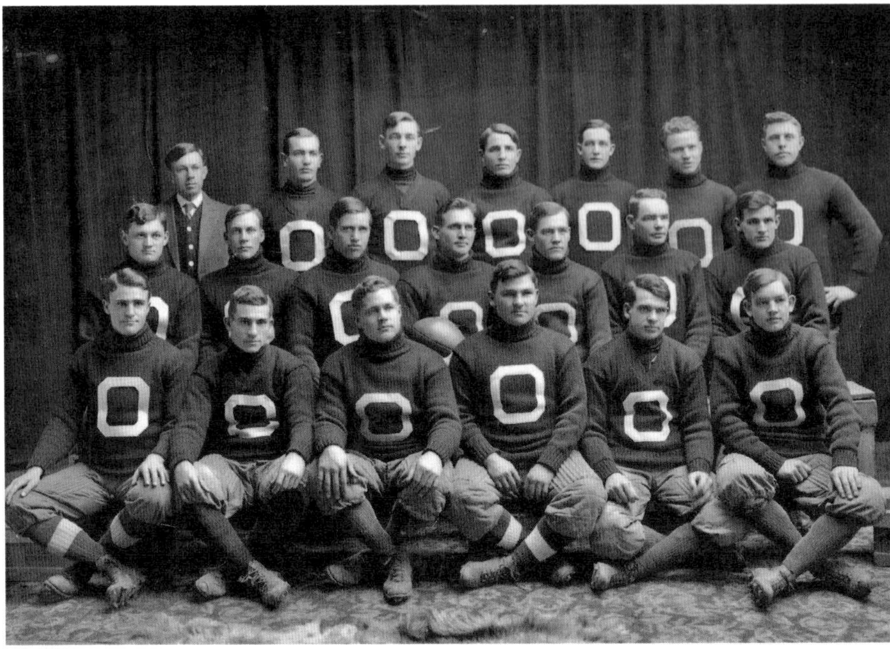

The OU 1910 varsity football team had a record of four wins, two losses and one tie. *Courtesy of the University of Oklahoma's Western History Collection, OUPC 8.*

later the university's director of physical education. Thompson, OU's first-ever line coach, doubled as head coach of the Norman High School Tigers.

Apparently, word had escaped that Bennie Owen was going to have a very potent team in 1911 because Central Oklahoma, OU's first scheduled opponent, refused to play, saying, "They are too strong." So instead, they opened their season in Norman on September 29 against Kingfisher. The *Daily Oklahoman* said of this game:

> *The largest score ever piled up by the University of Oklahoma against an opponent or between any two colleges in the southwest and possibly in the entire country was recorded here Friday in the opening game of the season, Kingfisher College being smothered by a count of 104 to 0. It was virtually a game of giants playing against pygmies, the Sooners bullying their lighter opponents up and down the field at will. The great strength and machine work of the state school warriors showed clearly that Coach Bennie Owen has the best material and the best team ever developed at Norman, and one which has an unusual chance to defeat the heretofore unbeatables, Kansas and Missouri in the later games of the season.*

One has to feel sorry for the Kingfishers. They were purely and simply cannon fodder for the Sooners and presumably several other schools. Bennie Owen's teams played them fourteen times between 1905 and 1919 and shut them out on twelve of these occasions. The Sooners won this farcically one-sided series by the cumulative total of 1,045–11, which averages out to 74.6 points per game for OU and .79 for Kingfisher.

The 104 points Oklahoma scored against them in 1911 was by no means the worst whippin' it ever administered to the hapless Kingfishers. The Sooners beat them 157 to 0 in 1919, and in 1917, they won by a score of 179–0. In that "contest," Arlo "Skivey" Davis kicked twenty-three extra points, a record that will hopefully never be broken.

The Sooners' second victim was Oklahoma Christian College. The game had to be postponed because the Christians had problems getting to Norman from Enid. A freight train wreck on the Santa Fe tracks at Lovell about forty miles south of Enid caused them to miss their connections in Guthrie, and they did not arrive in Norman until late in the evening. When the game was played the following day, OU crushed them 62–0.

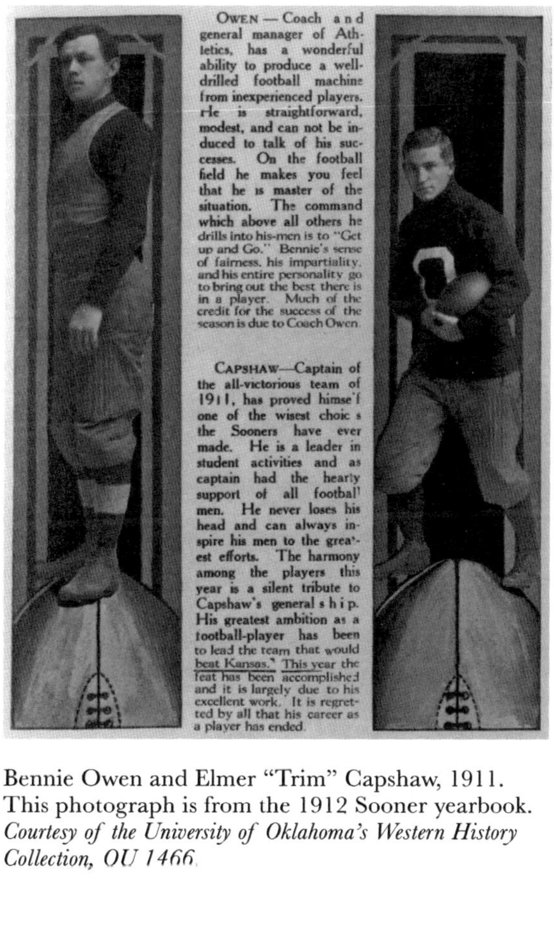

Bennie Owen and Elmer "Trim" Capshaw, 1911. This photograph is from the 1912 Sooner yearbook. *Courtesy of the University of Oklahoma's Western History Collection, OU 1466.*

Next up for Bennie's boys was Oklahoma A&M. While they were not nearly as hapless as Kingfisher, the Aggies were certainly dominated by OU. Owen's record against them was 16-2-2, and they failed to score against the Sooners in the first seven games they played. The score of the 1911 tilt was OU, 22; A&M, 0. Reeds scored two touchdowns and Courtright and Capshaw one each.

Then the Sooners disposed of Washburn by

the surprisingly lopsided score of 37–0. Now came the most difficult part of their schedule, back-to-back battles against Missouri and Kansas. These were the games they had been pointing toward since the first day of practice. The Sooners had played the Tigers only once but lost to them 26–0 the previous season, and Bennie had never beaten his alma mater in six tries.

Four thousand fans were on hand that chilly November day in Columbia, Missouri, to see their beloved Tigers take on the upstart Sooners from the windblown prairie of what just four years previously had been Indian Territory. The throng fully expected their heroes to prevail, especially after they saw the much lighter visiting team jog onto the field for pregame warm-ups in faded and raggedy uniforms.

However, they were soon disabused of this haughty presumption. Midway through the first quarter, the Sooners, living up to their reputation as "Speed Fiends," covered sixty yards in just three plays for the game's first score. The damage was done with two passes to end Glen Clark and a twenty-yard sprint by Capshaw for the TD. Capshaw also converted the extra point and, three minutes later, knocked through a thirty-yard field goal, which put the Sooners ahead 9–0.

The Sooners' defense kept the toothless Tigers at bay, and their offense, disdaining the huddle, kept up the relentless pressure as Ambrister shouted out his signals like a man firing a Gatling gun. With seven minutes remaining in the first half, Courtright took the ball on a cross buck and ripped off a beautiful thirty-five-yard broken field run for a touchdown. The extra point try sailed wide of the uprights, and the score stood at 14–0. Although no one would have suspected it at the time, OU did not score again and did not need to. With less than two minutes to play in the game, Missouri finally pushed across a consolation touchdown, but it was much too little and way too late. The final score was OU, 14; Missouri, 6.

This Missouri TD was the only one scored through OU's line all year. The only other points the Sooners surrendered that season were on a fumble return by Northwestern of Alva, Oklahoma, and a field goal by Texas. Back in Norman, the multitude that had been following the telegraphed accounts of the game assembled in front of Barbour's drugstore celebrated wildly, but after all the shouting and singing had died down, as they walked back to their homes and dorm rooms, the celebrants were consumed with one question, "Will this finally be the year we beat Kansas?"

Hoping to save on travel expenses, Owen kept his men in Columbia the following week rather than bringing them back to Norman. Undeterred by a steady rainfall, Bennie led his men on a ten-mile hike the day following the

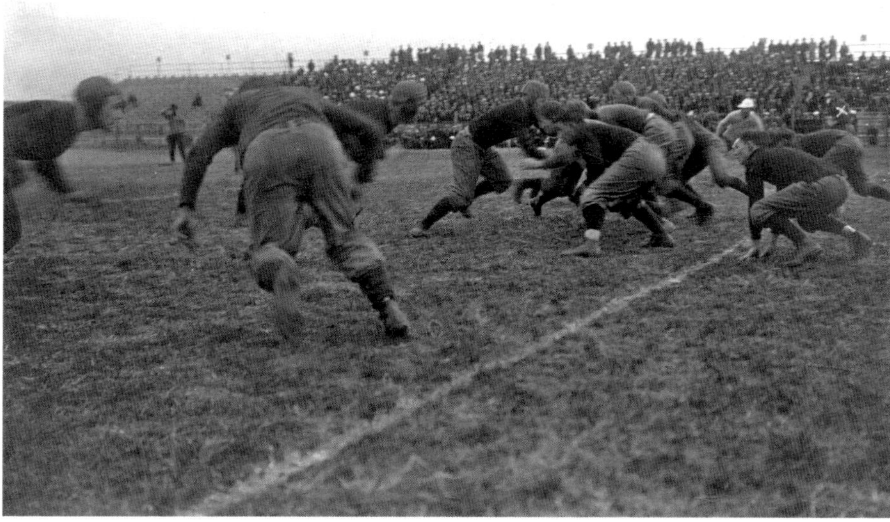

An action shot of the Sooners versus Missouri in 1911. OU won the game 14–6. *Courtesy of the University of Oklahoma's Western History Collection, Creel 1.*

game to "work out the stiffness." The Sooners held practices on the fairways of the university's golf course and twice scrimmaged against the Tigers, who were preparing for a game with Washburn.

Hiking and practicing were not all the Sooners did in Columbia. They also studied. At the urging of their coach, all eighteen men who made the trip brought their textbooks and worked on class assignments so they would not get too far behind in their coursework. Several Sooners even attended classes at the University of Missouri.

The Tiger student paper, the *University Missourian*, wrote: "We thank you Mr. Bennie Owen, for remaining in Columbia a week. Not simply, you understand, because it adds a touch of color to have those husky, good looking young men ambling around our classic thoroughfares, and not only because we like your smile, but it has been great to have a winning team among us for at least one week." A week later, the *Daily Kansan* published its reply: "You needn't be so swelled up about it Missouri. We had the same team with us over Saturday."

The Sooners spent Friday night in Kansas City and set out by train for Lawrence early the next morning. At first, the weather was so warm that they pushed open the windows of their day coach and took off their coats, but this was about to change. When they got off the train in Lawrence after a forty-mile journey, they were pelted with freezing rain. By game time, the rain had turned to snow, and the temperature had dropped to almost zero.

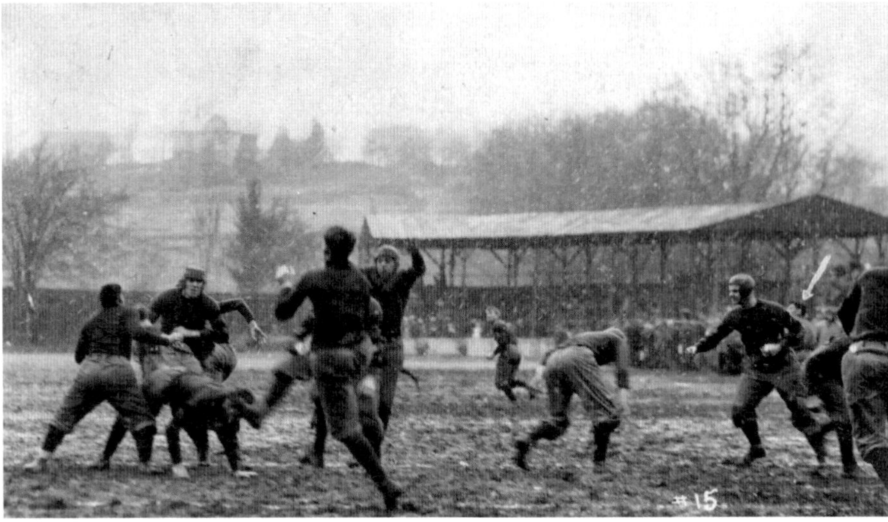

An action shot of OU versus Kansas in 1911. OU won the game 3–0. *Courtesy of the University of Oklahoma's Western History Collection, Creel 2.*

Less than two minutes into the first quarter, Capshaw nailed a twenty-two-yard field goal, which turned out to be the game's only score, although OU clearly dominated the Jayhawks, outgaining them 300 yards to 108. Immediately after the game, Owen received a telegraph from Oklahoma governor Lee Cruce that read, "The people of Oklahoma rejoice over your well-earned victory. You have shown the Oklahoma spirit."

At the urging of the student senate, OU president Julian Monnet canceled classes between 10:00 a.m. and noon the following Monday so that a rally could be held in the university's chapel to welcome back the conquering heroes. This is the *Umpire's* description of what followed:

> *A large tallyho* [a carriage drawn by four horses with the harnesses arranged so that one person can control all the horses] *had been secured and brought by the students to the campus. After the chapel meeting the players were carried on the rooters' shoulders to the vehicle. The band was also placed in the tallyho and the freshmen were given the honor of pulling it to town. The rooters formed in line behind the team which made a procession nearly two blocks long. When Main St. was reached two lines were formed on each side of the tallyho. In this position they marched to the east end of town and back to the First National Bank. Here each one of the players was called upon to make a speech and*

> *yells given for all. At about 12 o'clock the rally was dismissed and each one returned to classes in the afternoon as if nothing had happened, but feeling that they had fittingly shown their appreciation to the best coach and the best football team in the world.*

Ironically "the best coach in the world," was not there to accept these accolades because Bennie Owen had traveled from Lawrence to Ann Arbor, Michigan, to watch Yost's Wolverines beat Penn 11–9 and did not return to Norman until two days before the game with Northwestern. He probably would have been safe in taking off the whole week, as the Rangers proved to be no match for his Sooners, who crushed them 34–6. However, one more formidable foe remained for Bennie and his team. They still had to venture 375 miles south and play the Texas Longhorns. Owen took his team to Austin a couple days early so they could stretch their legs a little after the long train ride. On Friday, they packed picnic lunches and took a long hike along the banks of the Colorado River, which flows through the picturesque Texas Hill Country.

The *Daily Oklahoman* said of the game:

> *In spite of the fact that the first quarter belonged to Texas by long odds, Oklahoma came back and began a series of fast plays that showed their superiority over the Texas men at every point of the game. They went through the Texas line apparently with ease. Courtright and Capshaw were veritable demons at bucking the line. Time after time they hit it and went through for considerable gains with as many as five men hanging to them.*

This makes the victory sound a lot easier than it really was. In fact, when Texas kicked a twenty-seven-yard field goal in the first quarter the Sooners found themselves trailing for the first time all year. However, the perfect season was preserved when, fittingly, the Sooner's captain, senior Fred Capshaw, blasted over the goal line and then added the extra point just before halftime. Neither team could score in the second half, and the final score was OU, 6; Texas, 3.

This was really quite a remarkable year for the Sooners. Rarely does a team go through a season all-victorious when it has to play its three fiercest opponents on the road. Yet this was exactly what OU was able to accomplish in 1911, beating Missouri, Kansas and Texas on their home turfs. The Ivy League snobs like Walter Camp might not have been paying attention, but

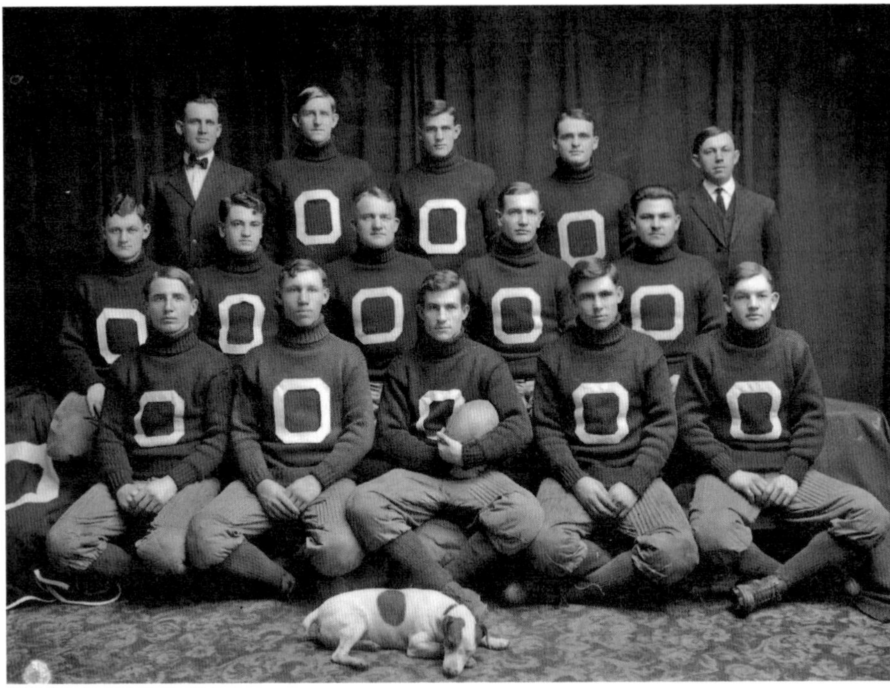

The OU 1911 varsity football team had a record of eight wins and zero losses. *Courtesy of the University of Oklahoma's Western History Collection, OUPC 9.*

most of the football cognoscenti living west of the Allegheny Mountains took notice of this feat.

These accomplishments become even more remarkable when one realizes that Bennie's men were truly students first and athletes second. One expense that Owen did not have was a recruiting budget. He did not proselytize. If he happened to meet a promising, broad-shouldered, barrel-chested prospect who could run one hundred yards in ten seconds flat, he might say, "I hope you will join us over in Norman next year." But that would be the extent of his "recruiting." "If they came, they came. If they didn't come they didn't come," he would explain several years after he retired from coaching.

Ten of the eleven starters on this team graduated from OU and several earned advanced degrees. Roger Berry, Fred Capshaw, Glen Clark, Ray Courtright and Ed Meacham were Phi Beta Kappas. Harold Keith's closing commentary on this season was that "Owen was then building what was the most truly amateur collegiate sports dynasty the university had ever known. His emphasis on sportsmanship, scholarship, clean living and scrupulously clean play made the Oklahoma team popular on every foreign campus it visited."

GEYER AND MORE GEYER

In 1914, Norman's Main and Boyd Streets were paved and the new bridge across the South Canadian River was open for traffic. Many locals had decided to trade in their horses and buggies for automobiles. Bennie Owen made a major decision this year also. He decided to live or die with the forward pass. He did this for two reasons. He thought his defense was not going to be strong enough to shut down the likes of Kansas, Missouri and Texas, and therefore, he needed to take some risks in order to put more points on the board. And he had the kind of athletes to make the aerial game work.

In 1914, Owen returned only four starters from the previous year: guard Curry Bell, tackle Billy Clark and backs Neil Johnson and Elmer "Trim" Capshaw, the younger brother of 1911 team captain Fred "Bink" Capshaw. But he had Forrest "Spot" Geyer.

Geyer had not been a stalwart on the 1913 squad, but when Claude Reeds went down with an injury, he stepped in and performed well in the Missouri game. The gangly Geyer was an unlikely looking football player. He scored only three rushing touchdowns in his collegiate career (against major opponents), but he could throw the football. Oh, how he could throw the football, and like a lot of other players in this era, his accomplishments were not limited to the gridiron. His longtime friend and Sooner halfback Montford "Hap" Johnson said, "He never had a dime while he was in school, but he was good at everything—dramatics, writing, sign painting, opera stage hand, or playing in the band. He was a smart kid and a wonderful mixer." Geyer may have had an impoverished childhood, but after graduating from OU with a degree in geology, he fashioned quite a career in the booming oil industry, eventually becoming the president of Marland Oil Company.

With Geyer aiming his accurate aerials at the Johnson brothers Neil and Hap, Glen Clark and Homer Montgomery, the Sooners reeled off a record of 9-1-1. An all-victorious Texas team that defeated each of its victims by at least two TDs pounded the Sooners 32–7. The following week, OU battled its old nemesis Kansas to a 16–16 draw in a game that the man who refereed it, John Grove, called "a double barreled, triple hammered, thriller from whistle to whistle…one I'll never forget."

The decisive loss to the Longhorns notwithstanding, many pundits believed Bennie Owen may have done his best coaching job ever with the 1914 team. Given his lack of proven talent, had he not made the bold decision to rely so heavily on the forward pass, the Sooners easily could have lost several more games. At a time when the eastern football establishment still shunned forward passing, OU was throwing the ball as often as thirty or thirty-five times a game.

Along with Owen's great coaching there is one other feat for which this season will be remembered—Lee Field's race against the train. On November 20, OU defeated Arkansas at Oklahoma City's Fair Park by a score of 35–7. When the Sooners prepared to board the interurban for the trip back to Norman, the sub Field found that no ticket had been purchased for him. In a fit of colossal pique, he decided to show his disdain for this unjust treatment by beating the electrically powered train back to Norman on foot. He removed his hat and coat, handed them to a teammate and, with a jaunty wave of goodbye, began running along the railroad tracks in his mufti and army brogans.

Although it was eighteen miles to Norman, Field sincerely believed he could beat the train. He had a thirty-minute head start and a cool north wind at his back, and most significantly, he was an accomplished runner. He had already set several school records and would eventually become the champion of the Southwest Conference in the mile run.

The tenacious Field stayed ahead of the train for seventeen of the eighteen miles. Despite his heavy shoes, he averaged just a little over six minutes a mile on his jaunt. After college, he opened a service station/restaurant in Pauls Valley, Oklahoma. Although the restaurant has been closed for many years, Field's frozen pies are still sold in grocery stores all over Oklahoma.

In what Harold Keith described as "the university's golden year of football," the Sooners of 1915 fulfilled the promise they had shown the previous year and posted a perfect 10-0-0 record. In this era, football was clearly the biggest thing on campus; in fact, it was just about the only thing on campus. There was no golf course (Bennie Owen had not built it yet), no pool halls, no movie theater, no soda fountains and certainly no bars or nightclubs. Throngs of fans always came to Norman's Santa Fe depot to greet the team when they returned from such exotic and faraway places as Lawrence, Kansas; Columbia, Missouri; and Fayetteville, Arkansas, and it

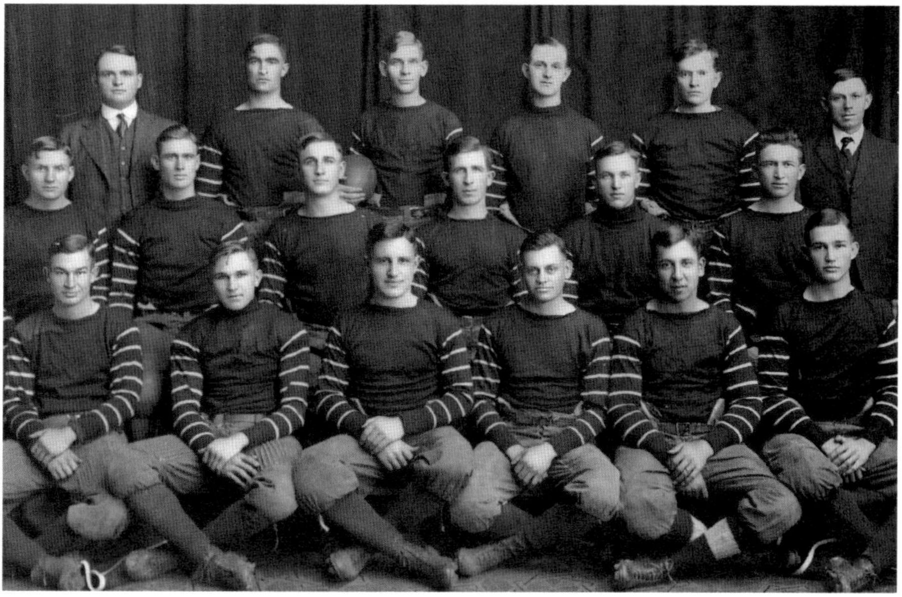

The OU 1915 varsity football team had a record of ten wins and zero losses. *Courtesy of the University of Oklahoma's Western History Collection, OUPC 15.*

was quite common for several students to gather around old Boyd Field on mild Indian summer afternoons and watch Bennie drill his charges.

The Ruf Neks booster organization was formed in 1915. One of the student yell leaders was Josh Lee, who later served as U.S. congressman from 1935 to 1937 and as a senator from 1937 to 1943. Lee was not the only person on campus that fall that went on to a successful career in politics after he left OU. Bennie's left guard on the 1915 squad, Leon "Red" Phillips, served one term as governor of Oklahoma, from 1939 to 1943.

The Sooners' leader on the gridiron that year was, of course, Forest Park "Spot" Geyer. To say that he was versatile would not be giving him his just due. He ran, he passed, he kicked extra points and field goals and he played defense. He even wrote a summary of the season for the school yearbook.

His favorite receiver was his right end Homer Montgomery, but he also aimed a lot of aerials at Trim Capshaw, Ray Foster, Frank McCain and Mike Swatek, who alternated as halfbacks. Bennie's long punt formation looked a lot like today's spread offenses from the shotgun. The Sooners split their ends and put three fast receivers who ran short patterns near the line of scrimmage. Geyer would take the snap from center about seven yards deep, roll out to his left or right, then pick a guy and let it fly. The line was anchored by the

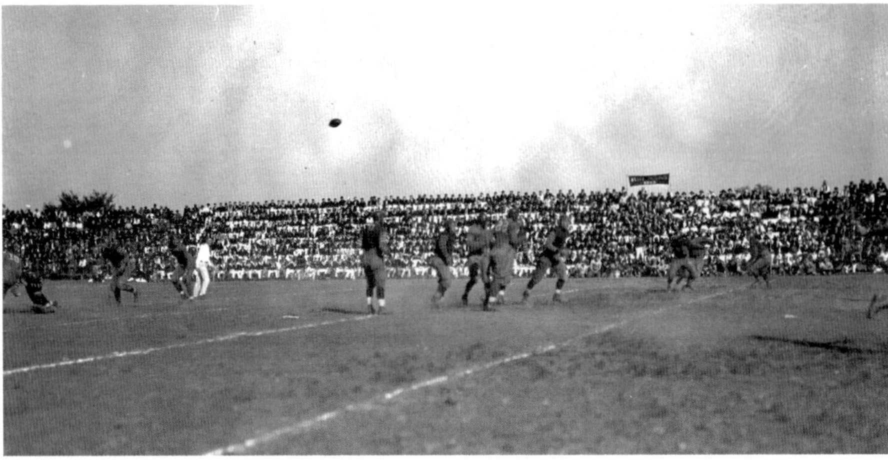

Forrest Park "Spot" Geyer uncorks a long pass at Boyd Field in 1915. *Courtesy of the University of Oklahoma's Western History Collection, OU 347.*

Hott brothers—Willis "Big Hott" and Oliver "Little Hott"—at tackles. Their elder brother Sabe (with the glass eye) had achieved nearly legendary status as a member Bennie's great 1911 squad. The Hotts were so popular the yell leaders had a special cheer for them: "Big Hott!, Little Hott!, Red Hott!, Too Hott!, Wow!"

After disposing of Kingfisher College 67–0, Southwestern Oklahoma 55–0 and Northwestern Oklahoma 102–0, OU was ready for the meat of its schedule: Missouri, Texas and Kansas. The Sooners had no trouble taming the Tigers in Columbia. On the third play of the game, McCain caught a pass from Geyer and ran 80 yards before he was dragged down on Missouri's 5-yard line. He scored on the next play, an end sweep, and the rout was on. Geyer completed sixteen of thirty-three passes for 260 yards, and the Sooners prevailed 24–0.

Hall-of-fame pitcher Kid Nichols, whom Bennie Owen had come to know during his time in Topeka, saw the game and remarked, "Hell Bennie, that isn't fair. That Geyer throws a football around like I throw a baseball." Nichols threw the horsehide around well enough to win 361 games, the seventh-highest total in major-league baseball history.

The *Columbia Globe-Democrat* stated:

> *Using the most variegated assortment of forward passes ever uncovered on Rollins Field, Oklahoma University defeated Missouri today 24–0...The long forward passes advanced the ball to striking distances*

> *for three touchdowns, two in the first quarter and one in the fourth quarter. Geyer kicked goals from all three touchdowns and in the second period made a field goal placement from the 65-yard line* [a 35-yard field goal, apparently, according to today's terminology].

OU had a much tougher time with Texas in Dallas the following week. Although Santa Fe arranged for a special train to carry Sooner fans to Dallas, the "exorbitant" round-trip fare of $9.15 was beyond the reach of most OU students, so many resorted to the "hobo" method of riding atop boxcars or passenger coaches. Several of these determined youth were arrested in Purcell, and others were stranded in Atoka due to high water. But some made it all the way to Dallas and were numbered among the eleven thousand who witnessed the game. This was, at that time, the largest crowd to ever attend a game in the state of Texas. The contest figured to be a low-scoring affair as neither team had allowed so much as a field goal, let alone a touchdown, thus far.

The Longhorns carried a 13–7 lead into the fourth quarter. Then Geyer went to work passing for 140 yards in the final period. Late in the game, he connected with Hap Johnson for a touchdown that tied the score at 13–13. The Sooners now had to make a decision. Since Johnson was just barely in fair territory when he crossed the goal line, under the rules of the day, OU had to attempt the potential game-winning kick at an extreme angle, or the Sooners could try to execute the equally tricky "kick-out."

The kick-out would involve executing a punt from the corner of the end zone, which hopefully would be fielded by one of the Sooners' own. If so, the ball would be spotted at that point, which presumably would give them a better angle from which to attempt the crucial extra point try. Geyer did not hesitate, "Aw, I can kick it," he said. He did, and the Sooners went home with a 14–13 victory.

Willis Hott was the defensive star of the game. He ranged far and wide, smashing Longhorn runners to the turf of Fair Park Field. He once made the stop singlehandedly on six consecutive plays.

The Texans outrushed the Sooners 206 to 100 yards, but Geyer's passing (completing ten of thirty passes for 232 yards) did them in. Their coach, Dave Alderdice, said, "It was the most thrilling exhibition of forward passing ever seen in the West!" The Longhorn's captain, K.L. Berry, said, "The forward pass beat us. That was our specialty but we acknowledge your superiority." The Texans apparently thought they had a good passing game because they threw the ball forty-one times. However, they completed only twelve passes for 130 yards.

The next day, four thousand faithful fans were crowded around the depot when the team's train arrived back in Norman. Also there to meet the Sooners was a genuine Texas Longhorn steer, decorated in burnt orange and white, which marched at the head of a parade through downtown Norman. On Monday, the steer was sacrificed, and the multitudes feasted on ice cream cones and barbecued longhorn sandwiches at Boyd Field.

"Homecoming, that modern football bacchanalia, was born at Norman the following week when the Kansas Jayhawkers invaded," Harold Keith wrote. Previously, attempts to lure alumni back to campus had been held in conjunction with spring commencement exercises. University registrar Errett R. Newby was given credit for recognizing that football would be a much more popular attraction for grads, thus establishing the tradition at OU.

The *Daily Oklahoman* said of the KU contest, "Superior straight football, superior forward pass plays, and superior endurance, overcame weight Saturday afternoon on Boyd Field, and Bennie Owen's fleet Sooner eleven downed the invading Kansas Jayhawkers in a beautiful gridiron contest 23–14. Six thousand persons, the largest crowd ever to have witnessed an athletic event in Oklahoma, saw the defeat of the beefy Kansans."

Geyer completed eleven passes for 288 yards, the most memorable of which traveled 55 yards in the air. This is how his modest receiver Howard McCasland, the great basketball center, recalled the play: "It was old 72. I glanced over my shoulder and saw the ball coming yards over my head, I remember Bennie saying, 'Try guy, you might be surprised.' So I jumped as high as I could, reached as far as I could and the darn ball lit right in my hands! Damn! I sure was lucky!" According to *Spalding's Guide*, this was the longest forward pass completed in America that season. McCasland did not make it into the end zone, but on the next play, McCain did. Geyer kicked the extra point, and this tied the score 7–7 just before halftime.

In the second half, KU scored one more TD, but Johnson and Geyer both tallied touchdowns for the Sooners. Geyer added a field goal to make the final score 23–14. Even though OU had four games remaining, the *Daily Oklahoman* confidently proclaimed, "All Victorious Eleven Now Assured." As it turned out, the newspaper was right, but Bennie and his boys got quite a scare from Henry Kendall College in Tulsa the following week.

Late in the game, trailing 14–13, with the ball on OU's eighteen-yard line, the Presbyterians inexplicably passed on a field goal, and the Sooners held on downs. Easy victories over Arkansas (24–0), Kansas State (21–7) and Oklahoma A&M (26–7) preserved the perfect season.

Several Sooners garnered individual honors that season. *St. Nicholas* magazine named Trim Capshaw to its All-Ameircan team, and Homer Montgomery and Geyer made the All-American squad chosen by *Outing* magazine. Missouri Valley coaches named Montgomery, Jess Fields, Johnson and Geyer to their All-Valley team. Johnson, Capshaw, Geyer, the Hott brothers and Montgomery were picked on the All-Southwest Conference team. Willis "Big Hott" was named guard of the year in the Southwest Conference.

Most significantly, Geyer became the first Sooner ever named to an All-American squad by an eastern sports writer when Brown Holmes of the *Newspaper Enterprise Association* picked him in his backfield. Holmes wrote, "Geyer of Oklahoma is touted as the passingest thing in football this year. His ability with the forward pass would make him a star wherever he might be dropped." Presumably, this meant that Geyer would have been a standout even if he had played in the Ivy League. Park H. Davis of the *New York Herald* called Geyer "one of those wonderfully developed all-round players whose exceptional ability with the forward pass has been a factor in the Oklahoma team's success." Indeed, it was many, many years before another passer with Geyer's skills would wear the Crimson and Cream.

FABULOUS FRESHMEN

In the fall of 1918, the Great War was winding down, but college football teams across the nation had seen their ranks greatly diminished because so many veteran players had volunteered for service. Texas University canceled its game with the Sooners, and Missouri was forced to cancel its entire season. Bennie Owen suffered great losses to his squad as well. He had awarded eighteen letters the previous season. Of these, only three reported for practice in 1918, and only one of these would play the full season. Almost every former player was soon in service somewhere.

Several of these men saw action in Europe. George Anderson (1914–15) was killed in action on July 22, 1918, during the battle of Chateau-Thierry in France. Also serving in combat were Hubert Ambrister (1910–13), Oliver Hott (1913–16), Cleve Thompson (1906), Neil (1913–14) and Hap (1014–16) Johnson, Tom Lowry (1912), Bill Clark (1912–14), Tommy Brownfield (1918) and Sam Montgomery, who as a marine sergeant in France, won a *Croix de Guerre* for his heroic action in the battle of Belleau Wood.

More devastating even than World War I was the great influenza pandemic of 1918, which is estimated to have taken the lives of as many as 20 to 40 million people worldwide. Known widely as "Spanish flu" or "La Grippe," it is still regarded as the most lethal epidemic in history. It is estimated that this scourge killed 675,000 Americans, which was ten times the number who died in the war. One of those who lost his life was Ralph Campbell, Bennie's great tackle on the 1908 squad, who, ten years later, was teaching mathematics at a small college in South Dakota.

OU students were put under quarantine from October 25 through November 1. University president Dr. Stanton Brooks decreed that students would not be permitted to go downtown, nor were they to spend time anywhere except in their rooms, boardinghouses, classrooms or the library. The pandemic peaked during the fall of 1918 and declined rapidly in the winter and spring. By the summer of 1919, it had run its course.

With so many veteran players signing up for military service, Bennie Owen was fortunate to have perhaps his best freshman class ever. These fabulous frosh, eight of whom became starters, formed the heart and soul of the all-victorious 1918 team as well as the undefeated 1920 squad.

The mother lode of this youthful bonanza matriculated to OU from Oklahoma City High School, whose team, by averaging more than a point a minute, romped through its schedule all-victorious. In the state championship game, Oklahoma City High School blew away Marshall High School 74–0. All seven seniors on this juggernaut chose to cast their football fortunes with Bennie Owen. Four of these seven composed OU's starting backfield. They were Russell "Stub" Hardy, Roy Swatek, Phil White (who, at 190 pounds, was extremely large for a halfback in this era) and Herschel "Bud" Graham. The other members of this magnificent seven were end Myron "Little Tub" Tyler, tackle George Cole and center Dick Lawrence.

There were some very good freshmen from other schools as well, such as Howard Marsh of Madill, Dow Hamm of Muskogee, Harry Hill of Chickasha, Roy Smoot of Lawton, Fred Martin of Wagoner and J. Adair "Big Boy" Lawrence of Tahlequah. Lawrence, at six feet, seven inches tall and 230 pounds, was undoubtedly the biggest man Owen ever coached at OU.

And Bennie did have a smattering of upperclassmen who contributed. There were Lawrence "Jap" Haskell, a sophomore who later became OU's baseball coach from 1927 to 1941, and juniors Page Belcher, who would later serve as a U.S. congressman from 1951 to 1973, and Dewey "Snorter" Luster, who coached the Sooner football team from 1941 to 1945. One veteran Owen did not have was his captain-elect, Hugh "Scottie" McDermott, who

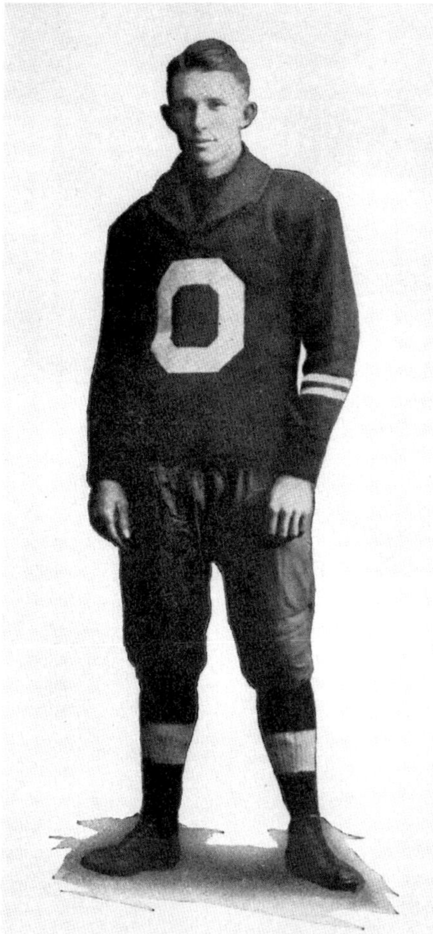

Hugh "Scotty" McDermott was the 1917 team captain. McDermott also starred in basketball for Bennie and later was the head coach of the Sooner basketball team from 1922 to 1938. *Courtesy of the University of Oklahoma's Western History Collection, OU 1480.*

was serving in the army air corps at Kelly Field in San Antonio, Texas. McDermott would go on to coach the OU basketball squad from 1922 to 1938.

Because of the logistical problems created by World War I and the influenza epidemic, the Sooners played only an abbreviated six-game schedule in 1918. The first four games (if you can call them that) were complete blowouts as they trounced Central Oklahoma 44–0, Post Field 58–0, Kansas 33–0 and Arkansas 103–0.

Their only test that season came at Allton Field in Enid on November 23, twelve days after the armistice ending the Great War was signed. Johnny Maultbetsch had put together a strong squad at Phillips University. The undefeated Haymakers had crushed the Haskell Indians 27–0, Fairmont 58–0 and Weatherford Normal 109–0, and they were not the least bit intimidated by the mighty Sooners. The Phillips line was anchored by 205-pound guard Steve Owen (no relation to Bennie), who later played for and coached the New York Football Giants. Their backfield stars were quarterback Franklin Cappon and fullback Douglas Roby, both of whom subsequently played for Feilding Yost at Michigan.

OU quickly realized it was in for a tough game when it saw that running the ball against the Haymakers was going to be difficult. Late in the second quarter, Roby completed a long pass and, on the next play, raced thirty-five yards for a touchdown (the first and only TD scored against OU all season).

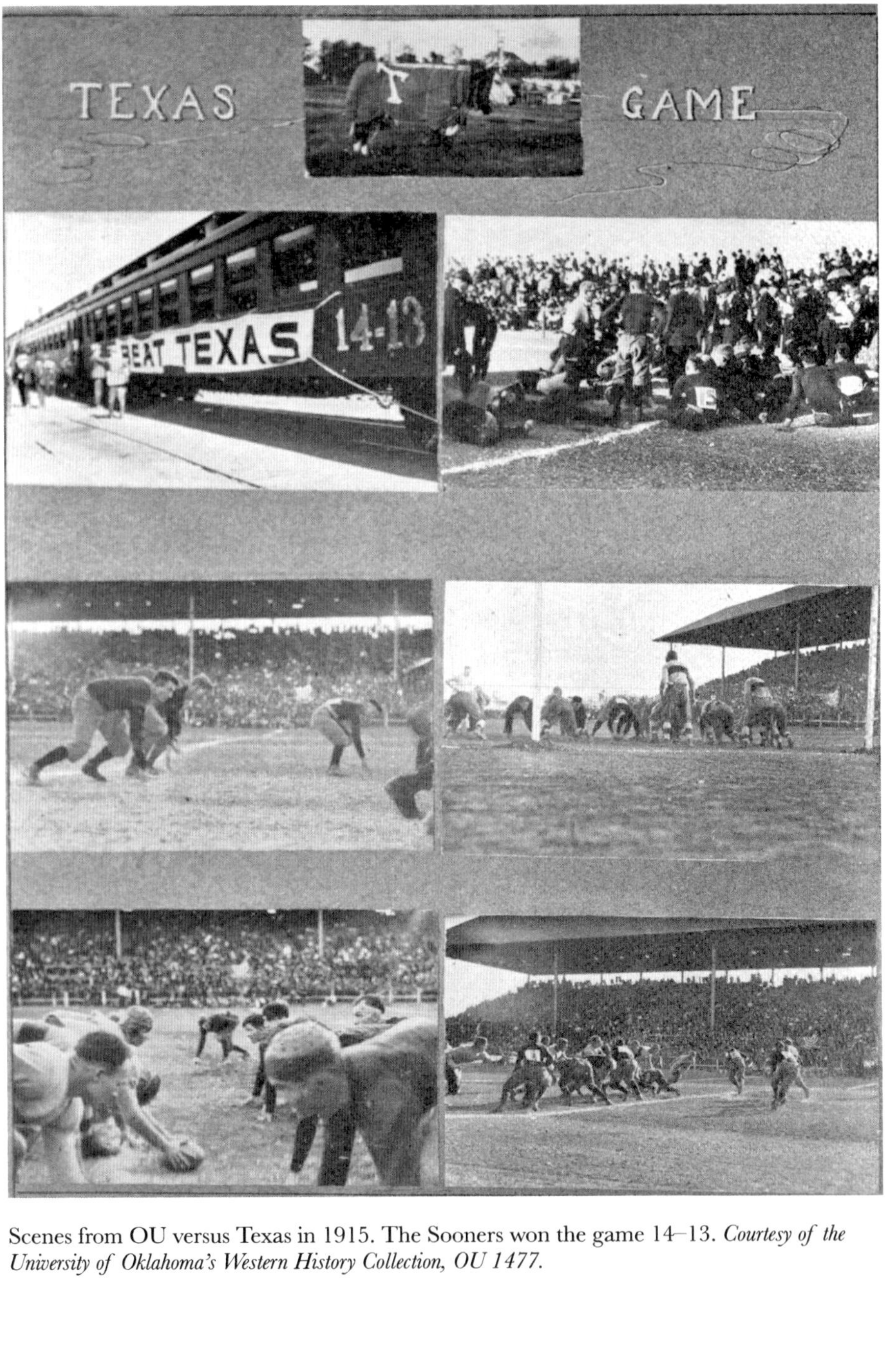

Scenes from OU versus Texas in 1915. The Sooners won the game 14–13. *Courtesy of the University of Oklahoma's Western History Collection, OU 1477.*

At this point, Owen inserted Stub Hardy as quarterback. Hardy marched confidently onto the field and yelled out to his teammates, "Come on you big dubs! Let's get goin'!" And they did.

A thick snow was making it difficult for Sooner runners to get traction, so they took to the air and quickly moved the ball into the red zone. Hardy called play No. 38 from the Owen playbook, and it worked to perfection. Right end "Little Tub" Tyler went in motion to the left and began calling out for Hardy to throw the ball to him. Then "Jap" Haskell, the left end, blocked down on the Phillips tackle, delayed for a couple of seconds and then sprinted across the middle. Hardy hit him with a perfect spiral that he snagged in the end zone. The extra point was good, and the score was tied 7–7 at halftime.

The two teams battled on even terms throughout the third quarter, but in the last period, the Sooner line began to dominate the Haymakers and free up Roy Swatek and Harry "Dutch" Hill for long gains. OU scored its last touchdown on the same play as the first, except this time, Hardy passed to the man in motion, Howard "Tarz" Marsh, who had replaced the injured Tyler. The extra point attempt was wide, and it looked as though this might cost the Sooners the victory as Phillips mounted a relentless ground game. But with time running out and the ball on OU's

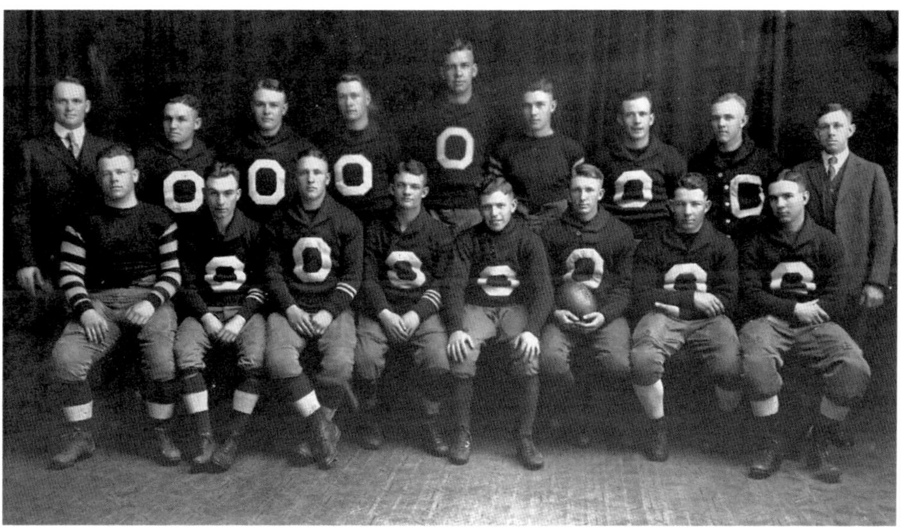

The OU 1918 varsity football team had a record of six wins and zero losses. The season was shortened due to World War I. *Courtesy of the University of Oklahoma's Western History Collection, OUPC 21.*

ten-yard line, Sooner center Dow Hamm pushed his counterpart back into the ball carrier Newt Weatherly, knocking him off balance. Earl Deacon broke free and finished him off, thus preserving the victory. Bennie's players, as gracious in victory as in defeat, were always quick to praise their opponents. "They had old heads," Tyler said. "I believe they'd have beaten us on a dry field."

Only one game remained, the annual Thanksgiving affair with Oklahoma A&M, which was to be played at Fair Park in Oklahoma City. The previous year, the Aggies had defeated OU (9–0) for the first time ever, and they saw no reason why they should not be victorious again this year. But alas, it was not to be. The Sooners received the opening kickoff and marched seventy-five yards. Haskell scored the TD on an end around, and the rout was on. The final score was OU, 27; A&M, 0.

If not for a talented group of freshmen, 1918 could have been a very forgettable year at OU with the double whammy of the First World War and an influenza epidemic. But under the calm and resourceful leadership of Bennie Owen, a young team gave Sooner fans a lot to celebrate.

Missouri Valley Champs

The Sooners claimed their first victory of the 1920 season in a rather disappointing fashion, 16–7 over Central Normal of Oklahoma, and were preparing for their first-ever Missouri Valley Conference game. They would be traveling to St. Louis to meet the Washington University Pikers.

Earl "Deke" Deacon, a 192-pound guard, was held out of action against Central in hopes that his injured knee would be ready for the Washingtonians. The knee was crushed in an oil field accident the previous summer, and Deacon thought his football career was probably over. But his good friend Sooner end Dewey "Snorter" Luster talked him into giving it a try.

Bennie was afraid the knee was not healing well, but Deke assured him that he was OK. Owen was not so sure. After a bit of verbal jousting, Deacon bet his coach a quarter that he could beat him in a foot race to prove the point. Bennie readily agreed and, in fact, gave his big lineman a twenty-yard head start.

Deke was so sure he could beat Bennie that he started out by doing an exaggerated imitation of a sprinter, but the old man was faster than he thought. Try as he might, Deke could not pull away from the coach.

Owen ran up literally on his heels, and although he could have passed him at any time, he made the big man keep running for another one hundred yards just to test him. Then the forty-five-year-old coach tapped him on the shoulder and sprinted by. Although he lost the race and the bet, Deacon had convinced his coach that his knee was sound enough to play against the Pikers.

Relying mostly on screen passes, Washington took a 14–3 lead into halftime. Then it began to rain. Harold Keith wrote, "With the clouds thickening, the field began to grow as dark as Oklahoma's blighted hopes. Back at Norman, eight hundred miles away, the hundreds of Sooner students listening to the returns in the bright sunshine in front of Barbour's Drug Store, wore long faces. It looked like a Washington victory."

Sooner fans were not just sad, they were also shocked. They had expected great things from their team this season, and why not? Bennie's 1920 edition was packed with big strong veteran players. Ten of the eleven who started the Washington game were lettermen, and many were holdovers from his all-victorious 1918 squad. Although Washington was clearly no pushover (they were undefeated thus far in the current season and had won the conference championship two years ago), its team was not thought to be the equal of Bennie's husky Sooners.

Owen inserted Phil White at halfback in the second half, and the big man (six feet, one inch tall and 190 pounds) became the star of the game. The *Oklahoma Daily* said of his play:

> *Tearing off long end runs, booting the ball as far as sixty-five yards, playing havoc with the opposition's passes and generally injecting 'fight' into the team, Phil White, 21, played his best game in Sooner football against Washington University Saturday…A week ago coach Bennie G. Owen had nearly given up hope of using White on account of Phil's trouble with his left arm which easily gets jerked out of joint. He kept the arm carefully at this side Saturday and it gave him no trouble.*

White said that he figured out how to keep his shoulder in place while following the wheat harvest north perched on the top of a boxcar the previous summer. It suddenly came to him, as in a vision, that he should sew a looped strap onto the left hip of his moleskins. Then he could insert his left wrist through this loop and keep his arm firmly anchored to his side. Apparently, this solved the problem because thanks primarily to his heroics, the Sooners scored three TDs in the second half (one of these on a pass from White to "Little Tub" Tyler) and defeated the Pikers 24–14. Actually, the rain may have been a blessing in disguise for OU because Norman had received heavy showers the previous week so they were used to a muddy field.

White, a member of the fabulous frosh of 1918, was a brilliant but headstrong young man who liked to do things his own way. "You could lead Phil anywhere, but you couldn't drive him" was the way his teammates described him. He often slept through classes and football practice too unless one of the other Sooners roused him out of his bed in the basement of the Owen home. Apparently Bennie liked to have him close by so he could keep an eye on him.

One could hardly blame White for not wanting to attend football practice because before he devised the strap for his arm, his shoulder caused him considerable pain. If the troublesome appendage slipped out of joint (as it frequently did), someone would have to put a shoe under his shoulder and, while White lay on his back writhing in pain, yank on his arm until they could force the shoulder back into its socket. One such episode would be enough to drive most men from the game. Perhaps it was this experience that led him to a career as a physician to relieve the suffering of others. However, White always made sure his appointment schedule was flexible enough so that he could work in an occasional round of golf.

Another standout for the Sooners in St. Louis that day was Roy "Soupy" Smoot, their 215-pound tackle who recovered a fumble and, flashing tremendous speed for one so large, ran it in for OU's second touchdown. Smoot, because of his rich tenor voice, was known as the "Sooner Caruso." Despite getting several teeth knocked out in the Washington game, the tenor-tackle earned his livelihood as an opera singer for many years after college.

Four days after the Sooners made their triumphant return from St. Louis, they again boarded a train and headed back to the state of Missouri. Their destination was the city of Columbia, where they would meet the Tigers of the University of Missouri on Rollins Field, and on this trip, they had plenty of company. Accompanying Bennie, his assistant coach Grover Jacobson and twenty-one players were their trusty tan-and-white bulldog mascot, Mex, and the Jazz Hounds, a thirty-two-piece pep band. The Jazz Hounds brought with them a prairie schooner, a cow and fifty pigeons. At halftime, they attached a sign to the cow that read, "This ain't no bull, we'll beat the Tigers" and paraded him around the field

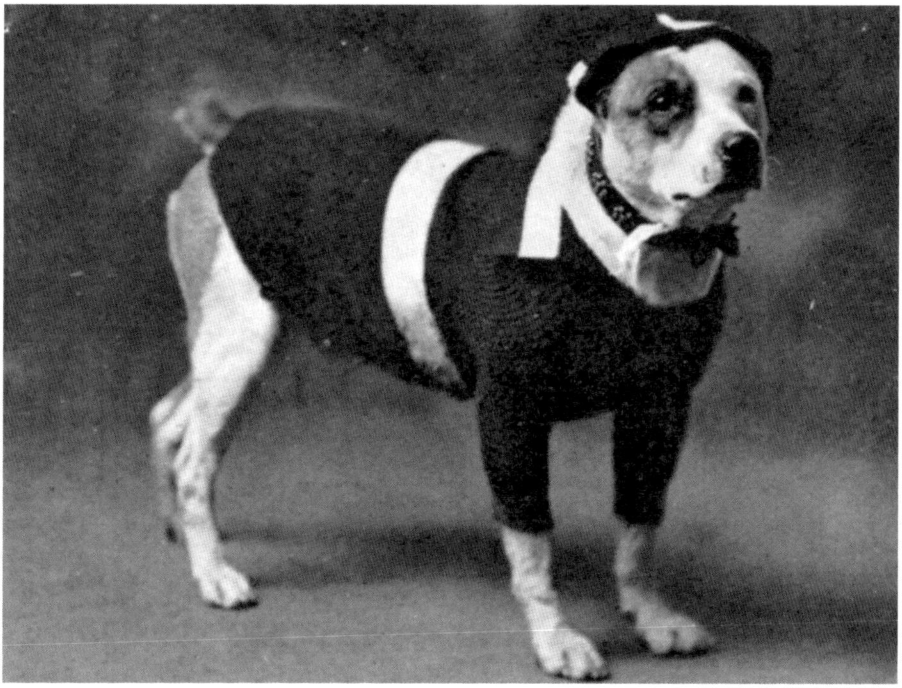

Mex was the Sooner mascot from 1919 to 1928. *Courtesy of the University of Oklahoma's Western History Collection, OU 1192.*

behind the schooner. Nowhere in Sooner lore is there any record of what they did with the pigeons.

It was obvious that Missouri's coach, John F. Miller, was taking the game seriously. "Tiger supporters must realize that the game with the Oklahoma is the crucial contest of the season," he said. "Last year the Sooners had the strongest eleven we met during the entire season. [The two teams had battled to a 6–6 tie in 1919.] They are equally versatile in using straight football or gaining yardage by the aerial route. With practically the same men back and a few additions, Bennie Owen may be counted on to turn out a first class team."

Bennie Owen also understood the significance of the contest because he did something he had never done before. Just before kickoff, he walked down the bench and shook hands with every player. This simple gesture, coming as it did from the coach they all loved, caused many of these big strong men to begin to cry. Most of them were too choked up to speak.

Roy Smoot, one of the few who could find his voice said, "Dawgone, we'll get 'um for you, Bennie." And they did.

The game was played in the brilliant sunshine of a cool October day. "The grassy gridiron was fast and in the background, stained by the alchemy of autumn, the trees wore their multicolored dresses" is the way Keith described the scene.

With Phil White again displaying his triple-threat talents, OU prevailed 28–7. For the second game in a row, a Sooner tackle scored a touchdown. This time it was Paul Johnston intercepting a pass and returning it thirty-five yards for Oklahoma's last score.

Next up for the Sooners were the Kansas Jayhawkers in Norman. This was homecoming weekend and the *Oklahoma Daily* published Draconian guidelines on how OU students were to conduct themselves before, during and after the game. The freshmen girls were to wear white skirts and sweaters, and the boys were to wear their caps, red sweaters and white trousers for Freshman Friday.

Game day rules were as follows:

> *All students must sit in the east bleachers. Freshmen will be grouped and upperclassmen will be grouped. The idea is that every available rooting unit must be centralized for the game. The ROTC will appear in full uniform, and will occupy a section of the bleachers unless other plans are made tomorrow.*
>
> *POSITIVILY NO DATES WILL BE PERMITTED TO THE GAME. WOE UNTO THE STUDENT WHO VIOLATES THIS RULE. This applies to all classes and rooting organizations will be ready for work with violators.*
>
> *Alumni and visitors will occupy the west bleachers.*
>
> *And furthermore—*
>
> *WHEN THE GAME IS OVER—*
>
> *The band will play Boomer Sooner. The entire student group should remain on the bleachers with hats removed until the band has finished, and the team is carried off the field. The Boomer football squad* [i.e., the freshman team] *will carry the team off the field. Then you may go.*
>
> *Remove your hat when Boomer Sooner is played. Common decency demands that.*
>
> *And help beat the Jayhawkers.*

Kansas was coached that year by Forrest Clare "Phog" Allen, DO. Dr. Allen will always be remembered more for his contributions to the sport of college basketball. He earned three letters in basketball at KU (1905–07) playing for the legendary Dr. James Naismith. He later coached his alma mater for thirty-one years. Known as the "Father of Basketball Coaching," his overall record was 771-223. However, for the season of 1920, and only for that one season, he coached the Kansas football team and led them to a record of 6-2-1.

A few days before he brought his team to Norman, he made an address to the KU student body warning them of the evils of betting on college football. He said this practice was "disloyal to the team and a selfish means of profiting from the loyalty of others. Horse racing, former king of sports, is a sideline; boxing is in the gutter; and baseball, America's greatest national game is kept alive only by its soul living in the breast of the six or seven year old child. All this is the result of gamblers. And now they are after the greatest intercollegiate sport—football. Don't bet on your team, don't bet against your team; assure them of your support by your undying loyalty to them."

When asked for his thoughts on Dr. Allen's statement, Bennie Owen agreed, wholeheartedly. He said, "Betting will ruin any sport there is... This mess we've had just come to light in world's series baseball [the 1919 "Black Sox" scandal] ought to be enough to show us that it's time to stop betting on any sport that we want to keep a real sport. Betting does not show pep or school spirit. It works just the other way. It destroys school spirit."

The game, a 21–9 Sooner victory, witnessed by a crowd of ten thousand, was proclaimed "unquestionably the greatest exhibition of football ever witnessed in Oklahoma" by the student paper. As usual OU was led by the great Phil White. The *Oklahoma Daily* was ecstatic in its praise of the halfback:

> *To star in a game where team play is predominant is not easy; but it was accomplished in the Sooner-Jayhawk game by Phil White. In every play the Kansans pitted two or sometimes three men against the six-foot, 194 pound runner. He was never stopped by one man. He punted for an average of 51 yards...and most of Oklahoma's winning passes were Phil's handiwork.*
>
> *Last year there were men who believed Phil was "yellow." It's a cinch he isn't now. He has to play with his left arm strapped at his side to protect his*

> *loose left shoulder joint. He can't stiff arm a tackler as other halfbacks can, but he has to let them hit him, then shake them off by the sheer hardiness of his flesh and the powerfulness of his muscular legs…"We just have to take off our hats to that man Phil White," said the Jayhawk players as they dressed after the game.*

After this victory, both the *Oklahoma Daily* and the *Norman Transcript* proclaimed that OU had won the Missouri Valley Championship even though they still had two conference games left to play. As things turned out, they were right, but it was not quite as easy as these scribes, and probably the Sooners themselves, expected. Their next game was a nonconference tilt at Stillwater with Oklahoma A&M, which OU won easily 36–0. Then they encountered a severe speed bump at Manhattan, Kansas, in their race for the title. Kansas State Agricultural College, which did not win a single conference game that season, played the Sooners to a 7–7 final score when OU, on three occasions, was held on downs inside the two-yard line.

"Overconfident and pepless? Or overtrained and stale?" the *Oklahoma Daily* asked. "Whichever or whatever accounts but poorly for a 7–7 score where there should have been a Sooner victory over the Kansas Aggies Saturday. Battling against 15 pounds per man superiority the Farmers plainly outfought, outkicked, and outplayed the touted all-victorious varsity eleven, and won what was from their standpoint victory with which to sugarcoat a whole season of defeats."

The *Daily Oklahoman* was a little less caustic in its analysis: "The Oklahomans played good football at times but could not put forth the necessary punch when a yard or two more would have meant a touchdown and additional points for Oklahoma. A strong south wind made punting dangerous, and White, giant Oklahoma City lad, averaged only eighteen yards on his boots that in other games this year have averaged around the forty-five yard mark."

The following week, the Sooners found their old form and slaughtered the Drake Bulldogs 44–7 in Des Moines, Iowa, on Thanksgiving Day and claimed the Missouri Valley Conference Championship in their freshman season. Shortly before the Drake game, Owen had received a telegram from Ohio State coach J.W. Wilce asking him if he would be interested in matching his Sooners against the Buckeyes, who were the undefeated champions of the Big Nine Conference. Wilce wanted to play OU on the Saturday following Thanksgiving. Since this would give the

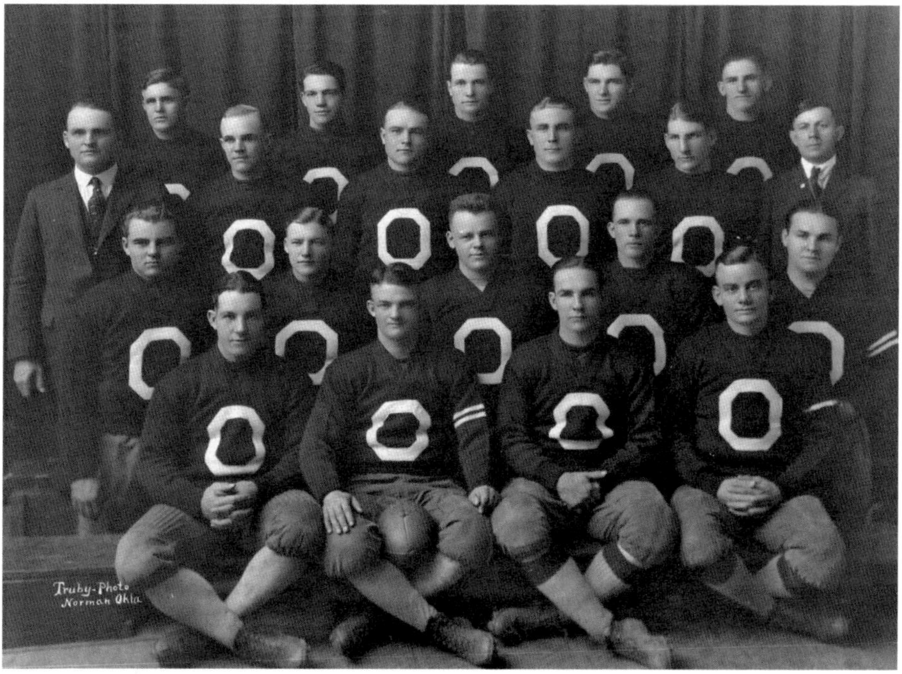

The OU 1920 varsity football team had a record of six wins, zero losses and one tie. Holding the ball in the front row is Dewey "Snorter" Luster, who later was head coach at OU (1941–45). *Courtesy of the University of Oklahoma's Western History Collection, OUPC 24.*

Sooners only two days' rest after the Drake game, Owen replied that he was indeed interested in the matchup but asked if it would be possible to play the game on the following Monday or Tuesday, thus giving his team four or five days' rest.

However, after shellacking the Bulldogs, Bennie and his boys were so confident that he wired Wilce and told him that the Sooners would leave Des Moines immediately and play the Buckeyes on their home field in Columbus on Saturday after only a two-day rest. But alas, it was not to be. Shortly before he got Owen's wire, Wilce had received an invitation to meet the University of California in the Rose Bowl on New Year's Day, so he canceled out on OU. He may have regretted this decision because the Buckeyes were soundly defeated by the Golden Bears 28–0.

In those days, each coach in the Missouri Valley was asked to pick his All-Conference team. Twelve Sooners were named by at least one coach, and three were selected by the Newspaper Enterprise Association as All-Americans. These were Roy "Soupy" Smoot the tenor/tackle, left guard

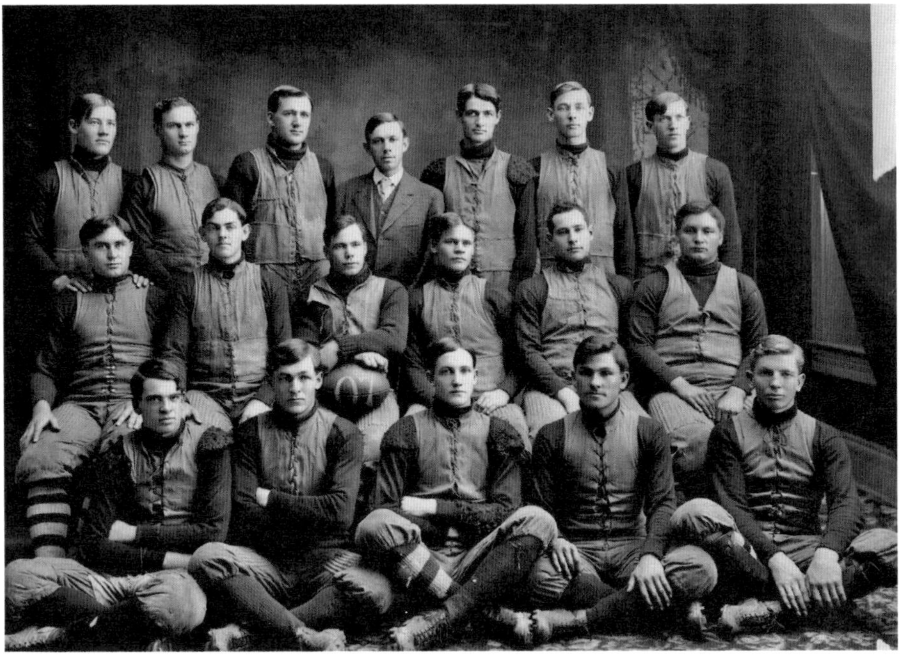

The OU 1907 varsity football team had a record of four wins and four losses. *Courtesy of the University of Oklahoma's Western History Collection, OUPC 5.*

James "Bon" Tolbert and, of course, the remarkable Phil White. Joining White in the All-American backfield that season was a young man from Notre Dame by the name of George Gipp.

The Sooner yearbook of 1920–21 stated:

> *Ben G. Owen, director of athletics, came to the university in 1905 when the total enrollment was less than half the size of the present freshman class. In fifteen years Owen has produced three all-victorious football elevens* [as well as the 1920 squad that was undefeated], *two* [actually there had been three] *all victorious basketball quintettes, and succeeded in introducing Oklahoma into the Missouri Valley conference in the winter of 1920. It was a fitting tribute to his genius to produce the champion football team in the first year of the university's participation in the Missouri Valley conference.*

Bennie Owen would coach football at the University of Oklahoma for six more seasons, but he had begun to plan well beyond that.

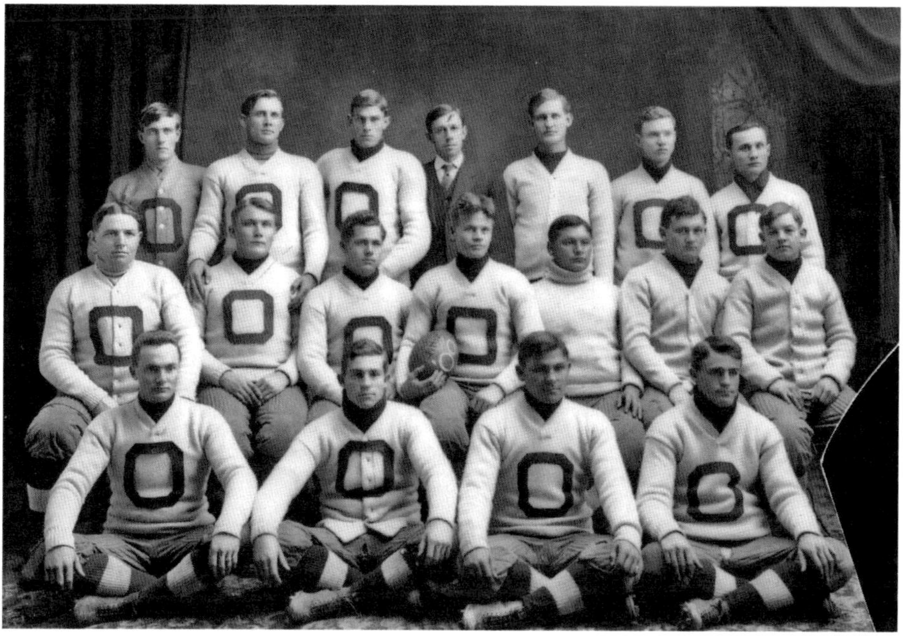

The OU 1909 varsity football team had a record of six wins and four losses. *Courtesy of the University of Oklahoma's Western History Collection, OUPC 7.*

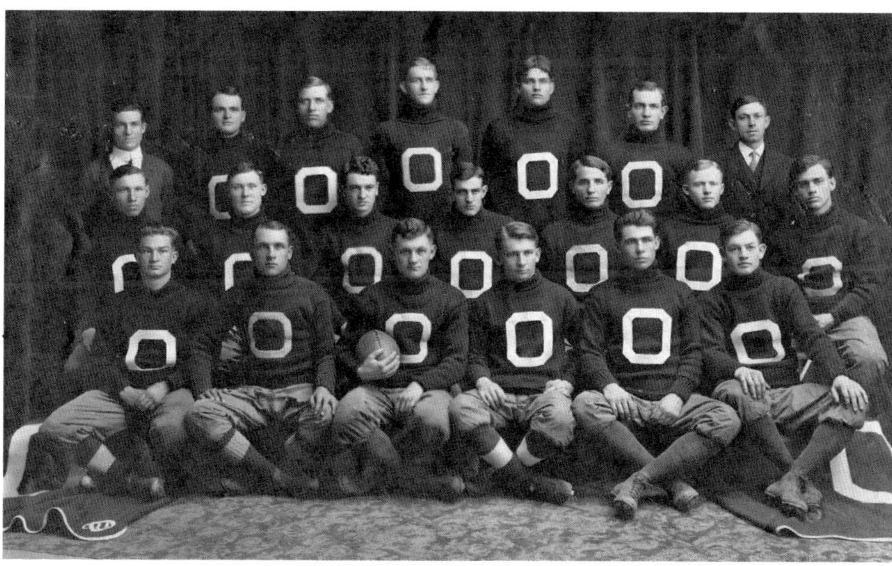

The OU 1912 varsity football team had a record of five wins and four losses. *Courtesy of the University of Oklahoma's Western History Collection, OUPC 10.*

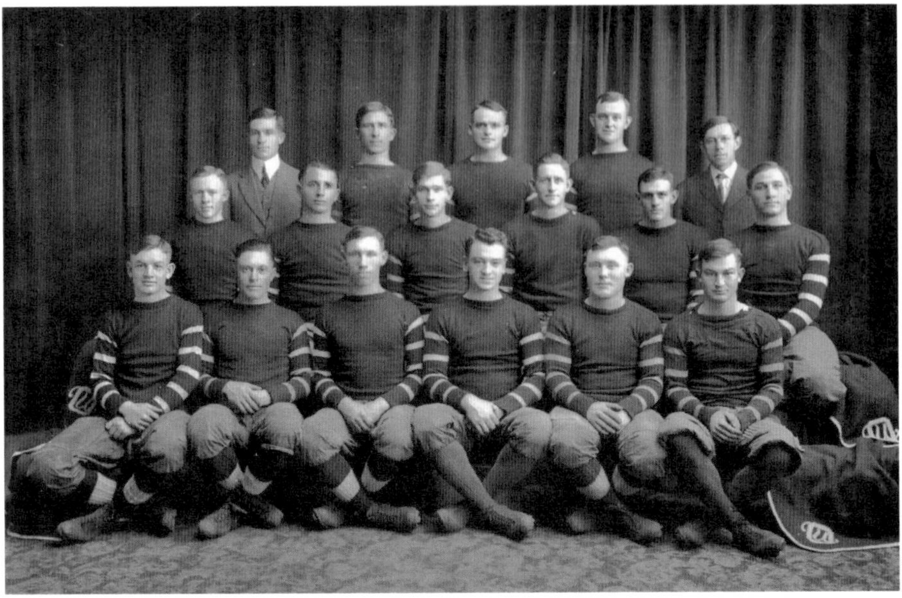

The OU 1913 varsity football team had a record of six wins and two losses. *Courtesy of the University of Oklahoma's Western History Collection, OUPC 12.*

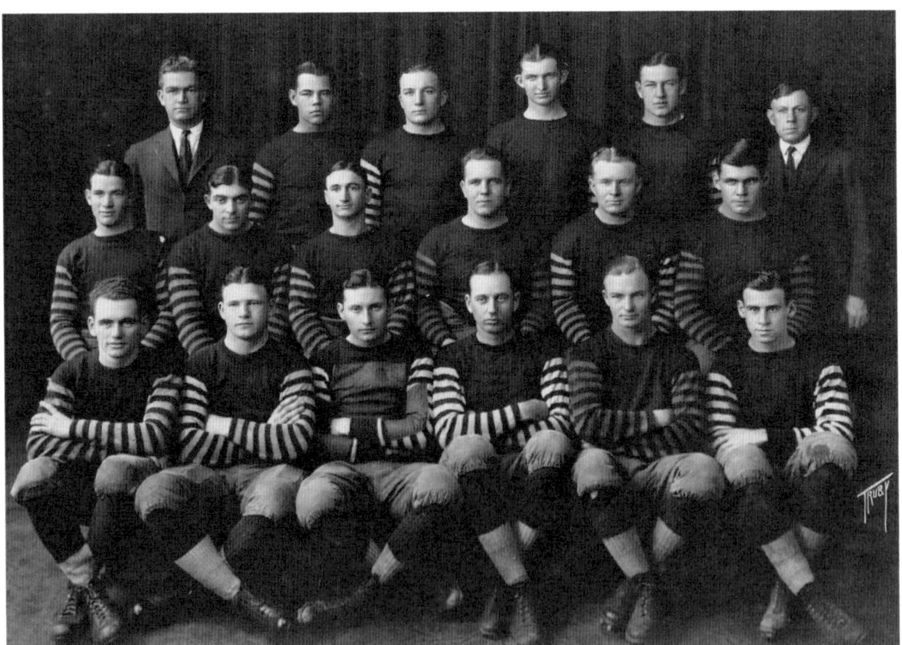

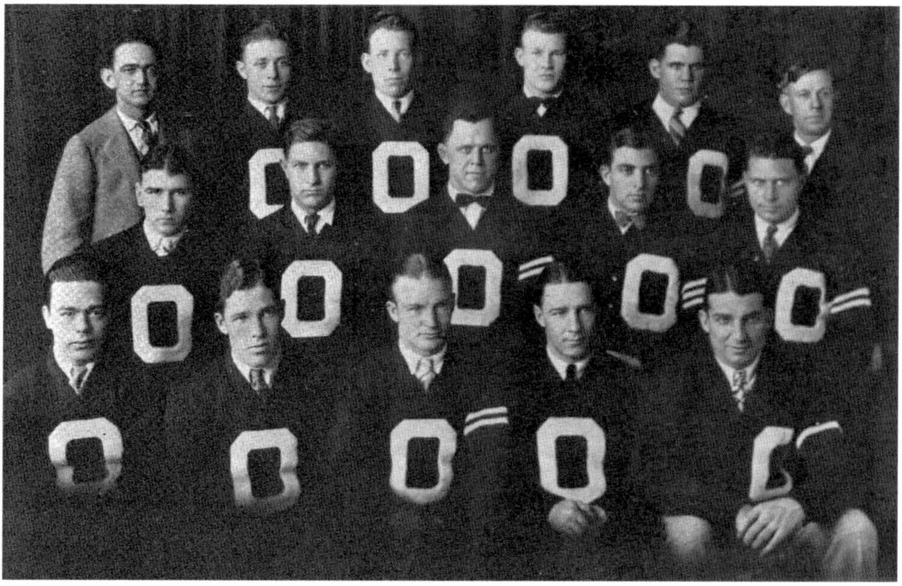

The OU 1925 varsity football team had a record of four wins, three losses and one tie. *Courtesy of the University of Oklahoma's Western History Collection, OU 1500.*

Opposite, bottom: The OU 1923 varsity football team had a record of three wins and five losses. *Courtesy of the University of Oklahoma's Western History Collection, OUPC 25.*

11

THE ARCHITECT OF SOONERLAND

THE HOUSE THAT BENNIE BUILT

Bennie Owen had a vision. This was not just a personal vision but a vision that would profoundly change the University of Oklahoma. No other single individual in the history of that institution would conceive of and bring to fruition such spectacular and long-lasting changes. Or to paraphrase Winston Churchill, never did one man (at OU) do so much for so many.

Bennie thought the university needed a new football stadium, and when Bennie Owen had an idea, he would not rest until that idea became a reality. On November 13, 1920, according to the *Oklahoma Daily*, he announced that he would ask the 1921 state legislature for $350,000 to build modern athletic facilities, including a football stadium and a gymnasium. Apparently, the legislature was not very receptive to this idea because a year later, the student paper reported that on December 15, 1921, he addressed an assembly of OU students and told them that the only way the stadium drive would be successful would be for the university student body, alumni and people in Oklahoma with a special interest in "Soonerland" to get behind it. The plan was for these students, over the upcoming Christmas break, to go back to their hometowns and drum up support for the project. Owen closed the meeting by saying, "The first gun has been fired in the stadium campaign and now we need every Sooner to get behind the movement and put it across."

Owen also got the faculty involved and, over the next two summers, organized university clubs around the state that gave contributions to the project. He believed, however, that the success of the campaign depended on the students. He said, in the *Oklahoma Daily* on May, 9, 1922, "Every student wants a stadium and every student knows the need of a stadium, and if we are to get one it is up to the student body to show the state how great that need is by coming through with a substantial subscription toward the realization of that need. With the student body pledging its quota, and the first payment paid the first section of the stadium can be begun."

"Will Oklahoma come through 100% for the stadium?" The student paper asked on May 18, 1922. It continued:

> *That depends on the individual student. Bennie Owen is doing his part, the team captains are doing their part and the final question is, "Are you doing your part?" Every student is being asked for $100 in four payments but that is not iron-bound or a set and fast rule. If you are a junior this year and cannot see how you can meet the payment next fall, sign up for a small amount and make it later on. Arrange the payments to suit your convenience, but make a pledge.*

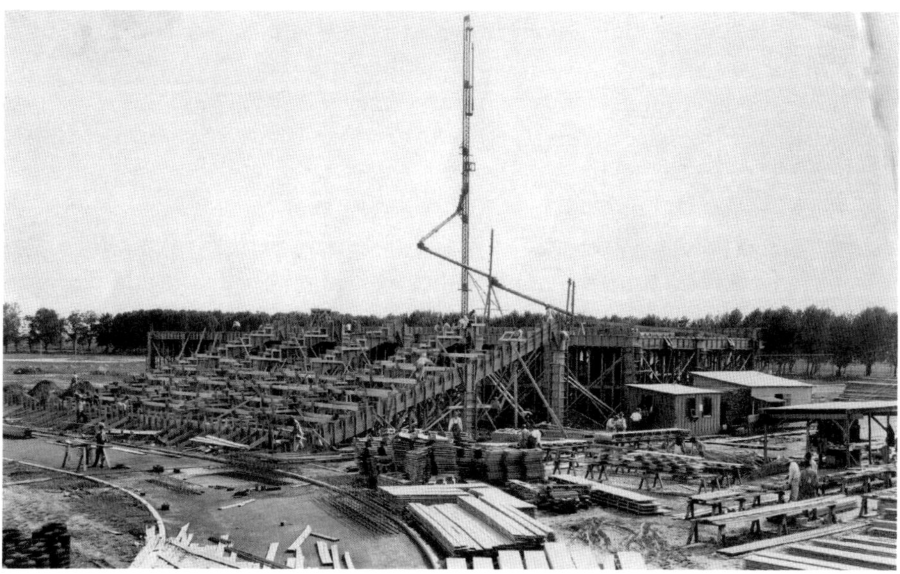

This image shows Memorial Stadium in an early phase of construction, circa 1922. *Courtesy of the University of Oklahoma's Western History Collection, OU 650.*

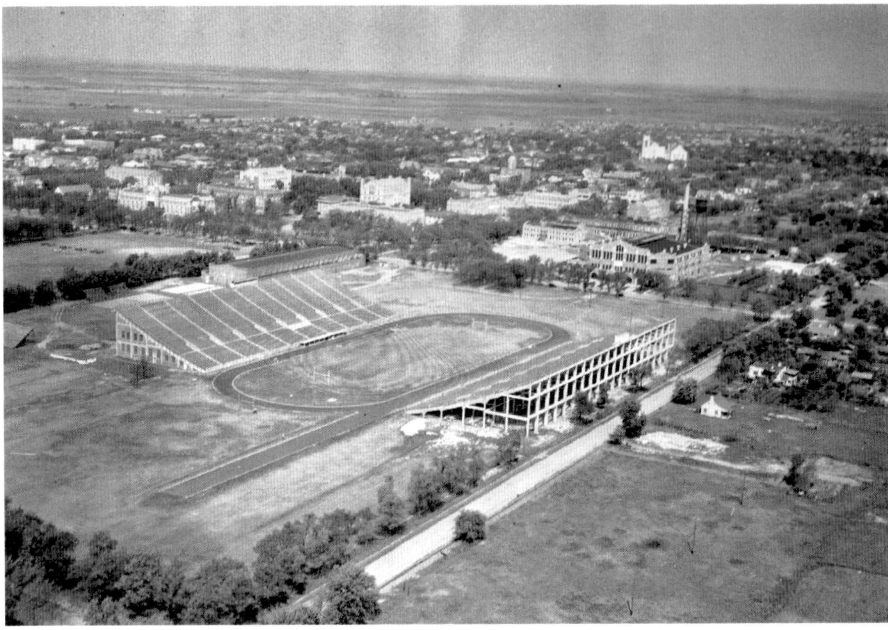

Memorial Stadium, 1929. *Courtesy of the University of Oklahoma's Western History Collection, OU 446.*

The students met their goal, and the first game, a 62–7 victory over Washington of St. Louis, was played in the new stadium on October 20, 1923. At this date, there was very limited seating, but by 1929, the capacity had grown to thirty-two thousand and would remain as such for twenty more years.

From the day it was opened through all its incarnations—even to the eighty-two-thousand-seat monster that it is today—many people have referred to this edifice as Owen Stadium. Although it was quite literally the "House that Bennie Built" because he laid many of the bricks with his strong left hand, that is incorrect. It was named Oklahoma Memorial Stadium in honor of the OU students who lost their lives in World War I. The actual playing field—the sod that strong legs churn up with their cleats and on which the players leave their sweat and blood—was then, is now and hopefully always will be known as Owen Field.

Before the stadium was enlarged in 1949, it contained a cinder track that encircled the field. Bennie Owen persuaded the Oklahoma Gas and Electric Company to give him the cinders for the track, and he talked the Rock Island and Santa Fe Railroads into hauling the cinders from Harrah to Norman for one dollar per carload. Then, with a little help from some students, he ground the cinders and spread them on the track. They also laid tiles for drainage and built cement curbs around the track.

The land just south of the new stadium was a low marshy area where Bennie had shot many a duck. He filled this in with cinders left over from the track and dirt that he hauled from the north oval (currently know as Parrington Oval), leveled it off and built a football practice field and a new baseball diamond.

NEW COACH, NEW RESPONSIBILITIES

A few months before the Sooners played their first game in the new stadium, Charles J. Brill, writing in the *Daily Oklahoman* asked, "Why not begin the new period with a modern organization as well as modern field?" He went on:

> *Oklahoma's athletic organization is as antiquated as the athletic field that is being abandoned. Everyone recognizes this; and Oklahoma cannot expect to become a factor in the Missouri Valley Conference until it does modernize. It is generous of Bennie Owen to go smilingly on his way, accepting without a whimper, the burdens which are being added from year to year. But it isn't fair. It isn't fair to the man who has given the best seventeen years of his life* [actually, at this time, Bennie was in his nineteenth year at OU] *to the upbuilding of athletics at the University of Oklahoma; and it isn't fair to the school and its supporters to have to shoulder the handicaps of an obsolete and inefficient system in their struggles for athletic honors.*
>
> *"Like all other universities of its rank, the University of Oklahoma should have an athletic director whose duties would be merely supervisory. He should not be called upon to shoulder the daily grind of personal coaching. For this post there is only one nominee: Bennie Owen.*
>
> *"Under him, each a specialist in his own line, should be organized a staff of coaches for the work of actual coaching. Each should be supreme in his own field with his associates forming merely an advisory council. It is a simple reorganization. It could be accomplished with practically no greater financial outlay than that required for the present system and until it is done, Oklahoma athletics will never reach their natural plane.*

It took three more years, but this is ultimately what happened. After the 1926 season, Bennie relinquished his coaching duties to Adrian "Ad" Lindsey and became OU's full-time director of athletics. Lindsey had followed much the same path to Norman that Owen had taken. He played his college football at Kansas and later was an assistant coach there. He had also coached at Bethany College. Unfortunately he did not enjoy the same success as his predecessor. In six seasons at OU, he compiled a 19-19-6 record.

The 1927 OU yearbook commemorated the close of Owen's coaching career with the following tribute:

> *After coaching Sooner football since 1905, Bennie Owen is retiring this year to become Director of Athletics. No more will the empty sleeve pinned to his coat flap before the fall winds that sweep across Owen Field, no more will his piercing call move men to action…He took his men off the raw, bleak plains, the Indian reservations, out of the blackjack country and out of large cities, molded them into stars, breathed the fire of his famous Sooner spirit into them. Although Bennie Owen is every inch a fighter, Oklahoma prizes the reputation of its Owen-coached teams for clean-playing and sportsmanship even more than its long ribbon of victories. One of the greatest achievements of his career is the Memorial Stadium, a project that Mr. Owen dared dream of back in the old days when the Sooner campus was mostly prairie and Oklahoma had just been made a state.*

Owen dared to dream about a lot more than a football stadium. His vision also included a new student union building, a field house, a golf course, a swimming pool, tennis courts and an intramural field. All these projects were funded essentially the same way the stadium had been, through Bennie's ingenuity and fundraising efforts with students, faculty, alumni and friends around the state.

The field house and student union building opened in 1928. Both are beautiful buildings featuring red brick trimmed with white stone. The architectural style has been described as "collegiate-Gothic." The original plans called for the union to be built as a part of the football stadium, but Owen said it would be best to build them separately. The total cost of both structures was $350,000. The Oklahoma Memorial Union has been enlarged and improved at least as many times as the football stadium. For over eighty years it has been the hub of all campus activity.

The field house, home of OU basketball until 1975, was constructed on what had been an apple orchard. Bennie instructed his football players to chop down the trees and dig out the stumps in lieu of their daily calisthenics.

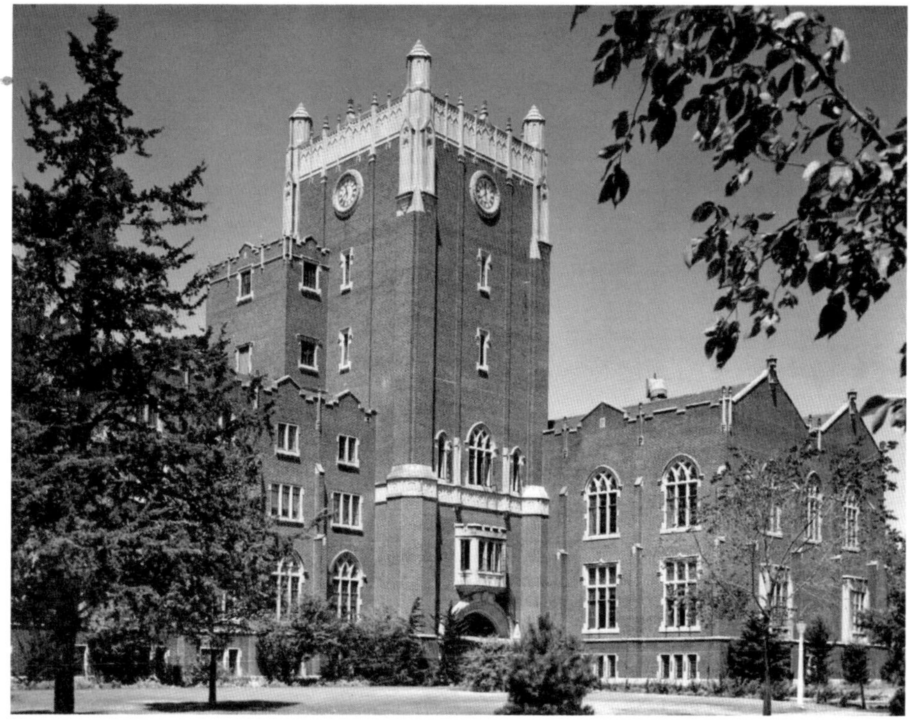

University of Oklahoma Memorial Union. *Courtesy of the University of Oklahoma's Western History Collection, OGS 2220.*

Its price tag was $186,000. However, Owen saved the university thousands of dollars by getting the indoor swimming pool in the north end of the building approved as a government project. With its seating capacity of 5,500, this grand old structure still serves as the venue for Sooner wrestling matches and volleyball games.

In the late 1920s, Owen purchased a fifty-seven-acre tract of land just east of the new football stadium from his friend Sam McBerney of Tulsa for the bargain-basement price of $16,000. Today, the official name for this area is Brandt Park (in honor of OU's sixth president, Joe Brandt), but it is much more commonly known as the Duck Pond. Later, Bennie would sell the land to the university for exactly what he paid for it. It was here that he built OU's first golf course, a quaint little nine-hole layout. Again he was able to save the university a considerable sum of money by designing the course and firing up his old tractor and moving most to the dirt himself. It would be difficult to verify, but this course is reputed to have been the first in the state to have grass greens. A lot of the old course has been covered over by

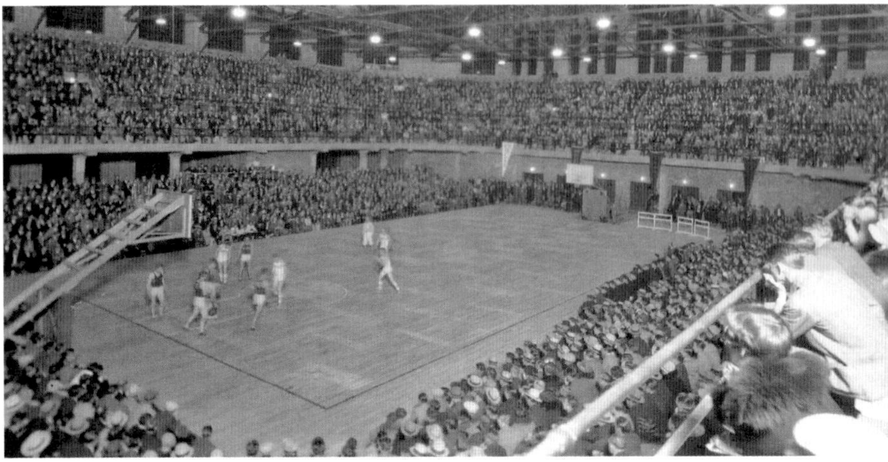

A basketball game is played in the field house, circa 1930. *Courtesy of the University of Oklahoma's Western History Collection, Kraettli 165.*

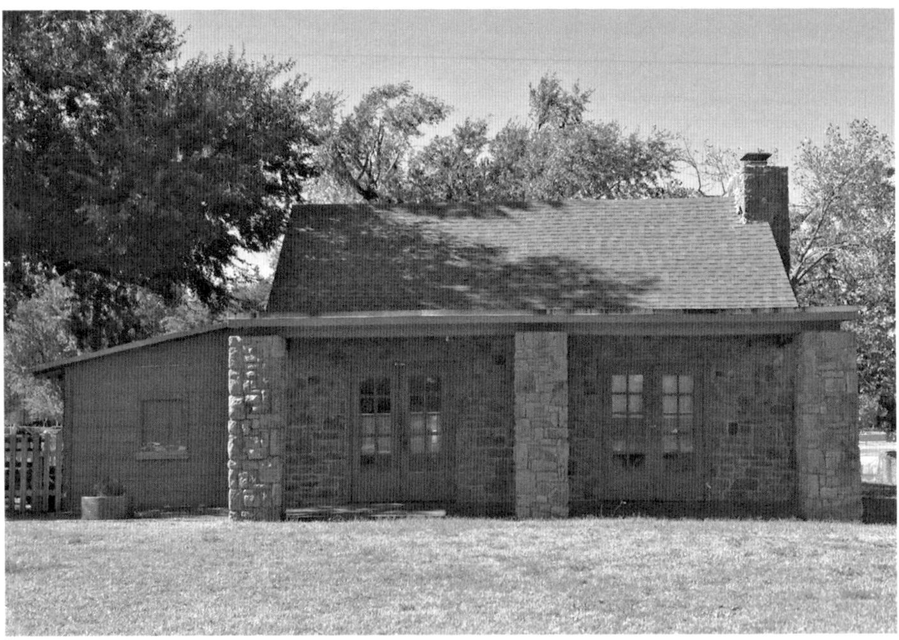

The clubhouse for the golf course that Bennie built. *Courtesy of Patricia King.*

buildings and parking lots, but if one looks closely enough, it is still possible to see where some of the tee boxes and greens used to be.

After seven years as OU's director of athletics, Bennie Owen's responsibilities changed in 1934 when he was given the title of professor of physical education/director of intramurals. He also served as the golf course superintendant and, of course, did the mowing himself. One day, he fell off the tractor and broke a couple ribs. The doctor who taped him up at the student infirmary gave him strict instructions to go home and rest, which he did but not for long. After about an hour, Nina could not find him anywhere. Soon he was located back on the tractor at the golf course. "I had to finish the mowing," he said.

Bennie had always believed intramural athletics were important, and finally, he had the facilities to promote the kind of program he had always wanted. He had these facilities—a swimming pool, a gymnasium, tennis courts, a golf course and a large field for intramural baseball and touch football games—because he had built them.

"I do not believe in the useless waving of arms and legs in coordination," Bennie Owen told a reporter for the student paper. "This is not my idea of physical education." Instead, the article said, "Owen would do away with the usual routine of the gymnasium exercises that is so commonly given in the colleges throughout the United States and substitute the keen rivalries and impetus of competitive games." This article further stated that a well-organized intramural program might "promote the desire to compete in sports whereby the wealth of material may be closely watched, trained, and in case of unusual development be drafted to participate in varsity sports." Indeed many of Owen's athletes in baseball, football and basketball had been drafted from the fraternity leagues.

Just twelve years after Bennie retired as OU's football coach, Harold Keith apparently feared that his accomplishments had been forgotten. In an article for the *Tulsa Tribune* on January 23, 1938, he wrote:

> *About the only reminder of Bennie's great football pigskin dynasty today are a few old brown footballs rotting peacefully on mantles in the homes of Bennie's boys who are now grey-haired men with sons of their own. As captains of the great Sooner teams that Bennie coached they kept those balls as trophies and have guarded and cherished them since. But today's fans don't know these graying men, nor do they know Bennie. Each year new Sooner football teams and new Sooner heroes crowd Owen's old-timers down a little deeper into nameless dust.*

Fortunately, Keith's fears were premature.

Celebrations and Honors

On February 24, 1950, there was a great celebration among the Owen clan. The occasion was the 100th birthday of Bennie's mother. "Mother Owen," as she was known to most, received 150 cards from friends around the nation as well as numerous flowers, potted plants and, of course, a lot of candy. She could not understand what the fuss was all about. "I haven't done anything to deserve it," she said.

Olivia—or "Ollie," as she was called—had lived with her son Ted, whose home was right behind Bennie and Nina's, since the death of her husband, George, in 1920. Ollie had out lived three of her seven children—Olivia, George and Roberta—but her sons Ted, Bennie and Bill and her granddaughter Frances Easterday were there to celebrate with her. Another son, Art, was unable to attend.

Mother Owen had not missed an OU home game in football, basketball or baseball until she was well into her nineties, and she still enjoyed watching sports on television. She was walking with a cane, and her vision and hearing were not as sharp as they once were; however, she remained an active member of the Maturitates Club, a neighborhood organization of "mature" women who met twice a month to discuss church affairs, recite scripture and poetry, sew items and make quilts for the needy.

Ollie Owen would live almost another five years. She died on December 3, 1954, at the age of 104.

On July 1, 1950, after forty-five years of loyal service, Bennie Owen retired from the University of Oklahoma. His pension benefits from the Oklahoma State Teachers' Retirement System were $79 per month. However, just prior to this date, Bennie received a letter from George L. Cross, the seventh president under whom he had served, informing him that the university was making "tentative arrangements" to provide a supplement that that would bring his total retirement package up to $100 per month. Assuming they followed through on these "tentative arrangements," this $1,200 per year would have been less than 25 percent of the $4,900 he had been earning as a full-time employee.

A year after his retirement, Bennie Owen became a charter member of the National Football Foundation's College Football Hall of Fame. Other members of this august class were Sammy "Slingin' Sammy" Baugh, Walter "the Father of Football" Camp, George "the Gipper" Gipp, Red "the Galloping Ghost" Grange, Bronko Nagurski, Knute "Rock" Rockne, Amos Alonzo "the Grand Old Man of Football" Stagg, Jim "Bright Path" Thorpe and Pop Warner. Unbelievably, Owen was not inducted into the Oklahoma Sports Hall of Fame until 2001, fifty years later.

On Saturday, March 28, 1953, Bennie Owen was the guest of honor in Lindsborg, Kansas, at the "Golden Football Reunion" of his "Terrible Swedes" of 1902–04. First, there was a luncheon in the Bethany cafeteria. One of the main topics of conversation at the meal was the 36–9 thrashing the Swedes had administered to the University of Oklahoma Territory in 1904.

After lunch, several of Bennie's former players—including Dr. Win Banbury and his brother Quince, Alfred and Leonard Petterson and Elmer Peterson, men now in their seventies—donned their old uniforms and sauntered out onto the practice field to have some pictures taken. When the photographers were finished, the old Swedes could not resist lining up and "running" through some of the plays they had used with such great success so long ago. The sight of these paunchy, gray and bald old men in their ill-fitting uniforms huffing and puffing around the field must have been a strange spectacle. The *Lindsborg News-Record* reported that "a crowd of curious on-lookers gathered to watch the 'boys of fifty years ago' go through their paces."

Most of the old warhorses actually seemed to remember the plays pretty well, but they appeared to have trouble handling the streamlined modern football. No forward passes were attempted, as that was against the rules when these men played, but there were several fumbled handoffs and dropped laterals. No one was critical of these mistakes, least of all their coach, Bennie Owen, who soon called a halt to the "practice" because he wanted his charges to be in good shape for the dinner that evening. When Bennie blew his whistle, the men headed back to the dressing room accompanied by cheers and applause from the crowd. "All in all it was a great day for the 'Terrible Swedes' who love football just as much as they did fifty years ago—but in a different way," the Lindsborg newspaper observed.

That evening, 360 people turned out for the banquet, which had been planned and promoted by Arthur Gustafson, the president of the Lindsborg Downtown Quarterback Club. The invocation was given by Reverend Ervin C. Malm, pastor of the Bethany Lutheran Church and chairman of the board of directors of Bethany College. Elmer T. Peterson was the master of ceremonies and, according to reports, "was in top form for the occasion and kept the large crowd quite alive and alert by his dry witticisms."

Roger Thorstenberg, a member of the Bethany faculty, played a trumpet solo and Otto Hansen, from nearby Marquette, led the crowd in a roaring rendition of the recursive "Yon Yonson":

My name is Yon Yonson,
I come from Wisconsin,
I work as a lumberjack there,
The people I meet when I walk down the street,
They ask me my name and I say…
My name is Yon Yonson,
I come from, etc. etc. etc.

Apparently Hansen must have brought this never-ending song to an end at some point because eventually the man they all came to honor was introduced. Bennie Owen was given a standing ovation as he approached the podium. He said that when he came to Bethany in 1902, the college president, Dr. Carl Swensson, welcomed him with open arms and never interfered with his football program. Bennie then launched into a humorous and entertaining history of college football as he had lived it, recounting stories from the days of limited substitutions, forty-five-minute halves and no helmets. When he had concluded his remarks, his former players presented him with a plaque

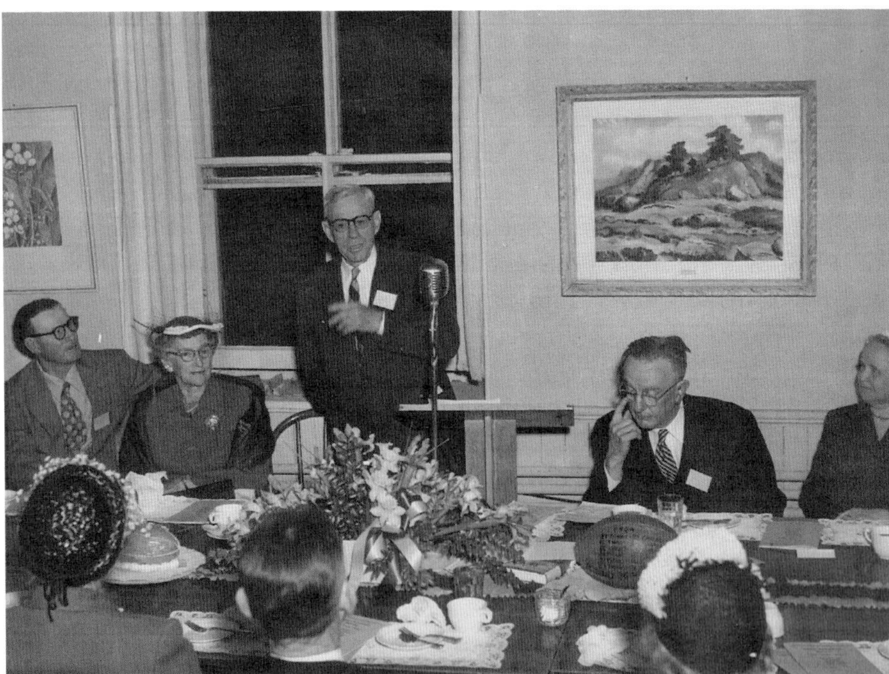

Bennie speaks at the "Golden Football Reunion" at Bethany College. *Courtesy of Jan Howard.*

commemorating the occasion. The evening ended with the assembled multitude standing and singing the Bethany alma mater song.

Two years later, on November 25, 1955, another "Golden Football Reunion" was held at the University of Oklahoma as five hundred of Bennie's friends, family, former players and other OU football fans gathered for a dinner at the Memorial Union to celebrate the fiftieth anniversary of his arrival on the Norman campus. The toastmaster Dewey "Snorter" Luster, Lawrence "Jap" Haskell and Hugh McDermott had played prominent roles in planning the soirée. Their promotional letter promised this would be "an evening for reminiscing" with "no long speeches." Nine speakers, each from a different era of Bennie's long tenure, made their way to the dais and told their favorite stories from the "good old days." They were Bill Cross, 1905 quarterback; Artie Reeds, 1909 fullback; Charlie Orr, 1911 quarterback; Neil Johnson, 1914 fullback; Howard McCasland, 1915 end; Paul X. Johnston, 1918 tackle; Dow Hamm, 1920 center; Granny Norris, 1926 tackle; and U.S. senator Mike Monroney, who described his brief career on the OU freshman team of 1920.

Luster announced that the program would be fought under Marquis of Queensberry rules—three-minute rounds. Several of the old-timers went a little over the prescribed time limit, but none of the diners asked for a refund of the $2.50 they had paid for a ticket. Senator Monroney said, "Overemphasize the home, motherhood or the Baptist Church, but not football at Oklahoma. I know of no other asset of Oklahoma as great as this Bennie Owen to [the] Bud Wilkinson tradition. The teams represent the best in American manhood. As the Chinese proverb says, 'When you drink the water, don't forget the spring from which it flows,' and Oklahoma will never forget Bennie Owen."

The final speaker was Charles "Bud" Wilkinson, then OU's football coach, who said, "I'm a fortunate person to be able to come to Oklahoma and be adopted as an Oklahoman. I hope I'll be here a long time." Then he listed three reasons why OU owes so much to Bennie Owen. First, the facilities he built were "the finest here I've ever seen." Second, the support from the institution and the state he garnered was there "because of the type of program Bennie established." And third was the tradition he created: "Bennie has given that to Oklahoma too. I'd like to thank Bennie for being able to come here and inherit the tradition that Bennie Owen built."

Then Bennie was called to the dais, where "Jap" Haskell presented him with a certificate that commemorated the occasion and Ram Morrison (1921 fullback), on behalf of all Owen's former players, presented him and Nina with a full set of luggage. Finally, it was the eighty-year-old Bennie Owen's turn to speak.

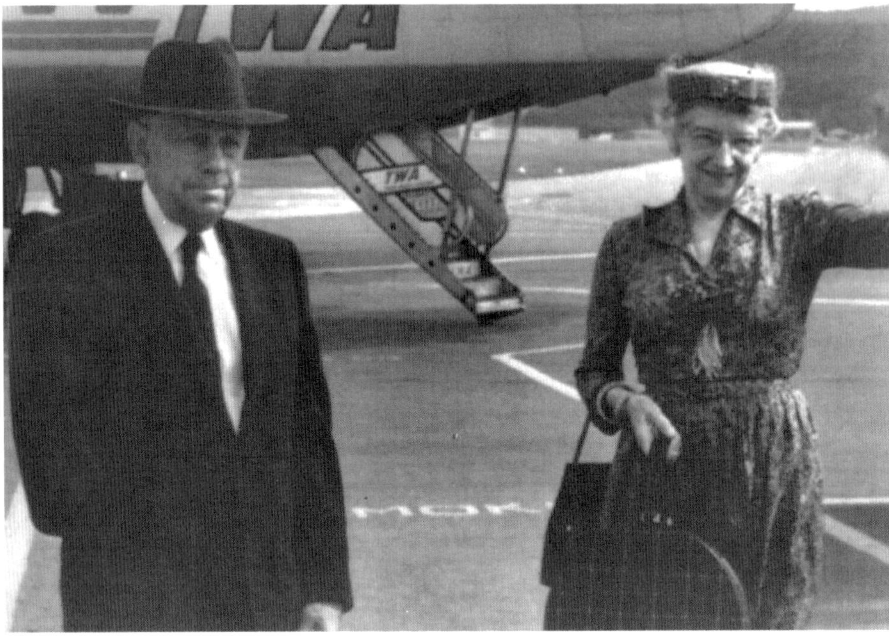

Bennie and Nina prepare to leave on a trip to Europe, circa 1958. *Courtesy of Jan Howard.*

> *I just can't express my appreciation. It's a lot more than we deserve. We all appreciate Bud Wilkinson and his staff and that we're number one. It's wonderful that you all could remember back to our small beginnings.*
>
> *But when I think of the meager equipment we had and the cooperation you boys gave us, oh boy! You guys are the cause of it. It doesn't seem possible that we could get where we are when I think back to our beginnings.*

Several gray-haired men were observed dabbing handkerchiefs to their eyes during these brief remarks. The following afternoon, Owen and several of "his boys" were introduced during halftime of the Sooners' game with the Oklahoma Aggies. Fittingly, OU prevailed in this contest 53–0.

In his retirement, Bennie and his wife, Nina, continued to attend football games and other athletic events on the OU campus. Norman residents spoke respectfully, even reverently, about the small man with his coat sleeve pinned to his side when he was seen around town. His many friends and admirers were very sorry to see him leave in 1964.

LEAVING PARADISE

Both Bennie, who was, at the time, ninety years old, and Nina, who was seventy-nine, hated to leave Norman, but the time, ineluctably, had come. There had been an accident, a car wreck. Nina, who had been driving, was not seriously injured, but Bennie had been thrown through the windshield and had suffered severe facial lacerations. The *Norman Transcript* reported that he had also suffered a broken hip, but his granddaughter Jan Page Howard did not think so. "When I went to visit him in the hospital, he was just totally bruised and black and blue, but I don't think he had any broken bones. That's the reason Mother insisted they move to Houston. She didn't want my grandmother driving any more. She wanted them close to her. Pretty soon after he got out of the hospital, they moved to Houston."

"We're really sorry to go," Nina told Jack Bagby of the *Norman Transcript* on July 20, 1964. "This is the only home we've ever had, and we're reluctant to give it up. We built this house when we were married in 1912 and it's hard to make the break."

"Norman was a paradise when I came. I shot quail in the back yard and ducks where the stadium is now," Bennie said. This was a time when the only hunting regulations were that the hunter split his take with the farmer who owned the land.

As Bennie Owen crossed the sandy South Canadian River on the four-lane bridge on his and Nina's drive out of Norman, he thought about how many times in the old days he had forded this capricious old river on horseback or in a buggy. He looked to his left and saw the place where he had lost his right arm in the hunting accident so many years ago. How long had it been? Fifty, fifty-five? No, fifty-seven years ago. This trip to Houston completed a southerly journey that had begun in Chicago almost twenty-five years before the dawn of the twentieth century when he was still a very young child. It was a journey that had taken him to St. Louis, to several stops in Kansas (Arkansas City, Lawrence, Topeka and Lindsborg) and then to Norman, Oklahoma Territory.

Bennie may have considered Norman a paradise, but to a lot of people, it was just a windy prairie hamlet of 2,500 people when he arrived in 1905. Fewer than 500 students were enrolled in its fledgling university then. Bennie had watched Norman grow to a fair sized city of 55,000, and the university boasted an enrollment of 12,000. The OU football squad had also grown. In fact, several years earlier, Bennie had remarked, "We've got more football players now than we used to have students. We played Missouri in 1910 with just 96 boys enrolled in school and eligible to play."

He was taking lot of memories with him to Houston. Memories of his great teams and the tough, determined young men he had coached and on whose lives he had made such lasting impressions, as well as memories of hunting quail and ducks and of fishing in the ponds and rivers nearby. Now he was leaving, and he would not be back.

Bennie was departing, but memories of him would remain in the town he had loved so much. The OU campus itself was essentially a memorial to the man. The football stadium, field house, union building and Owen Field were lasting memorials to the genius and vision of Bennie Owen.

FOURTH QUARTER

Bennie and Nina settled into an apartment in the Dilson House complex at 7900 Westheimer Road. The courtyard surrounded by the white apartments gave the place a sort of antebellum look and feel. Bennie's daughter Ruth Page; her husband, J.W.; and her children, Bill and Jan, lived just five minutes west of him at 10011 Ella Lee Street.

Ruth looked in on her parents almost every day and took them to do their shopping. Jan, who was sixteen when Bennie moved to Houston (her brother, Bill, was twenty), remembered her parents and grandparents playing bridge together frequently. She also liked to visit Bennie and Nina at their apartment. "Grandmother was always baking," she said. "I loved to go down there when she was making homemade bread and rolls."

Bennie made a quick and seemingly complete recovery from his injuries. Although he never went hunting and fishing again, as soon as he got to Houston, he was walking around the courtyard at his apartment complex. "I was amazed that he recovered so well," Jan said. "That's another reason that I don't think he had any broken bones because he recovered too fast."

In fact, the Pages were afraid Bennie would be bored in Houston because in Norman he was always tinkering with things in his big basement. But if he missed Norman, he never said anything about it. "I never heard him complain one time," Jan said. "I never saw him get mad and never heard him say a rude word."

On December 31, 1968, OU lost to Southern Methodist University 28–27 in the Astro-Bluebonnet Bowl. The previous day, the *Daily Oklahoman* reported:

Oklahoma's Big Red football team undoubtedly numbers many ardent fans in the Houston area for its New Year's Eve meeting with Southern Methodist in the Astrodome, but none whose support is more unwavering than the Ben G. Owen of Westheimer Road in Houston. Bennie Owen "the grand old man" of Sooner football and namesake of Owen Field in Norman, celebrated his 93rd birthday November 25th. He has followed the team's exploits with interest through newspapers and on television during the year and may view Tuesday evening's clash on television his wife Nina said. Mrs. Owen will attend the game with relatives.

Although the paper got Bennie's birthday wrong (he had celebrated his ninety-third birthday six months earlier on July 24), it provided a pretty strong clue that his health was failing. Otherwise, he would have certainly attended the game with his wife and "other relatives" (most likely the Page family).

The cause of Bennie's decline was diabetes. "I know he developed diabetes late in life," Jan Howard said. "I don't remember him having any health problems until shortly before he died. He was always walking around and talking. He was never senile."

A little more than one year after the Astro-Bluebonnet Bowl game, Bennie went into the hospital to have a leg amputated due to complications from diabetes. Just before the surgery, he told his daughter Dorothy Bryan, "Don't worry about me. I'll be fine."

"We all thought he did fine during the surgery," Jan said. "But there were complications either that day or the next." Benjamin Gilbert Owen died on February 26, 1970. He was ninety-four years old.

Immediately, the tributes began to pour in. OU president Dr. J. Herbert Holloman said, "The death of Bennie Owen is sad news for every member of the University family. Although I did not have the pleasure of knowing Mr. Owen, I share the pride of OU faculty and staff members, students and alumni in his outstanding contributions, which brought OU to the forefront of intercollegiate football. His story will always be an important part of the history of the University of Oklahoma."

A man who did know Owen personally, OU president emeritus Dr. George Lynn Cross said, "Mrs. Cross and I were deeply saddened to learn of the death of Bennie Owen. He was a true friend to us and his contributions to the University athletic program can never be measured. He was a legend in his own time and his name will always be synonymous with football."

Harold Keith and his former players declared their love and admiration for Bennie and praised his innovative genius as a coach and his visionary

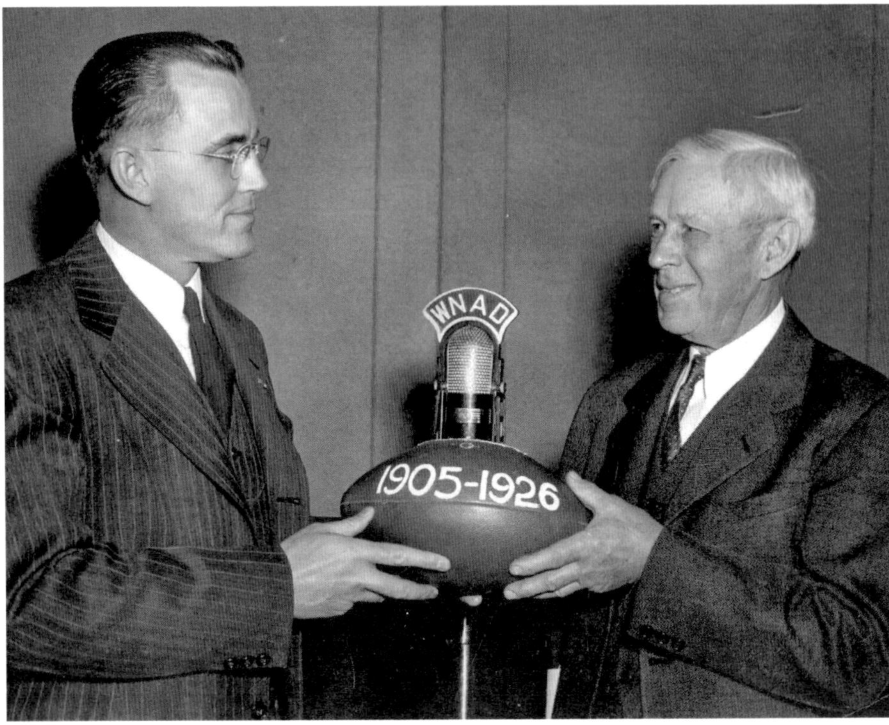

OU president George Cross on the left and Bennie Owen in 1955. *Courtesy of the University of Oklahoma's Western History Collection, OU 49.*

prescience for the university, but it was the Reverend Kenneth Feaver of Norman's First Presbyterian Church who most eloquently and insightfully described the essence of the man. In his eulogy, Dr. Feaver said:

> *Bennie Owen came to the University of Oklahoma in 1905 before he was thirty years of age. It was just six years ago that he left, physically, this community. During all those years his presence has been felt and his shadow of influence has fallen across not only the University community but also across the whole town and its far reaching environs. You know his story...*
>
> *He was a man of quality, who let this quality shine through the characteristics that marked him. The first of these, and one that showed through all his living, was a basic and penetrating stubbornness, a pervading tenacity. Genial man that he was, he made it clear to all about him that he knew who he was and who he was not, and no one should question this. With a grace that could disintegrate any would-be challenger, through the*

ripples of a smile across his face he communicated with utmost clarity that he believed in himself and no one, with impunity, debated this. It was a fascinating suggestion of strength.

Supporting this tenacious trait was a contagious congeniality. To sit in conversation with Bennie Owen was to enjoy every minute of it. He made it very clear that he was open. He had nothing to hide and so while we are together, let's enjoy each other. This made everyone who sat with him very comfortable and relaxed. He opened himself to others. He thus communicated the suggestion that others could open up to him. This characteristic contributed greatly to the impact he made not only upon the men on his many teams, but also those who stood behind these teams.

Bennie Owen was an honest man. This honesty related to every facet of his being: the way he thought, the feelings he felt, the decisions he arrived at, the actions he engaged in. He had no patience with cover-up or deceit. He believed that straightforwardness, however blunt it might have to be, was a basic condition for good human relationships and production.

One other characteristic: Bennie Owen was imaginative. He respected the past. He enjoyed the present. But also, he had the imagination to probe the territory beyond the established boundaries. He was intrigued by the prospect of bringing the future into today. Life for him did indeed have a past, and a demanding present, but it likewise ought to have upon it the alluring grasp of the future.

Epilogue

Bennie Owen was buried in Norman's IOOF Cemetery. When Nina died on November 1, 1977, she was laid at his side. However, Dorothy Bryan, unhappy with the way the graves were being maintained, in September 2004 had her parents disinterred and moved to Memorial Park Cemetery in Oklahoma City.

On November 13, 2010, 105 years after Bennie Owen coached his first game at OU, statues of him and Bud Wilkinson were unveiled in Norman. Bennie's only surviving daughter, Dorothy, then ninety years old, and forty-nine other family members were on hand for the ceremonies. The two bronze statues were created by Mario Grijalva. The renderings of the men are nine feet tall and each stands on a four-foot base.

Bennie's statue faces Owen Field, which is less than fifty yards away, just to the west across Jenkins Street. The inscription on this monument reads:

> *A winner as a quarterback and one of the nation's most promising young coaches, Bennie Owen turned his hand to establishing the University of Oklahoma as a winning football program when he arrived in Norman in 1905.*
>
> *A soft-spoken but tenacious competitor, Owen quickly transformed the Sooners into a force, compiling a 7-2 record in his first season. Six of those victories were shutouts including a 2–0 conquest of Texas. Owen, whose overall coaching record is 155-60-19, emphasized innovation, speed, conditioning, and sportsmanship in compiling a 122-54-16 record*

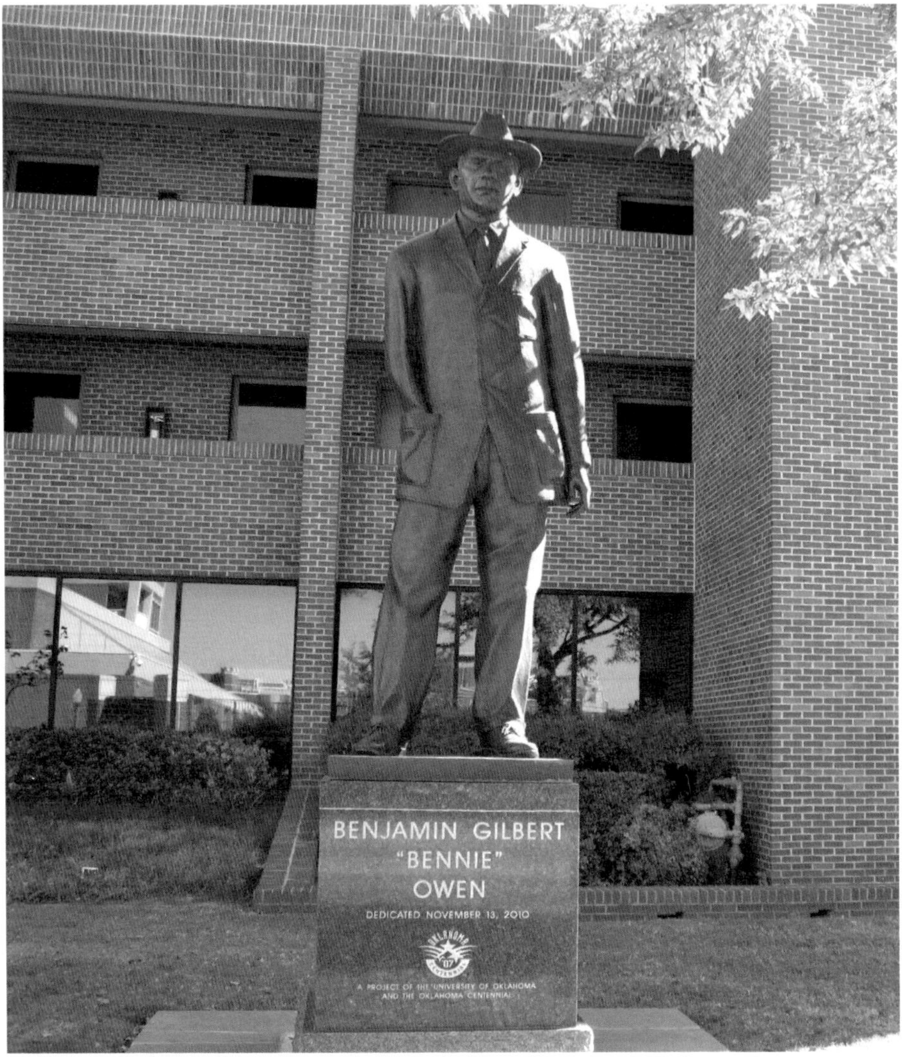

The statue of Bennie Own. *Courtesy of Patricia King.*

in 22 seasons at OU. His Sooners were unbeaten in 1911, 1915, 1918 and 1920.

Owen's insightful adaptation of new tactics included the deceptive "spinner" play, the forward pass, and running plays off a direct snap from center. Owen's teams outscored the opposition 5,031–1,470 laying OU's foundation as the highest scoring football program of all time.

Despite losing his right arm in a hunting accident in 1907 Owen also coached basketball until 1921. He went 113-49 in 13 seasons on the hardwood to become the only Sooner coach to achieve 100 victories in each sport.

As athletic director, Owen in 1922 began a fund-raising campaign to build a football stadium and student union. His Sooners won the first game ever played on what would become Owen Field in 1923. He also pushed through construction of the field house, a baseball stadium, tennis courts, a swim area and OU's first golf course.

A charter member of the College Football Hall of Fame and a member of the Helms Foundation Hall of Fame and Oklahoma Sports Hall of Fame, Bennie is remembered as a true gentleman and creative pioneer who relished challenges while promoting clean play, a love of the game and good sportsmanship.

Bennie Owen was a leader of men.

Bennie Owen's Coaching Records

Football

Washburn University: One Season, 6-2-0

1900 (6-2-0)		
11	vs. Haskell	0
24	vs. Kansas	0
80	vs. Fort Riley	0
29	vs. Colorado College	6
0	vs. Denver A.C.	5
5	vs. Haskell	11
29	vs. Kansas	0
16	vs. Ottawa	0

Bethany College: Three Seasons, 22-2-2

1902 (8-1-1)		
42	vs. Wesleyan	0
105	vs. Hoisington	0

56	vs. Pratt	0
17	vs. Otttawa	5
11	vs. Washburn	12
0	vs. Haskell	0
17	vs. Ottawa	0
40	vs. KSAC (Kansas State Agricultural College)	0
72	vs. Washburn	5
11	vs. Haskell	0
	1903 (7-1-1)	
40	vs. Wesleyan	0
21	vs. Cooper	0
23	vs. Kansas City Medics	11
18	vs. Kansas State	0
0	vs. Glasco	0
11	vs. Emporia	5
6	vs. Washburn	12
21	vs. Cooper	13
12	vs. Oklahoma	10
	1904 (7-0)	
23	vs. Chilocco	0
17	vs. Fairmont	0
16	vs. Kansas State	0
82	vs. Cooper	6
28	vs. Kansas State	5
71	vs. Ottawa	0
39	vs. Oklahoma	9

Oklahoma University: Twenty-six Seasons, 122-54-16

1905 (7-2)			
October 9	at Central Oklahoma	W	28–0
October 16	Haskell	W	18–12

October 23	at Kansas	L	34–0
October 25	Kansas City Medics	W	33–0
October 28	Washburn*	L	9–6
November 3	Texas*	W	2–0
November 12	at Kingfisher College	W	55–0
November 19	Central Oklahoma	W	29–0
1906 (5-2-2)			
October 6	Central Oklahoma	W	12–0
October 13	Kingfisher Collete	W	11–6
October 19	at Oklahoma A&M	W	23–0
October 26	at Kansas	L	20–4
November 2	Texas*	L	10–9
November 9	at Central Oklahoma	W	17–0
November 16	Pawhuska	T	0–0
November 23	Sulphur	W	48–0
November 28	at Washburn	T	0–0
1907 (4-4)			
October 4	at Kingfisher College	W	32–0
October 11	Chilocco	W	43–0
October 19	Kansas	L	15–0
October 25	Epworth	W	29–0
November 9	Oklahoma A&M	W	67–0
November 12	at Texas A&M	L	19–0
November 15	at Texas	L	29–10
November 28	Washburn*	L	12–0

1908 (8-1-1)			
September 25	at Central Oklahoma	W	51–5
October 3	at Oklahoma A&M	W	18–0
October 10	Kingfisher College	W	51–0
October 17	at Kansas	L	11–0
October 23	at Kansas State	W	33–4
October 30	Arkansas	W	27–5
November 5	Epworth	W	24–0
November 13	Texas	W	50–0
November 19	Fairmont	W	12–4
November 24	at Washburn	T	6–6
1909 (6-4)			
September 23	Central Oklahoma	W	55–0
October 2	Kingfisher College	W	46–5
October 9	at Kansas	L	11–0
October 13	Northwest Oklahoma	W	23–2
October 20	at Arkansas	L	21–5
November 5	Washburn	W	42–8
November 12	at Washington	W	11–5
November 17	Texas A&M at Dallas	L	14–8
November 19	at Texas	L	30–0
November 29	Epworth*	W	12–11
1910 (4-2-1)			
October 7	at Kingfisher College	W	66–0
October 17	at Central Oklahoma	W	79–0
October 21	Oklahoma A&M	W	12–0

October 28	Missouri	L	26–0
November 12	Kansas*	L	2–0
November 28	at Texas	W	3–0
December 2	Epworth	T	3–3
1911 (8-0)			
October 7	Kingfisher College	W	104–0
October 14	Oklahoma Christian	W	62–0
October 20	at Oklahoma A&M	W	22–0
October 27	Washburn	W	37–0
November 4	at Missouri	W	14–6
November 11	at Kansas	W	3–0
November 22	Northwest Oklahoma	W	34–6
November 30	at Texas	W	6–3
1912 (5-4)			
October 5	at Kingfisher College	W	40–0
October 11	Central Oklahoma	W	87–0
October 19	Texas at Dallas	W	21–6
October 26	Missouri	L	14–0
November 2	at Kansas	W	6–5
November 9	Texas A&M at Houston	L	28–6
November 16	Oklahoma A&M	W	16–0
November 23	at Nebraska	L	13–9
November 28	Colorado	L	14–12
1913 (6-2)			
September 27	Kingfisher College	W	74–0
October 4	at Central Oklahoma	W	83–0

October 11	Northwest Oklahoma	W	101–0
October 18	at Missouri	L	20–17
October 31	Kansas	W	21–7
November 10	Texas at Houston	L	14–6
November 21	at Oklahoma A&M	W	7–0
November 27	Colorado	W	14–3
1914 (9-1-1)			
September 26	Central Oklahoma	W	67–0
October 3	at Kingfisher College	W	67–0
October 9	East Central	W	96–6
October 17	Missouri	W	13–0
October 24	Texas at Dallas	L	32–7
October 31	at Kansas	T	16–16
November 6	Oklahoma A&M	W	23–6
November 13	at Kansas State	W	52–10
November 20	at Arkansas	W	35–7
November 26	Haskell	W	33–12
November 30	at Henry Kendall	W	26–7
1915 (10-0)			
September 25	Kingfisher College	W	67–0
October 2	at Southwest Oklahoma	W	55–0
October 9	Northwest Oklahoma	W	102–0
October 16	at Missouri	W	24–0
October 23	Texas at Dallas	W	14–13
October 30	Kansas	W	23–14

November 6	at Henry Kendall	W	14–13
November 13	Arkansas	W	24–0
November 20	at Kansas State	W	21–7
November 25	Oklahoma A&M*	W	26–7
1916 (6-5)			
September 23	Central Oklahoma	W	27–0
September 30	at Shawnee Normal	W	107–0
October 7	Southwest Oklahoma	W	140–0
October 14	Henry Kendall	L	16–0
October 21	Texas at Dallas	L	21–7
October 28	Missouri	L	23–14
November 4	at Kansas	L	21–13
November 11	at Kingfisher College	W	96–0
November 18	Kansas State	L	14–13
November 25	at Arkansas	W	14–13
November 30	Oklahoma A&M*	W	41–7
1917 (6-4-1)			
September 22	at Central Oklahoma	W	99–0
September 29	Kingfisher College	W	179–0
October 6	Phillips*	W	52–9
October 13	at Illinois	L	44–0
October 20	Texas at Dallas	W	14–0
November 3	at Missouri	W	14–7
November 10	Kansas	L	13–6
November 17	Arkansas	T	0–0
November 24	Henry Kendall	W	80–0

November 29	Oklahoma A&M*	L	9–0
December 15	at Camp Doniphan	L	21–7
1918 (6-0)			
October 26	Central Oklahoma	W	44–0
November 2	Post Field	W	58–0
November 9	at Kansas	W	33–0
November 16	at Arkansas	W	103–0
November 23	Phillips*	W	13–7
November 28	Oklahoma A&M	W	7–0
1919 (5-2-3)			
September 27	at Central Oklahoma	W	40–0
October 4	at Kingfisher	W	157–0
October 11	Henry Kendall	L	27–0
October 18	Texas at Dallas	W	12–7
October 25	at Nebraska	T	7–7
November 1	Missouri	T	6–6
November 8	at Kansas	T	0–0
November 15	Arkansas	L	7–6
November 22	at Kansas State	W	14–3
November 27	at Oklahoma A&M*	W	33–6
1920 (6-0-1)			
October 9	Central Oklahoma	W	16–7
October 23	Washington	W	24–14
October 30	at Missouri	W	28–7
November 6	Kansas	W	21–9
November 13	at Oklahoma A&M	W	36–0
November 20	at Kansas State	T	7–7
November 25	Drake	W	44–7

1921 (5-3)			
October 8	at Central Oklahoma	W	21–0
October 15	Oklahoma A&M	W	6–0
October 22	Washington	W	28–13
October 29	at Nebraska	L	44–0
November 5	Kansas	W	24–7
November 12	at Missouri	L	24–14
November 19	at Kansas State	L	14–7
November 24	Rice	W	27–0
1922 (2-3-3)			
October 14	Central Oklahoma	W	21–0
October 21	Kansas State	T	7–7
October 28	Nebraska	L	39–7
November 4	at Kansas	L	19–3
November 11	Missouri	W	18–14
November 18	Texas	L	32–7
November 25	Oklahoma A&M	T	3–3
December 2	at Washington	T	0–0
1923 (3-5)			
October 13	at Nebraska	L	24–0
October 20	Washington	W	62–7
October 27	Oklahoma A&M	W	12–0
November 3	Kansas	L	7–3
November 10	at Missouri	W	13–0
November 17	at Texas	L	26–14
November 24	at Kansas State	L	21–20
November 29	Drake	L	26–20
1924 (2-5-1)			
October 4	Central Oklahoma	L	2–0

October 11	Nebraska	W	14–7
October 25	at Drake	L	28–0
November 1	at Oklahoma A&M	L	6–0
November 8	Missouri	L	10–0
November 15	at Kansas	L	20–0
November 22	at Washington	W	7–0
November 27	Kansas State	T	7–7
1925 (4-3-1)			
October 3	at Kansas State	L	16–0
October 17	Drake	W	7–0
October 24	at Southern Methodist	W	9–0
October 31	at Nebraska	L	12–0
November 7	Kansas	T	0–0
November 14	at Missouri	L	16–14
November 21	Washington	W	28–0
November 26	Oklahoma A&M	W	35–0
1926 (5-2-1)			
October 9	Arkansas	W	13–6
October 16	at Drake	W	11–0
October 23	Kansas State	L	15–12
October 30	at Washington	W	21–0
November 6	Missouri	W	10–7
November 13	at Kansas	L	10–9
November 20	St. Louis	W	47–0
November 25	at Oklahoma A&M	T	14–14

(*) indicates games played in Oklahoma City

Combined Football Coaching Record

Thirty seasons

150-58-18

.704

Basketball

University of Oklahoma: Thirteen Seasons, 113-49, .698

1908–09 (3-3)		
Edmond Teachers	W	93–7
Emporia Normal	L	37–33
at Chilocco	L	27–20
at Emporia Normal	L	45–19
Blackwell Baptist	W	31–21
Tonkawa Prep	W	28–26
1909–10 (8-0)		
Edmond Teachers	W	90–1
Chilocco	W	24–7
Washburn	W	55–20
at Chilocco	W	51–12
Oklahoma A&M	W	46–15
at Oklahoma &M	W	41–24
Texas	W	59–26
Texas	W	63–23
1910–11 (1-5)		
Blackwell Baptist	L	29–28
Edmond Teachers	W	65–3
at Winfield KS	L	53–34
Friends	L	26–24
at Blackwell Baptist	L	26–12
Winfield KS	L	41–40

1911–12 (7-2)		
Shawnee Baptist	W	78–12
Chilocco	W	45–36
Chilocco	W	38–29
Oklahoma A&M	W	59–17
at Oklahma A&M	W	30–24
at Chilocco	L	31–26
at Blackwell Baptist	L	22–21
Tonkawa Prep	W	37–18
Winfield KS	W	35–22
1912–13 (8-0)		
Blackwell Baptist	W	46–26
Blackwell Baptist	W	50–26
Chilocco	W	32–29
at Chilocco	W	29–28
Bethany	W	48–32
at Bethany	W	42–38
Edmond Teachers	W	78–12
Oklahoma A&M	W	46–16
1913–14 (7-1)		
Weatherford	W	43–15
at Weatherford	W	43–11
Edmond Teachers	W	68–13
at Chilocco	L	45–29
Chilocco	W	32–9
Edmond Teachers	W	47–27
Weatherford	W	34–13
At Weatherford	W	39–19

1914–15 (7-5)		
Tonkawa Prep	W	36–19
at Bethany	L	36–6
Emporia Normal	L	41–40
Bethany	L	32–30
Edmond Teachers	W	52–18
Henry Kendall	W	46–26
Henry Kendall	W	52–19
Chilocco	L	39–28
at Chilocco	W	37–27
Weatherford	W	49–10
at Henry Kendall	L	21–19
at Henry Kendall	W	40–30
1915–16 (19-7)		
Weatherford	W	37–31
at Weatherford	W	39–24
Oklahoma A&M	W	35–33
at Oklahoma A&M	W	57–49
Henry Kendall	W	40–20
at Henry Kendall	W	57–29
at Chilocco	W	34–17
Chilocco	L	39–38
Alva Teachers	W	41–26
at Alva Teachers	W	42–39
Edmond Teachers	W	59–29
Emporia Normal	L	38–33
at Emporia Normal	L	35–30
Kemper Military	W	61–23
Central Missouri	W	42–26

at Missouri	L	20–50
Missouri	W	29–28
Warrensburg, MO	L	44–43
at Warrensburg, MO	L	58–41
Springfield YMCA	W	60–46
at Springfield Y	L	59–30
Henry Kendall	W	46–33
at Henry Kendall	W	43–33
Edmond Teachers	W	68–26
at Oklahoma A&M	W	50–30
Oklahoma A&M	W	59–30
1916–17 (13-8)		
Weatherford	W	53–26
at Weatherford	W	37–35
at Oklahoma A&M	L	58–11
at Oklahoma A&M	W	24–23
Henry Kendall	L	46–45
Henry Kendall	W	41–29
at Durant Teachers	W	65–22
Durant Teachers	W	74–20
at SMU	L	43–20
Hardin School	W	23–8
SMU	W	45–33
Terrell School	W	40–19
Baylor	W	42–28
Oklahoma A&M	L	35–25
Oklahoma A&M	W	22–21
at Chilocco	L	37–35

Chilocco	W	56–33
at Henry Kendall	L	37–27
at Henry Kendall	L	31–22
Edmond Teachers	W	50–41
at Edmond Teachers	L	46–35
1917–18 (11-1)		
OK Methodist	W	68–27
OK Methodist	W	63–22
Oklahoma A&M	W	45–28
Durant Teachers	W	116–13
Durant Teachers	W	91–19
at Chilocco	L	33–29
Edmond Teachers	W	52–32
Chilocco	W	37–32
at Oklahoma A&M	W	27–19
at Henry Kendall	W	51–20
Henry Kendall	W	83–23
Edmond Teachers	W	62–20
1918–19 (12-0)		
Shawnee Baptist	W	82–30
Shawnee Baptist	W	82–16
Edmond Teachers	W	65–20
at Oklahoma A&M	W	44–33
at Oklahoma A&M	W	38–34
TCU	W	91–34
Kansas	W	91–34
at Edmond Teachers	W	62–29

at Edmond Teachers	W	52–26
Oklahoma A&M	W	51–33
Oklahoma A&M	W	45–36
at Chilocco	W	43–37
at Chilocco	W	52–27
1919–20 (9-7)		
at Kansas State	L	37–18
at Kansas State	L	21–14
Edmond Teachers	W	35–24
Edmond Teachers	W	25–12
at Missouri	L	33–21
at Missouri	L	51–18
at Washington (MO)	L	46–39
at Washington (MO)	W	26–22
Kansas State	W	37–28
Kansas State	W	28–26
At Oklahoma A&M	W	36–13
At Oklahoma A&M	W	32–16
Oklahoma A&M	W	37–25
Oklahoma A&M	W	50–11
at Kansas	L	32–28
at Kansas	L	42–26
1920–21 (8-10)		
Oklahoma A&M	W	42–10
Oklahoma A&M	W	54–15
at Kansas State	L	28–16
at Kansas State	L	23–9
Missouri	L	47–24
Missouri	L	34–19

at Creighton	L	27–16
at Nebraska	L	34–20
at Nebraska	L	32–22
at Drake	W	35–32
at Drake	L	22–16
at Grinnell	W	25–22
at Grinnell	W	23–20
Washington (MO)	W	44–23
Washington (MO)	W	44–27
at Oklahoma A&M	W	46–15
Kansas	L	33–30
Kansas	L	37–32

Baseball

University of Oklahoma: Fifteen Seasons, 142-102-4, .581

Year	Won	Lost	Tied
1906	10	6	0
1907	12	5	0
1908	No team		
1909	13	4	0
1910	11	9	0
1911	11	6	0
1912	6	6	1
1913	11	6	0
1914	12	7	1
1915	17	4	0
1916	7	9	0
1917	No team		
1918	10	6	0
1919	6	7	0

1920	5	8	1
1921	6	9	1
1922	5	10	0

BIBLIOGRAPHY

ARTICLES

Evans, Harold C. "College Football in Kansas." *Kansas Historical Quarterlies* 9, no 3 (August 1940).

Watterson, John S. "Gridiron Crisis of 1905: Was It Really a Crisis?" *Journal of Sport History* 27, no. 2 (2000): 291–98.

BOOKS

Alexander, Charles E. *John McGraw*. Lincoln, NE: Bison Books, 1995.

Angell, Roger. *The Summer Game*. Lincoln, NE: Bison Books, 2004.

Asinof, Eliot. *Eight Men Out*. New York: Holt Paperbacks, 2001.

Brent, J. *Sooner Century: 100 Glorious Years of Oklahoma Football*. Coal Valley, IL: Quality Sports Publications, 1995.

Brooks, Phillip. *The Forward Pass: The Play That Saved Football*. Yardley, PA: Westholme Publishing, 2007.

Cross, George Lynn. *Seeds of Excellence*. Norman, OK: Transcript Press, 1986.

Hetrick, Thomas J. *Chris Von der Ahe and the St. Louis Browns*. Lanham, MD: Scarecrow Press, 1999.

Keith, Harold. *Oklahoma Kickoff*. Norman: University of Oklahoma Press, 1984.

Leerhsen, Charles. *Crazy Good: The True Story of Dan Patch*. New York: Simon & Schuster, 2008.

Levy, David. *The University of Oklahoma: A History, Volume I*. Norman: University of Oklahoma Press, 2005.

Lindquist, Emory K. *Smoky Valley People: A History of Lindsborg, Kansas*. Lindsborg, KS: Bethany College, 1953.

Lundgren Robert A. *Bethany in Kansas: The History of a College*. Lindsborg, KS: Bethany College, 1975.

———. *A Century of Bethany Football, 1893–1993*. Lindsborg, KS: Bethany College, 1993.

Oldroyd, Bess Riley. *Between the Rivers: Stories of the Eighties and Nineties in Arkansas City, KS*. Arkansas City, KS: Home National Bank, 1975.

Price, Jay M., ed. *Cherokee Strip Land Rush*. Charleston, SC: Arcadia Press, 2006.

Ritter, Lawrence S., ed. *The Glory of Their Times*. New York: Harper Perennial Modern Classics, 2010.

Robinson, Ray. *Rockne of Notre Dame: The Making of a Football Legend*. Oxford, UK: Oxford University Press, 1999.

Spinney, Robert. *Big Shoulders: A History of Chicago*. DeKalb: Northern Illinois University Press, 2000.

Yost, Fielding. *Football for Players and Spectators*. Gloucester, UK: Dodo Press, 2010.

MEDIA GUIDES

Bethany College: Football 2009.

Kansas University: Baseball 2009, Basketball 2009 and Football 2009.

Michigan University: Football 2009.

Nebraska: Football 2009.

Oklahoma University: Baseball 2009, Basketball 2009 and Football 2009.

Washburn University: Football 2009.

Newspapers Archives

The actual articles are noted in the text.

Bethany Messenger
Chicago Tribune
Daily Kansan
Daily Oklahoman
Denver Post
Denver Times
Detroit News
Kansas City Star
Kansas University Weekly
Lincoln Star
Lindsborg News
New York Times
Norman Transcript
Oklahoma Daily (and the *Umpire*, as it was once known)
Topeka State Journal
Tulsa Tribune
Washburn Review

Personal Communication

Dorothy Bryan
Michael Grant
Anne Haynes
Joe Haynes
Jan (Page) Howard
William Gilbert Page
Ann Stussi
Sandy Trudgeon

Special Collections

Selected items from Bennie Owen's personnel file at the University of Oklahoma.
Bennie Owen's transcripts from the University of Kansas.
Feaver, Kenneth E. "Eulogy of Bennie Owen." Unpublished manuscript, February 1970.

Yearbooks

Bethany College, 1902–04.
Kansas University, 1897–1900.
Oklahoma University, 1905–1926.
Washburn University, 1901.

Websites

"About Haskell." Haskell Indian Nations University. http://www.haskell.edu/about.html (accessed January 15, 2010).

"Charles Comiskey Biography." National Baseball Hall of Fame. http://baseballhall.org/hof/comiskey-charles (accessed September 15, 2009).

"George Woodruff Biography." College Football Hall of Fame. http://www.collegefootball.org/famer_selected.php?id=90022 (accessed September 11, 2009).

"Grover Cleveland Alexander." Cubs History, http://chicago.cubs.mlb.com/chc/history/chc_feature_alexander.jsp (accessed November 14, 2009).

The Hudson Super Six. http://www.hudsonsupersix.com (accessed October 12, 2009).

Kansas University. http://www.ku.edu (accessed, June 19, 2010).

"Missouri Valley League (D)." Baseballreference.com. http://www.baseball-reference.com/minors/league.cgi?code=MOVL&class=D (accessed July 7, 2010).

"The Paris 1900 World Exposition." History of World Expositions. http://www.expo2000.de/expo2000/geschichte/detail.php?wa_id=8&lang=1 (accessed July 16, 2010).

"University of Michigan Athletics History." Bentley Historical Library. http://www.bentley.umich.edu/athdept/football/bowls/1902rose.htm (accessed July 25, 2010).

Washburn University. http://www.washburn.edu/main/index.html (accessed June 19, 2000).

INDEX

H

J

K

L

M

About the Author

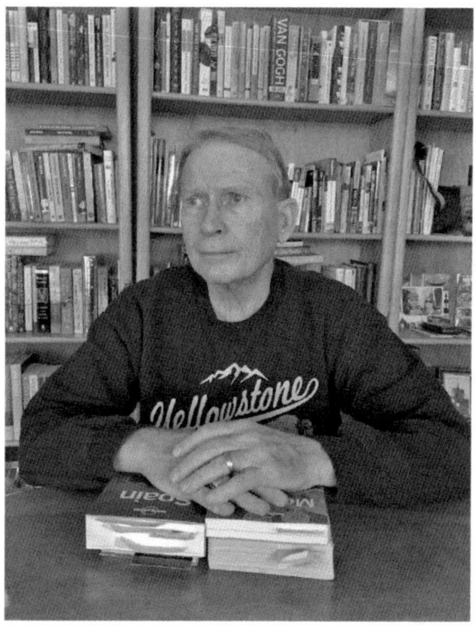

Courtesy of Patricia King.

Gary King was a professor of psychology at Rose State College in Midwest City, Oklahoma, for thirty-five years before his retirement in 2007.

He has published articles in several journals and papers—such as the *Oklahoma Observer*, *Sooner Magazine*, *Sooner's Illustrated*, *Oklahoma Prep*, *Distinctly Oklahoma*, *Norman Magazine* and the *Dallas Morning News*—as well as short stories in *Pegasus*, *Aethlon: The Journal of Sports Literature* and a nonfiction piece in the United States Golf Association's *Golf Journal*.

His first book, *An Autumn Remembered: Bud Wilkinson's Legendary '56 Sooners*, was published by the University of Oklahoma Press in 2006.

He currently resides in Norman, Oklahoma, with his wife, Patricia.